JIM ROUSE

Capitalist/Idealist

Paul Marx

University Press of America,® Inc.
Lanham · Boulder · New York · Toronto · Plymouth, UK

Copyright © 2008 by
University Press of America,® Inc.
4501 Forbes Boulevard
Suite 200
Lanham, Maryland 20706
UPA Acquisitions Department (301) 459-3366

Estover Road
Plymouth PL6 7PY
United Kingdom

All rights reserved
Printed in the United States of America
British Library Cataloging in Publication Information Available

Library of Congress Control Number: 2007937983
ISBN-13: 978-0-7618-3944-6 (paperback : alk. paper)
ISBN-10: 0-7618-3944-5 (paperback : alk. paper)

∞™ The paper used in this publication meets the minimum requirements of American National Standard for Information Sciences—Permanence of Paper for Printed Library Materials, ANSI Z39.48—1984

*To my wonderful wife, Jeannette,
Who has shared the joy and the frustration*

Cover drawing by Amy Marx

CONTENTS

Preface vii

Acknowledgements xi

Chronology xiii

1. What's the Purpose 1
2. Huck on the Chesapeake 11
3. Jim at School 21
4. A Poor Relation 31
5. The Ace 43
6. The Fights Against Blight and War 49
7. Stepping Stones 63
8. The Company and the City 77
9. Bad Mall, Good Mall 89
10. The Summer of 1963 99
11. The Village of Cross Keys 109
12. Columbia: The Dream, the Plans 119

13.	Columbia: The Next America	131
14.	Columbia and the Vietnam War	147
15.	A Downward Turn	155
16.	Festival Marketplace: Boston	171
17.	Festival Marketplace: Baltimore	179
18.	The Social Entrepreneur	187
19.	Back to Baltimore	201
20.	Last Years	213
21.	Columbia Fully Grown	221
22.	Legacy	231
Bibliography		237
Index		239
About the Author		249

Preface

I detest consumerism. I hate the whole apparatus by which people are made to believe they need more and more and more. More ways to adorn their bodies. More ways to make their homes distinctive. More ways to tickle their palates. The Rouse Company's malls are gilded palaces of consumerism. Yet a few years ago I married a woman who lived in a high-rise across the street from just such a palace, the Towson Town Center, in Maryland. Jeannette, my new wife, liked wandering around in that palace. But I resisted. I wouldn't step inside the place. On rainy days, though, it seemed like a good place to get my walking done. I discovered that the Towson Town Center was a happy place. People were there to buy but also to hang out. Friends met and sat around with coffees. Seniors with newspapers sat on comfortable benches. The place was bright with sunlight and greenery. In its way it was like a market plaza in Madrid, Rome, Bologna, or Nancy. I began to like going over there. It was then that I learned that Towson Town Center is owned by The Rouse Company. Who was this Rouse?

Normally the life and career of an American multi-millionaire real estate developer like Jim Rouse would be of no interest to me. The term that best describes my political and economic philosophy is democratic socialism. Unlike most of my countrymen, I have never aspired to have for myself the wealth and power of a big-time capitalist; being a tenured professor with a modest but guaranteed income was wealth and power enough for me. Unlike capitalism's faithful, I've had a hard time with the notion that free enterprise is the most sensible system for organizing a nation's economic life. During my politically formative years, through the reading I did, the classes I took, the political talk all around me in the vibrant Brooklyn neighborhood in which I lived, I was exposed to sharp criticism of the way things were. That was not the case with Jim Rouse, a member of the generation before mine, a member of "the greatest generation." Rouse grew up on Maryland's Eastern Shore, which—let's face it—is (or, maybe, was) an intellectual backwater. Neither in school, town, or home did he encounter discussions of alternatives to capitalism—or even the desirability of trade unions.

I grew up in a working-class immigrant home in the Brighton Beach section of Brooklyn. In boxer shorts and undershirt, my father, in a millinery factory on West 39th Street, in the old garment center of Manhattan, worked with steam and rope to give shape to ladies' hats. On the Brighton Beach boardwalk on pleasant evenings in the 1940s, clusters of working men, most of whom were union members employed in the garment industry, argued about the issues of the day. They were of the left, socialists and communists of one stripe or another. They'd denounce cheating bosses, politicians who lined their own pockets, landlords stingy with heat. I would hover on the fringe, absorbing it all. After college, I tried to get a job as an organizer for the United Millinery Workers.

So I grew up not having much faith in capitalists or businessmen in general. They were all liars and cheats, trying to make a buck out of you however they could. I knew you couldn't take advertising at face value, and you had to watch every move a shopkeeper made in waiting on you. I learned at first hand the meaning of exploitation when, as a teenager, I worked as a vendor in Ebbets Field, home of the old Brooklyn Dodgers. In order to sell and earn a 10% commission, you had to be at the ballpark six hours before game time to do odd jobs for the concessionaire without pay. If a game was later rained out after your six hours of work, that was tough; there'd be no pay.

And my dislike of the system was held even more strongly after majoring in economics at the University of Michigan. I still don't believe the market should be the main factor in how income is distributed and who then has access to comfortable living space or dental and medical care or to an education at Harvard, Yale, or Williams. If I had my way, income disparities would be much smaller. If I had my way, I'd see to it that everyone able to work had a job and that everyone had a decent place to call home. I'd cap incomes of CEOs at ten times what their janitors get paid. I'd pay a university president no more than twice what the highest-paid professor makes. "I've got mine and I don't give a damn about anyone else" is an attitude I despise. The Donald Trumps of the world are not my heroes.

Still, it was an unlikely route that led to my decision to invest a big chunk of time learning about Jim Rouse. I had spent a year researching and writing *Utopia in America,* a project that resonated deeply with my beliefs. I had immersed myself in the ways of several literary utopias and several real 19th century planned communities—the Shakers, New Harmony, and Oneida. I also studied and wrote about several late 20th century communities, especially Twin Oaks, the Virginia community that was founded in 1968 and after more than thirty years was still very much alive. The leaders of these communities had put their minds to the question of what would be the best kind of community for human beings to live in.

Jim Rouse, it turns out, had wrestled with the same question. The builder of suburban malls really cared about how people lived. And he took actions that would improve the living conditions for large numbers of people. This capitalist was an idealist!

Although many Americans may enjoy sharing and cooperating, what they do as members of a community is usually quite limited. Most Americans want their privacy. They have problems with the notion of economic equality; they don't want to be in situations in which they end up doing more work than somebody else yet get the same amount of praise or income. They definitely don't believe in the idea that each person should contribute according to his ability and get rewarded according to his need. Mainstream America doesn't do well in encouraging sharing—or in satisfying the longing for community. Yet a significant number of Americans are unhappy with modern American culture. They refuse to aspire to ownership of the gaudy, unneeded things American advertising says they should want. They refuse to stifle their minds and go along with everyone else. They enjoy being a part of a community; they enjoy community life, they enjoy knowing their neighbors and doing things with them, having common experiences and acting as a team.

Regarding the Endnotes

Jim Rouse was a pack rat. He seems to have saved every piece of paper he ever touched: correspondence with U.S. presidents but also letters from ordinary people making a donation or seeking a favor, business correspondence of all kinds, typescripts of all his many speeches, annual reports of his companies, clippings from newspapers and magazines, adolescent love poems, all the writing he did in high school. A few years after Jim died, Patty Rouse, his widow, helped form the Columbia Archives, located in the town center of Columbia, Maryland. She gave the Archives a huge amount of material, all of it saved by Jim. Some of the material in the Archives came from other sources. The total Rouse collection in the Archives is formally called The James W. Rouse Papers.

With a few exceptions, all the primary sources in this book are in the Columbia Archives, indicated by CA in the notes. Unless otherwise indicated, the source document is in the Archives. The most frequently used sources are Rouse's letters, memos and speeches; all are filed by type. Much also came out of the autobiography Rouse attempted to write, with the help of journalist Jerry Buckley, in the last years of his life. The work was never finished and remains unpublished. The typescript of the autobiography, indicated in the notes by "Autob," presents a special problem in documentation. Most pages are unnumbered; some are single-spaced, others double-spaced. Numbering doesn't begin until fifty-seven pages into the typescript. Where there is numbering, the numbering starts all over again with the beginning of a new chapter. I chose to ignore that unhelpful numbering, and numbered the pages consecutively for the whole typescript, beginning with 1 for the first page and continuing through page 187.

Another unpublished document is an anonymous 48-page biography of Rouse by an author, who, it is thought, produced the work to meet requirements for a degree. The high quality of the writing and the author's perspicacity make the document totally credible. It begins with a chapter on Jim's early life, and, in four additional chapters, takes the reader through 1963 and the start of construction at Columbia.

Acknowledgments

I am grateful to the founders of the Columbia Archives and to Patty Rouse for her donation of Jim's papers to the Archives. Barbara Kellner, the manager, and Robin Emrich, the archivist, were of great help. Nancy Rouse made available to me a copy of the Rouse family genealogy that she had compiled. I have to offer a very special thank you to Jim Holechek, who made available to me his copy of the unpublished autobiography. Throughout the book, I have made use of information developed by Joshua Olsen for his *Better Places, Better Lives: A Biography of James Rouse.* For his superb book, Olsen interviewed many of the top people who worked for Rouse, and I have made use of his reports of those interviews. *Creating a New City: Columbia, Maryland,* edited by Robert Tennenbaum, was an indispensable source of information about Columbia. I also have made use of two oral histories done for the Maryland Historical Society. The one by Barry Lanman deals with political influences on the young Rouse. The one by Patricia J. La Noue deals with a variety of personal issues.

Chronology

1914 Wilson Richardson Rouse born on April 26

1930 Lydia Rouse, mother, dies, early in year; Willard Rouse dies in August. In September Jim enrolls in Tome School

1931-32 at University of Hawaii

1932-33 at University of Virginia

1933-35 at University of Maryland Law School (in Baltimore)

1935-36 works for Federal Housing Administration in Baltimore and on Eastern Shore

1936-39 works for Title Guaranty & Trust in Baltimore

1941 marries Elizabeth Winstead on May 3

1949 on Baltimore Mayor D'Alesandro's Housing Commission

1953-54 on President Eisenhower's Advisory Committee on Housing

1955 writes, with Nathaniel Keith, *No Slums in 10 Years*

1955 develops Mondawmin Mall in inner-city Baltimore

1955 starts development of enclosed Harundale Mall, which opens in 1959

1960 loses bid to develop Charles Center

1961 purchases 68 acres in Baltimore for the development of Village of Cross Keys

1961 Cherry Hill Mall opens

1962 approaches Connecticut General for funding of Columbia

1963 July 23 writes "ultimate purpose" memo. Vacations with family in Europe and visits New Towns. In September gives the first Berkeley speech

1964 Cross Keys opens

1967 Columbia opens

1976 first building of Boston's Faneuil Hall Marketplace opens

1978 referendum approval for development of Baltimore's Harborplace

1979 on May 23, Jim Rouse retires as CEO of Rouse Company

1980 Rouse begins Enterprise Foundation

1990 on May 24, second Berkeley speech, delivered by Jimmy Rouse

1996 on April 9, Jim Rouse dies

Chapter 1
What's the Purpose?

Baltimore is uncomfortably hot and humid in summer. Most who can afford it, try to get away from the city for at least a week. In the summer of 1963, Jim Rouse, famous within the real estate industry for his development of enclosed malls, had plans to take his family to northern Europe for five weeks. But he was right in the middle of a novel project, developing a planned community within the city of Baltimore. And he was in the crucial beginning stages of a much bigger venture—the building from scratch of a whole new city. He was in the process of acquiring the land on which it would be laid out, ultimately about 16,000 acres between Baltimore and Washington. The new city dominated his thinking. This was not to be just another large-scale suburban development with minimal amenities. Rouse had come to despise piecemeal development in suburbia, with every developer bent on maximizing his profit, doing his houses, roads, and infrastructure with little or no coordination with anyone else. He also chafed at the limitations imposed on black people when it came to finding places to live. He wanted his new city to be as good a place to live as he could possibly make it. He wanted to see white people and black people living harmoniously on the same street. He wanted his brand-new city to be a real city, with inhabitants at all different income levels. He wanted the new city to be the very best kind of place for bringing out the very best in people. He was being guided by his favorite maxim: "Think no small thoughts. Make no small plans."

From his boyhood on Maryland's Eastern Shore, Rouse had always been interested in public affairs. November of '63 was to be bad, but the first half of the year already had him in despair about his country. The news was dominated by the black civil rights struggle in the South and by the increasing commitment of the United States to defend the corrupt government of South Vietnam. The Cuban Missile Crisis in the fall of 1962 had almost turned the Cold War hot.

Now, President Kennedy was sending more and more soldiers to Vietnam. Rouse, a strong advocate of world government and peaceful solutions, thought the American intervention wrong.

But it was the civil rights struggle that he could do something about. As a boy on the Eastern Shore he willingly had been part of the system of enforced segregation. Later, settled in Baltimore and trying to make his way in the real estate mortgage business, he saw the miserable housing in which poor blacks lived. He decided he would do whatever he could to improve those conditions. In 1954 the U. S. Supreme Court had ordered an end to racial segregation in schools and on interstate buses, and black leaders began their fight to end all Jim Crow laws. In Mississippi in 1962, 5,000 troops were brought in to protect James Meredith when he enrolled at the university. In the city of Birmingham, Alabama, in April and May 1963, daily clashes were occurring between civil rights demonstrators and police. Police commissioner Bull Connor was attempting to stop peaceful marching and picketing with powerful firehoses and attack dogs. At the University of Alabama on June 11th, Governor George C. Wallace personally attempted to block desegregation "today, tomorrow, and forever." That night President Kennedy addressed the nation and asked, "Are we to say to the world . . . that this is the land of the free except for Negroes?" The next day Medgar Evers, the head of the Mississippi NAACP, was shot dead.

Jim Rouse was forty-nine years old and had come far from that bad stretch when, in his late teens, he was parentless and dirt poor. He had been financially dependent on his older brother Willard and his sisters. He hadn't been able to continue at prep school because of the burden its expense put on Willard. He was able to get through two years of college only because two brothers-in-law found ways in which he could be subsidized. But he hated being dependent. He worked long hours at a Baltimore parking garage to get himself through the night law school of the University of Maryland. He then worked with mortgages for the Federal Housing Administration and for a leading Baltimore bank, culminating that stage of his career by becoming a member of the board of the National Mortgage Bankers Association.

He had acted against Baltimore customs by developing an in-city mall that welcomed both black and white shoppers. He had developed a dozen enclosed malls that he hoped would become focal points of suburban community life. Under way was the Village of Cross Keys, a community within the city of Baltimore that he hoped would be a showcase for enlightened urban planning, a community from which blacks would not be excluded.

Now, in July of 1963, he had bought over 100 parcels of land in the Maryland countryside. He had to take the new project into its next phase: deciding exactly what to do with the land. He had observed that it was just this phase that was slighted by developers. As he put it in the speech he was to give at Berkeley on September 23rd, "The biggest hole in the planning process in America . . . is right at the beginning of it. We aren't coming up with the right answers because we aren't asking the right questions." Rouse was determined to ask a lot of questions before any trenches were dug or concrete poured. So on

July 23rd, just two days before he and his family were to depart for a European vacation, he confined himself to his office at 14 West Saratoga, focused his mind, and brought together a wide range of thoughts. He had lots of questions about the purpose and design of new towns. He had taken note of the development of new towns in recent years and had not been very impressed. So he brought his observations and questions together in an intra-office memorandum to his four top aides at Community Research and Development. It was a lengthy memo for a man who exhorted his staff to keep their memos brief. He invited the four "to challenge, destroy, supplement or expand."[1]

Conveying Rouse's unique philosophy, the document is a surprising statement for a real estate developer—or for any American businessman. Rouse says he wants an answer to the question of what the basic purpose of a community is. The answer would seem obvious, but Rouse says what he wants to know is, "What would be the optimum results in the most successful possible community that man could conceive?" By "optimum results," he does not mean optimum financial results. He answers his own question when he states what a developer's ultimate purpose should be. It is "the improvement of mankind." And he goes on: "There really can be no other end purpose of planning except to develop better people. The most successful community would be that which contributed the most by its physical plan, its institutions and operation to the growth of people." We need to consider, he says, the kind of people we want to grow. We need to consider, "What would mark the greatest advance in our civilization?"

Once into the middle years of his career, Jim Rouse wanted his businesses to have a purpose beyond simply making money. He wanted his business pursuits to be a form of public service. To help appreciate the kind of man Jim Rouse was, it is instructive to take a brief look at two of America's most famous capitalists. Donald Trump, the country's best-known real estate developer, is Adam Smith's capitalist par excellence. In every business transaction his purpose is to buy as low as possible or sell as high as possible. Or if he holds onto a property, he wants to squeeze as much revenue from it as possible. He allows nothing to get in the way of those objectives. He has become a billionaire. For what purpose? The glory and pleasure of Donald Trump! As he says in his *Art of the Deal,* he builds and runs casinos in order to make "a ton of money." He builds the Trump Tower, on top of which he can live the life of the ultimate hedonist, in a triplex rivaling "the quality of Versailles." "When it comes to my own apartment . . .why spare any expense? I want the best whatever it takes." And so, sparing no expense, among other things, he had "the finest craftsmen in Italy hand-carve twenty-seven solid marble columns for the living room."[2] Rouse, on the other hand, could not care less about owning columns of the finest marble. He was a successful capitalist who liked to brag that the janitor and he lived in the same neighborhood.[3] About his city of Columbia, he would say, "Everyone feels equal here. . . . No one is upper class or lower class."[4]

Warren Buffett is another billionaire—but not known for extravagance or ostentation. Buffett, CEO of the vast Berkshire Hathaway holding company, is generally regarded as the paragon of American business ethics. Observers of corporate life cannot conceive of Buffett endorsing any behavior that would be other than 100% ethical. In a long article in the *New York Times,* precipitated by his possible connection to a scandal involving a Berkshire Hathaway subsidiary, Buffett is described as "a man widely regarded as a financial genius, a model for corporate integrity, and someone who has spent 74 years trying to integrate personal values such as honesty, trust and openness with the business, political and public worlds around him."[5] Timothy L. O'Brien, the *Times*'s writer, interviewed businesspeople in Omaha, headquarters city of Berkshire Hathaway. No one had a negative thing to say about Warren Buffett. If similar interviews were held in Baltimore and Columbia, Jim Rouse would be spoken of with comparable affection and appreciation. No one would question his integrity.

Jim Rouse and Warren Buffett knew and had the highest respect for each other. They were aware of each other as men driven by a strong zest for life. Rouse, though, focused on "the improvement of mankind." Buffett focused on financial returns for investors; Rouse produced houses and neighborhoods, villages and shops, woods and lakes. Except to the extent that it could limit his good works, Rouse did not care about financial returns. His worry was solvency, not increasing profitability. He had an abhorrence of selfishness.

In the July 23rd memo, Rouse wondered about the kind of people who would fulfill the highest potential of human beings. He thought they should be "inspired, concerned, loving people," who will live in a society that will dignify man. He hoped the individual citizen

> will find the ways to develop his talent; will put the fruits of his labor and intellect to effective use; will achieve brotherhood; eliminate bigotry and intolerance; will care for the indigent, the delinquent, the sick, the aged; seek the truth and communicate it; respect the differences among men.

These are the words of an idealist. But Jim Rouse was also a realist. His father had been a broker in the canning industry on the Eastern Shore, and Jim grew up accepting capitalism as a fact of life. Although his young manhood corresponded with the years of the Great Depression, Rouse did not, unlike other idealistic young men of the time, look to socialism or some variant as a solution to the country's ills. In 1938 when he first became a capitalist, with the formation of the Moss-Rouse mortgage company, he had no problem with the market system, and wanted to benefit himself to the maximum. Even as he became more idealistic and began to question the wisdom of allowing free enterprise to be completely free, he continued to believe in the necessity of the profit motive. As he was to say a few years later in an interview with *Life* magazine, "Profit is the thing that hauls dreams into focus."[6] With his work as a mortgage banker and developer, however, he saw how unjust the allocation of housing could be when left totally to the operation of the market. Later, with his creation of the city of Columbia, he tried to correct two major distortions of American capitalism. If the system worked the way it was supposed to, black people with money would have equal access to the housing market. But in 1963, in much of the country, even blacks with good incomes could not buy property wherever they wanted. Within Columbia, he would change that; he would insist that white people and black be able to live in the same apartment building or in single-family houses on the same street. Unalloyed individualism and social isolation were other harmful effects of American capitalism. Rouse would try to counteract them by devising ways to encourage social interaction and cohesive communities. President Bill Clinton had it exactly right when, at the 1995 presentation of the Presidential Medal of Freedom, he said Jim Rouse had been engaged in "healing the worn-out heart of America's cities" and had demonstrated that "we can build communities worthy of the character and optimism of our people." Rouse, Clinton said, had changed America.[7]

Jim Rouse was a man who would not allow his perceptions to be distorted in order to justify an ideology that benefited him. Faced with harsh truths, he would remain honest with himself, and formulate a plan of action to minimize the effects of bad circumstances. When he stepped into Baltimore's black slums, he was disgusted by what he saw and smelled. But he didn't just shrug and say that's the way they are or that it wasn't his problem. If he didn't like what he saw, and could do something about it—he'd act. He thought about those slums and fought to get housing codes enforced. He thought about how slums could be got rid of altogether. At the beginning of his career and also at the end, with his Enterprise Foundation, "No more slums" was a kind of mantra. In the 1960s, he was disgusted by the ugly sprawl he saw in the suburbs; while the suburbs had their advantages, there was no denying that they left the newly arrived disconnected and discontented. It made sense to him that regional malls would help stop suburban sprawl, bring people together, and give their unplanned towns some cohesion. In the 1970s, he produced his festival marketplaces on the waterfronts of Boston and Baltimore, hoping to generate uplifting intermingling of shopkeepers and patrons, of white and black. Then there was the world scene and the Cold War, which a simple miscalculation could turn hot. That mankind could be reckless with human life and permit wars to break out, that too was a problem to be worked on. For Jim Rouse, reason and ingenuity and will were powerful tools. They could make any problem less of a problem.

Rouse always listened patiently and respectfully to the other side's objections, complaints, anxieties, grievances. If they were valid, he attempted to correct the problem. If they were groundless, he would try to explain why. In his office, hung a banner that said, "There are no such things as enemies. The worst that there are are friends who are misinformed."[8] In the early days of the planning for Columbia, many citizens of Howard County were prepared to resist the grandiose scheme to build a city in the midst of their pleasant countryside. They liked Howard County just as it was; they were comfortable and didn't want any disruption. At the very first meeting between the company people and the county people, Rouse was fond of saying in later years, "There was a group which was absolutely furious because the proposed hospital would be too close to their homes." He heard them out, but still couldn't understand why they objected. "In any case, we said, 'OK, we'll move it,' and the problem was solved."[9] That kind of sensitivity melted resistance and built goodwill. It was a way of thinking Rouse employed in all his business relationships. This was the way of thinking Rouse attempted to imbue in everyone who worked for the Rouse Company. This also was the way of thinking that led him to take his strong position against the Vietnam War. He was certain it was possible to avoid the disaster of wars.

When he turned sixty-five, in 1979, Rouse decided to retire as CEO of his company. At the annual meeting to which he made his last speech as CEO, he said he was a believer in mandatory retirement. Continuing on indefinitely led chief executives to think of themselves as indispensable. Also, retirement at sixty-five gave others in the company an opportunity to make their contributions. The voluntary relinquishing of power was surprise enough, but Rouse went on to speak about what he considered the company's distinctive "way of thinking." The Rouse Company, he said, was a company that believes "people seek warm and human places, with diversity and choice, full of festival and delight: that they are degraded by tricky, tasteless places and oppressed by coldness and indifference." He concluded by saying proudly that the Rouse Company put the bottom line—where it belongs—"at the bottom." "It is when the bottom line is made the top line—the object of the enterprise—that business gets mixed up, off the track, loses its way."[10] The 250 shareholders present gave Rouse a standing ovation.[11] From the purpose-seeking memo of July 23, 1963 to that retirement speech, Jim Rouse, despite disappointments and defeats, had stuck to his distinctive way of thinking about how American capitalism should operate.

And then he entered a new phase of his life, one more obviously devoted to the public good. He became a social entrepreneur. The Enterprise Foundation, formed after his retirement from the Rouse Company, was to be the means through which every American would have a decent place to live. Rouse used his skills as a real estate developer to make money that was then funneled into decaying neighborhoods. During this period, he was greatly saddened by the conditions he saw at the bottom of society and the indifference to them of the country's leaders. He thought the injustices suffered by blacks put the country in danger of revolution; he actually used the word "revolution." A year and a half before he died, in a letter to his friend William Donald Schaefer, mayor of Baltimore 1971-86 and, at the time, governor of Maryland, Rouse wrote that the work he was doing to rehabilitate the inner-city neighborhood of Sandtown-Winchester "is the most important work I have ever undertaken in my lifetime. Patty [Mrs. Rouse] and I give it all of our available time and energy—days, nights, and weekends."[12]

Rouse made misjudgments. He failed to persuade some people he thought were a cinch. Within his lifetime some projects that he thought were cures for urban or suburban infirmities turned out to be little more than band aids. And in the decade after his death, the successes that Rouse was most proud of—Columbia and the renewed Sandtown took turns that made them into places different from the ones he left behind. Rouse could not have anticipated the upswing in the suburban real estate market in the first years of the new century that transformed Columbia from a city devoted to growing good people to an upscale suburb driven by values based on the good of the individual family rather than the good of the community. Rouse could not have imagined that the comprehensive rehabilitation of Sandtown that was turning it into a model of a rising black urban community would be bedeviled by a new crime wave.

Rouse saw himself as a winner. But even winners lose sometimes. As an ardent sports fan from early boyhood, Rouse was well aware of that rule of life. Sometimes another school's relay team is faster. Sometimes Babe Ruth strikes out. Sometimes the German heavyweight will beat the American. Rouse suffered his share of losses. The very organization of which he was a founder gave the contract for the development of Baltimore's Charles Center to another firm. When the new city of Columbia was desperate for a major corporate tenant, Rouse and his staff did everything they could have possibly done to persuade the Teachers Insurance and Annuity Association (TIAA) to move its headquarters from Manhattan to Columbia, but TIAA decided to stay put. After the successful development of Columbia, Rouse wanted to use that successful development plan elsewhere, and was not able to. Sitting on the eastern shore of Chesapeake Bay but a few miles from the area where he had spent his youth, Wye Island was ripe for development. Rouse was absolutely confident that the people of Queen Anne's County would see all the beneficial effects his plan would have on the county. When the county acted, Rouse went down to an inglorious defeat.

Rouse was able to handle his defeats and bounce back with renewed energy, with renewed exuberance. Rouse was a model of the exuberant person, the kind of person described by the renowned Johns Hopkins professor of psychiatry Kay Redfield Jamison in her *Exuberance: The Passion for Life*.

Defeat did not soften Jim Rouse's temperament. When he lost, he let himself feel his disappointment and frustration, resentment and anger, but then he let those pernicious emotions starve. Exuberance built again, and he would be ready to take on another project he thought would improve lives. "Exuberance," Jamison says, "is a fermenting, pushing-upward-and-forward force."[13] Exuberance is

> a powerful mix when its energy and opportunities come together. Exuberant people hold their ideas with passion and delight, and they act upon them with dispatch. Their love of life and adventure is palpable. Exuberance is a peculiarly pleasant state, and in that pleasure is power.

Jim Rouse's exuberance fell within the model. As Jamison defines it, exuberance "leaps, bubbles, and overflows, propels its energy through troop and tribe."[14] The exuberant person is usually full of assurance and optimism and new plans, and gets by with little sleep.[15] For a few, "exuberance is in the blood, an irrepressible life force. . . ."[16] Jim Rouse's father had that exuberance, going with minimal sleep, pursuing his intellectual interests through the night. Franklin Delano Roosevelt and Winston Churchill were exuberants, and so was Theodore Roosevelt. While they may border on it, most exuberants do not have manic-depressive illness. "Exuberance," Jamison says, "is far from a pathological state for most who have it. It is, instead, a highly valued and integral part of who they are and how they meet the world."[17]

Exuberance at its peak is contagious. "As it spreads pell-mell throughout a group, exuberance excites, it delights, and it dispels tension."[18] Rouse had that exuberance, and it was indeed contagious, spreading throughout the company, making the company special—innovative, adventurous, productive, trusted. It had given the company its special spirit—it's caring. In his retirement speech, he said,

> Rouse Company people create places that matter; that make a difference in the lives of men, women, and children—and their communities. These places lead us to create still better places as a result of our experience. And they raise up new ideas for others to see and follow. They set new standards for other developments. The impact of our work reaches far beyond our own projects.[19]

Jim Rouse was a real estate developer for whom real estate development was a means to an end—an end that was not primarily self-interested. More than a developer Rouse was a humanitarian, an exuberant human being who wanted to make other people as happy and optimistic as he was. He worked to improve the lives of the inhabitants of the other, poorer America. He wanted to bring diverse racial and income groups together, to generate feelings of love and community. He wanted decent, affordable housing for everyone. He wanted to build a brand-new city where all that could happen.

Because of Jim Rouse, America has the vibrant and aesthetically pleasing city of Columbia; it has, within the city of Baltimore, Columbia's forerunner in the Village of Cross Keys; it has, in urban neighborhoods that had been victims of blight, the regional landmarks of Boston's Faneuil Hall Marketplace and Baltimore's Harborplace; it has models of social entrepreneurship in the creation of the Enterprise Foundation and in the rehabilitation of the rock-bottom Baltimore neighborhood of Sandtown-Winchester.

Rouse did not gain everything he wanted, and there have been objections to what he did gain. He heard criticism during drawn-out approval processes, and he sometimes failed to get those approvals. But, overall, during his lifetime and since his death, relatively little negative criticism has been heard. The most comprehensive critique of Rouse's career as a developer is that of Nicholas since his death, relatively little negative criticism has been heard. The most comprehensive critique of Rouse's career as a developer is that of Nicholas Dagen Bloom in his *Merchant of Illusion*. Bloom, looking to European models, believes the people of the United States have been misled by capitalists like Rouse into thinking that only for-profit efforts will work in attempting to find solutions to the country's domestic problems. Bloom believes private-sector advocates such as Rouse have "proved to be such gifted promoters of the businessman's utopia" through "magnificent propaganda—spoken, textual, visual, and built" that they "have crowded out other visions."[20] In comparing American efforts to improve the lot of ordinary people with what has been done in the socialist and communist societies of Europe, Bloom believes many opportunities have been missed because of the American people's deep strain of hostility to involvement by the federal government. And he places Rouse "at the leading edge of the triumph of privatization, particularly on urban issues, that helped steer America away from the creation of a comprehensive urban social welfare state."[21]

As this book takes the reader through the highlights of Rouse's life and career, Bloom's insights will be addressed. The dominant thesis of this book, however, is that Jim Rouse was an exceptional businessman who demonstrated that much could be accomplished within the framework of American capitalism. The author proposes to show a man who tried to harness the energy of profit-seeking capitalism to serve the general welfare and produce effects that would make his country and countrymen better. But Rouse the idealist was also a realist. He aimed high, but knew his devotion to the public good would always be matched by others with equal devotion to their *own* personal good. He knew that if he did not work to make here-and-now capitalism serve the needs of people, those needs would be largely ignored. Europe had its culture and intellectual traditions, but America's, with its worship of private enterprise and personal success, were different. Rouse never thought there was an alternative to staying within the system. But he would bend the system he was born into and try to make it serve good purposes. Sometimes, though, his notions of what would make Americans better were not notions Americans agreed with. Still, it is important to understand the sources of Rouse's idealism, the uses he made of the system to temper capitalism's harsher effects, and the ultimate successes and failures of his efforts.

Chapter 1 What's the Purpose?

1. JWR memo to William Finley, with copies to Willard G. Rouse, Charles F. Jenkins, and Morton Hoppenfeld.
2. Donald Trump, *Art of the Deal* (New York: Random House, 1987), 30.
3. Susan Hlesciak Hall, "Now this I love. I just love talking about Columbia," *Columbia Magazine,* June 1987, 43.
4. Hall, 43.
5. Timothy L. O'Brien, "The Oracle of Omaha's Latest Riddle," *The New York Times,* April 10, 2005, 1BU.
6. Quoted by Hall, 43.
7. Quoted by Joshua Olsen, *Better Places, Better Lives* (Washington: Urban Land Institute, 2003), 361.
8. Hall, 44.
9. Hall, 44.
10. May 23, 1979.
11. *The Sun* (the morning paper of Baltimore), May 24, 1979, 15A.
12. Quoted by Olsen, 358-59.
13. Kay Redfield Jamison, *Exuberance: The Passion for Life* (New York: Knopf, 2004), 6.
14. Jamison, 4.
15. Jamison, 101.
16. Jamison, 5.
17. Jamison, 131.
18. Jamison, 7.
19. Rouse speech to the Annual Meeting of The Rouse Company, May 23, 1979.
20. Nicholas Dagen Bloom, *Merchant of Illusion: America's Salesman of the Businessman's Utopia* (Columbus: Ohio State University Press, 2004), xxii.
21. Bloom, xix.

Chapter 2
Huck on the Chesapeake

Even in the twenty-first century, "small town" is an apt description of Easton, Maryland. Easton is on Maryland's eastern shore, close to its Chesapeake Bay coastline. From Annapolis, the state capital on the western shore, Easton, the seat of government of Talbot County, is approximately twenty-five miles across the water to the southeast. At the beginning of the twenty-first century, its population is 10,000. When the boy James Wilson Rouse, born on April 26, 1914, roamed its streets and environs, the population was about half of that. The people Jim met were not strangers. If he were to need help, he could count on almost anyone to offer it. If a townsman asked him for some form of assistance, he would jump at the chance to lend a hand. To even a black person? Well, the black person was not supposed to let a white know help was needed. Young Jim's Easton, little more than 200 miles from New York City, was a small *Southern* town.

James Wilson Rouse, the youngest of the seven children fathered by Willard G. Rouse, was born and raised in a three-story, eight-bedroom Victorian home only a few blocks from the courthouse and the center of town. In boyhood, he could easily walk beyond the town limits and out into the country. Just as easily he could get to water of whatever width met the day's requirements—creek, branch, or river, all ultimately tracing back to Chesapeake Bay. It is hard to imagine a more suitable environment for a restless, curious, adventurous boy. Any boy not tied to apron strings would be out of the house for as many hours as possible, playing, exploring, trying things out, making mischief.

Jim Rouse's carefree, liberated boyhood, was a lot like the boyhood of the great Romantic poet William Wordsworth. For up in the northwestern corner of England, in the Lakes District, the boy Wordsworth too had freedom, and he used it to roam hills and sail lakes, and let his imagination store up all the beneficent effects of nature, which, he claims, were decisive in making him a worthy poet. Rouse's boyhood was also like that of Samuel Clemens, the creator of America's archetypes of carefree boys, Tom Sawyer and Huck Finn.

Sam Clemens, who grew up to become the writer Mark Twain, embodied in Tom and Huck his own experiences and those of his buddies in and around Hannibal, Missouri, a small town on the west bank of the Mississippi River. When he was four, Sam, born in 1835, and his family moved east to Hannibal from an inland village, and in the years that followed young Sam discovered the uses of water as playground and laboratory, just as Jim Rouse was to do. While the vessel accessible to young Sam was the jerry-rigged raft, young Jim had the benefit of a bought sailboat. With that boat he could explore all the nearby water, the Tred Avon River, and maybe even venture into the big bay. Afloat, both boys would take note of such things as the vegetation on the banks, the birds of varied size and color, the flashing fish, the changing sky. Up to their knees in wading pools, they would look down hard and observe the ways of minnows, tadpoles, daddy-longlegs, and such. They might swim or play pirate or gather turtle eggs. And not too far off there would be woods and their creatures to be observed or caught. "It was a heavenly place for a boy," the adult Sam Clemens said of Hannibal. It was part of the creed of the adult Jim Rouse that when people are exposed to a natural environment as he was as a boy—"the space and scale, the color and texture"—they are uplifted and made to feel comfortable and secure. He called his life as a boy in Easton "lyrical."

> Everything, including school, church, movie theater, post office, the drugstore, and downtown, was within walking distance. We all [except blacks] went to the same schools, shopped at the same stores. Everybody knew each other, and, to a large degree, looked out for each other."[1]

In pre-Civil War Missouri and, in the years before segregation came to an end, on the Eastern Shore, black people were always part of the background. From time to time the young Sam Clemens would catch a glimpse of slavery at its worst. He saw slave auctions on the town dock, and heard the wailing of mothers split by sale from their children or mates. He saw a master, just like that, kill a slave for a petty offense.

Until the last third of the twentieth century, the Eastern Shore, because of its relative isolation, was like a separate state, a Deep South state. Slavery had been as much of a presence on the Eastern Shore as it had been in Georgia or Alabama. That was not the case on the Western Shore, where slavery had been tempered by the voices of abolitionists in nearby Pennsylvania. On Eastern Shore plantations, battalions of slaves worked the crops—wheat, corn, vegetables, tobacco, tomatoes. In 1817 Frederick Douglass, the great African-American writer and abolitionist, was born into slavery on a Talbot County plantation. He was fortunate in being sent to work as a boy in Baltimore and in ultimately getting across the border to Pennsylvania. While Lincoln's Emancipation Proclamation of 1863 freed the slaves of the Confederate states, it was not until a year later that Maryland freed its slaves. But daily life on the Eastern Shore was not much affected. It was possible for a free black to take the ferry across the bay and try to get better-paying or more challenging work, but very few did. Most newly freed blacks continued to do the work they did before the war. Politically, most whites on the Eastern Shore remained with the Democratic Party, because the Republican Party was the party of Lincoln and the black man. Indeed, into the twenty-first century Maryland remained a Democratic stronghold.

When Samuel Clemens became the writer Mark Twain, he was haunted by what he had seen and knew of slavery. Slavery and racial issues turn up in his writing again and again. He saw that while the legal status of black people had changed, they were still subjected to injustice and, in an instant, could become the victims of wanton violence. Twain remembered his boyhood encounters with slavery: "I was not aware that there was anything wrong about it. No one arraigned it in my hearing; the local papers said nothing against it; the local pulpit taught us that God approved it, that it was a holy thing, and that the doubter need only look to the Bible."[2]

As a boy in the 1920s, Jim Rouse encountered black people every day. They worked as servants in his home. They did menial tasks in the shops of Easton. They tended the crops on nearby farms. Near the waterfront they shucked oysters, packed crabs, cleaned and cut fish. When the vegetable and fruit harvests were in, they worked in the canneries. They played a vital role in the economy of the Eastern Shore. But at the end of the workday they went home to barely habitable shanties. He was not aware that there was anything wrong with the black man's working a long and hard day and then going off to an awful place for rest and sleep. The imaginary Huck Finn had as his raft-mate on the Mississippi the escaped slave Jim. The real-life Jim Rouse says that his "earliest and closest friend" was a black boy named Bolton Goldsborough. "We were the same age and we played together all the time. His parents, Ida and George, worked for our family at one time or another."[3] While Rouse says they stayed friends, Talbott County's segregated schools kept the pals apart for most of the day and most of the year.[4]

No one in Easton spoke about segregation, and the papers rarely said anything against it. But there was one exception—H. L. Mencken in Baltimore's morning newspaper *The Sun*. In his seventy-fifth year, Rouse explained that H. L. Mencken had a lot to do with the animosity between Eastern Shore people and Western Shore people. Mencken had a low opinion of the former; they were a good example of what he called the "boobeoisie." "Eastern Shore people did feel some wrath toward the Western Shore and *The Sunpapers*," Rouse said. "

> H. L. Mencken used the Eastern Shore for some of his most cutting sarcasm. At one point, *The Sunpapers* couldn't deliver their papers to the Eastern Shore. A Sunpaper truck was picked up and thrown into the bay when it tried to land from the ferry at Claiborne in Talbot County.[5]

At any rate, there is nothing to indicate that young Jim or his parents ever questioned the system of segregation. But Rouse did say that his father would have been turned off by the idea of integration: "He would have thought it was unnatural and that it couldn't happen. And that's the way most everyone felt about colored people."[6] Never, for example, did a black person take a seat in Easton's Episcopal church, the church the Rouses attended. Thus, the boy Jim Rouse must have stored away quite a few contradictory memories of black life on the Eastern Shore. Those memories played a significant role in Rouse's determination twenty years after leaving Easton to do all he could to improve the lives of Baltimore's blacks.

The Rouses considered themselves Presbyterians. But there was no Presbyterian church in Easton. Jim was not baptized until the family could get over to the Presbyterian church in downtown Baltimore, when Jim was eight. Still, the family faithfully attended Easton's Episcopal church every Sunday. Jim went to its Sunday school, and "learned lessons there about being a Christian that have stayed with me all of my life."[7]

Sam Clemens had a father who was not a ne'er-do-well but came close. He wasn't shiftless but he was unpredictable. He didn't stay in one line of work for very long. When his father died, Sam was twelve; his father's influence on him had been only marginal. Jim Rouse's father was a college graduate, an attorney, a man admired by all who met him. By the time he died when Jim was sixteen, in 1930, he had had a profound influence on his youngest son. He had provided Jim with models of a well-informed citizen, the father of a happy household, and, in general, an exuberant human being. Willard Rouse was a voracious reader. In an age when radio was still primitive and there was no TV, Willard kept up with local, state, and national events through newspapers and journals. He wanted his children to keep up too. In the evening after dinner, father and children would sit around the living room—and discuss. After everyone had gone to bed, he would settle down to his reading. "It was not at all unusual for us to come down in the morning for breakfast and find him still in the living room, still reading."[8]

While the man definitely had his imperfections, young Jim Rouse was unaware of them and loved a father who seemed faultless. The feeling of affection for his father was strong enough to make the athletic, free-spirited Jim, around Christmastime 1928, sit down and write a poem entitled "To Daddy."

> To Daddy
> When Christmas time comes around each year,
> And all of us are filled with cheer
> That's good,
>
> When on Christmas morn we're sitting,
> Talking, joking, splitting
> Our sides with laughter,

II
Then's the time to think of one
　　All of us daughter's sons
　　　　Should think of Dad,

We laud and praise the mother,
　　In poetry, prose, and every other
　　Way we can,

III
Now the mother's quite deserving
　　Of all this praise we're serving
　　　　Out to her

But the father is neglected
　　When the tribute is directed
　　　　To the parents.[9]

Who was this neglected father? He was Willard Goldsmith Rouse, sixty-one at the writing of the poem. Before moving his family to Easton in 1910, Willard had lived most of his life on the western side of the Bay, in Bel Air, the county seat of Harford County, about twenty-five miles north of Baltimore and about the same size as Easton. Born in Cresswell, near Bel Air, on April 4, 1867, Willard was the eldest of seven children fathered by John Goldsmith Rouse, probably Harford County's most successful merchant. John Goldsmith was born in Joppa, Harford County, on March 14, 1844. His father, Christopher Chapman Rouse, was also a wealthy man, having made his money as both a farmer and a merchant. C.C.'s father, John Rouse, immigrated to Maryland from England. The maternal grandfather of John Goldsmith Rouse was a large landowner in Harford County, and at one time clerk of the county court. A brother of JGR, William C. Rouse became a partner in the Baltimore merchant firm of Rouse, Hempstone & Co.[10] With the exception of Jim Rouse's father, the Rouses of northern Maryland at the end of their lives were quite prosperous.

At twenty-one, in 1865, John Goldsmith Rouse, Jim's paternal grandfather, owned a small crossroads store. In 1877, he opened a bigger store in Bel Air, and eventually that store became the biggest in the county, and John Goldsmith became the owner of one of the finest homes in Bel Air. He became a director of the Harford National Bank and also was a director in various building and loan associations; in this, he was somewhat of a forerunner of grandson Jim, who was to make millions as a real estate developer. Jim's mother's sister Daisy became the wife of J. Wilson Richardson. James Wilson Richardson are the given names on Jim Rouse's birth certificate.

Willard Goldsmith Rouse, Jim's father, graduated, in 1887, from Johns Hopkins University in Baltimore. In 1889, he graduated from the law department of the University of Maryland, also in Baltimore. After practicing law in Baltimore for two years, Willard returned to the Bel Air area and formed a law partnership with Richard Dallam. Willard became State's Attorney for Harford County, and his partner later became Maryland's secretary of state.

With his family so rooted in Harford County, Willard's move to the Eastern Shore is puzzling. One reason might have been that Bel Air was too closely associated with loss and sorrow. For Bel Air is where Willard's first wife, Anna Stump Webster, died at the age of twenty-six. Anna had given birth to two children; the boy, John Goldsmith Rouse II, lived to a ripe old age, but the girl, Anna Stump Rouse, did not survive infancy. Her mother, Willard's first wife, died less than a month after giving birth to Anna in July of 1897. A year and a half later, baby Anna died. Within that year and a half, then, Willard lost both his wife and his daughter, and was left with a four-and-a-half-year-old son.

Anna Stump Webster had come from a well-to-do family. Her father prospered as a farmer, and, when he quit farming, became the director of the Mutual Fire Insurance Company in Harford County. Anna died in August of 1897. Willard married again three or four years after Anna's death; his new bride was Lydia Robinson, three years younger than the deceased Anna. The Bel Air wedding of Willard and Lydia was anything but quiet. *The Aegis,* the local newspaper, said that "Owing to the popularity of both bride and groom the edifice [the Union Chapel Methodist Protestant Church] was packed with interested friends."[11] Willard's first child by his second wife was born on August 16, 1902, and named Margaret Robinson Rouse. Two more daughters were born while the couple lived in Bel Air, Lydia and Mary Day. Jim Rouse and his older brother Willard were born in Easton.

Around the end of the nineteenth century, canning became an important industry in Maryland. Harford County and the Eastern Shore were the major centers. Metal containers for preserving food first came into use in the United States in the 1820s. Canning was first done in Harford County in the late 1860s. Over the next hundred years about 100 canneries operated in the county. Easy access to water and also to the populations of Baltimore, Philadelphia, and Wilmington contributed to the success of the industry. The principal crops canned were corn and tomatoes but also beans and fruit. Usually, the canner grew his own crops.[12]

In the archives of the Harford County Historical Society there is an interesting legal document relevant to the connection between Willard G. Rouse, successful lawyer, and canning. The document is a chattel mortgage, dated June 8, 1899. One Alex Smith has become indebted to the firm of Smith [Christian], Rouse & Webster for the sum of $10,091.97. The document states that if that sum is not paid, Smith, Rouse and Webster will be entitled to personal property owned by Alex Smith, specifically a total of 25,350 cases of tin cans to be found at four sites in Harford County: written up as, for example, "3600 cases of 2 lb tin cans, together with wooden cases for same." Obviously Smith, Rouse & Webster believed cash could be had in exchange for the cans—or that one or all of them would have a use for the cans. In 1911, there was an interesting note in *The Aegis* about C. C. Rouse, Willard G. Rouse's one brother:

Mr. C.C. Rouse, when he opened up his cannery a few days ago, having quite a lot of sugar corn and a car load of apples on hand, discovered that his boiler was leaking badly. This was all the more surprising because it had been severely tested a few days before. With his characteristic energy he soon accrued another boiler from Baltimore of undoubted capacity and rushed its installment to a rapid completion. Reports of similar trouble have come to us from several canneries in the county.

In any event, it would seem that almost anyone doing business in Harford County around the turn of the century would have had some contact with the canning industry. Willard G. Rouse, then, did not go cold into the canning business when, in 1910, he moved to the Eastern Shore. He brought a good deal of knowledge with him from his experiences in Harford County.

Twelve years earlier, Willard had learned still another business—soldiering. During 1898, the year of the Spanish American War, Willard was a lieutenant in the Army, in Company D from Harford County. A copy of a newspaper photo in the Columbia Archives shows Willard with two other junior officers sitting in front of their tent at an Army training camp in Atlanta, Georgia. Interestingly, on both sides of the tent stand "colored orderlies." The time is probably less than a full year after the death of his wife. Was the motivation to join the Army primarily patriotism or was it a desire to get away from Bel Air? Willard again served in the Army during World War I.

At the age of forty-four, with his second wife and four children, Willard moved across Chesapeake Bay, from Bel Air to Easton, and became a canning-industry broker. Typically, before a canning season, brokers would lend money to cannery operators so they could buy new equipment, get repairs done, pay their help, and buy fruits or vegetables. The collateral for the loans was the "pack" or possibly the cannery itself or other property, such as cans. If the canner couldn't pay back his loan and the interest on it, the broker would take over the pack and sometimes the cannery. The product would be sold to stores, restaurants, and hotels.[13] Jim Rouse remembered that twice his father tried to corner the canned-tomato market. He bought up all the tomatoes he could all over the East and beyond. Both times "he made a fortune" and both times he lost the fortune "when surplus canned tomatoes were released on the market, sending the prices down."[14]

Willard was in a risky business, dependent on factors that often would be beyond his control—the release of unknown supplies of the product, the regional and national economies, the weather, transportation availability, the honesty of others. For a time Willard made a lot of money. He was able to buy that eight-bedroom house and employ servants. But then much that he made was lost. And while Willard, in 1930, spent months in a Baltimore hospital with terminal cancer of the bladder, bill collectors were constantly calling at the house in Easton. The mortgage on the house went unpaid, the bank foreclosed, and the home the family loved was lost. Jim already had lost his mother. She suffered from chronic heart trouble and had gone back to Bel Air to the care of her parents and siblings. Jim's mother died in February. Willard died in August. During that bad stretch, Jim, finishing high school, lived in an Easton boarding house with his brother Willard. He might have been the only member of the Easton High School class of 1930 who did not have a parent present at graduation.

The sorrow and hardship of that year did not dim Rouse's view of his childhood in Easton. It had been idyllic. The good feelings he had about those years stayed with him all his life. Those memories led to his conviction that people grow best in small communities, communities of 5,000 to 10,000. He thought it important that the dominant forces in people's lives be "within the scale of their comprehension and sense of responsibility." He believed friendships and meaningful relationships are more likely to grow in a village or small town than in a city. On such a scale, people have more support, and self-reliance is promoted. He came to believe, though, that cities could be divided in ways that would produce a small town effect. In its central core, a city could provide the range of services, activities, and culture available only in cities while the support that human beings need would be provided by the smaller place. Baltimore's Village of Cross Keys was to be built to the specifications of a village. Columbia was to be a city, but within it would be neighborhoods and villages.

Chapter 2 Huck on the Chesapeake

1. Autob, 2.
2. Mark Twain's Autobiography, Chapter XIII.
3. Autob, 4.
4. Autob, 4-5.
5. JWR in a letter to his children and other family members, July 7, 1989.
6. Autob, 5.
7. Autob, 3.
8. Autob, 1.
9. "To Daddy," is dated December 23, 1928.
10. The biographical information on the Bel Air years of Willard G. Rouse and on his father John G. Rouse, and on their ancestors and relatives, comes from *Portrait and Biographical Record* (New York: Chapman Publishing Company, 1897), 449-50, 460-62. Additional information comes from *A Rouse Family Genealogy*, done in 1989 by Nancy R. Rouse, wife of John Goldsmith Rouse III. The *Genealogy* can be found in the Harford County Historical Society in Bel Air, Maryland.
11. The copy of *The Aegis* article in the Harford County Historical Society is undated.
12. Margaret S. Bishop, *Canning Industry in Harford County,* Harford Historical Bulletin No. 42, Fall 1989.
13. Information about the canning industry on the Eastern Shore was provided to the author by R. Lee Burton of Cambridge, Maryland.
14. Autob, 1.

Chapter 3
Jim at School

During prosperous times in the Rouse household in Easton, the children were taught by a teacher who came to the home. The teacher was not entirely on her own. The children's mother, Lydia Robinson Rouse, had herself been a teacher and the curriculum that was used was determined by the highly regarded independent Calvert School in Baltimore. Since 1906 the Calvert School has had its faculty prepare home-school materials based on what is done in its classrooms. Its home-school program was esteemed in the early decades of the twentieth century, and continues to be so into the twenty-first. Once they learn about Calvert School Educational Services, most parents who home-school turn to it. Jim Rouse did first grade at home with Calvert materials.[1]

At school, unless he was under very tight discipline, Jim let himself get interested in a lot more about the world than what was being studied in the classroom at any particular time. He learned the basics as well as anyone, but he wasn't devoted to keeping up with his assignments while there was plenty to command his attention in the real world. School records show him to be a slightly better than average student,[2] but he probably knew more than any kid his age in Easton. Not many, if any, of his peers were likely to be found hanging around the Chautauqua encampment that was set up in Easton every summer. A Chautauqua, named after its home city in upstate New York, was a program of lectures and high-brow entertainment. Many years later, in his seventies, Jim Rouse was invited to be a participant. Time pressure made him decline, but the very name Chautauqua was a dip into nostalgia. "Each year Chautauqua came to Easton," Rouse wrote to Chautauqua's president in 1988. The touring group "set up its tent on the school grounds, and provided lectures by great men, shows, and performance of all kinds. It was education, culture, fun of magical proportions to a young boy."[3]

Jim liked to write. His high school compositions show him to be an acute, straightforward observer with some zest for the vivid image. In college, his writing picked up a sophisticated tone. As a businessman, his memos and letters were always carefully considered and flawless in their language and grammar. As a president or chairman of a company, he sometimes commented on, and rejected, the writing of a subordinate in the manner of a stern English teacher.

Jim's school compositions were usually based on what he had seen. In a composition written in high school called "Background That Determines My Individuality," he defines that background in terms of the different groups he saw "gathered in one place talking." One group he called the "Country Politicians." Gathered in a local store was the group he called "the Country Sportsmen." Probably seen in the feed store were the people he called "the farming class." His sharp eyes picked out the "men about town types." He noted that Negroes "are scattered over the entire town and country." The wealthy occupy the big houses along the nearby Miles River. He was tuned in to political party affiliation. There were Republicans in Easton but, given the strong Democratic background of his father and of the whole area, he had the feeling that there was something strange about Republicans. "Democrats are predominant," he wrote. And in the 20s, 30s, and 40s, that was the approximate balance between the two parties in all the states in which enslaved blacks had provided the labor for plantations.

In "My Ancestors," Jim says the Rouses and the Robinsons, his mother's family, had been in America since the seventeenth century. Both grandfathers, he wrote, fought for the Confederacy in the Civil War. While Maryland had many supporters of the Confederacy, the state did not secede from the Union and become a member state of the new nation. One of his grandfathers was only sixteen, Jim wrote with pride and perhaps some envy too, when he "led a small group of cavalry and would have been in command longer but they fell into the hands of the North and were in prison for three weeks, after which my grandfather and one other escaped." Free, they went to the Rouse home and hid there. They wanted to return to the war, but their fathers would not let them. It was not to be too long before Jim overcame this early identification with Confederates.

Jim was the last of five children born to Lydia; three girls were followed by two boys. In "Being the Smallest in a Large Family," Jim says, "being the smallest in a large family is awful." He did not like it when he walked down an Easton street and somebody said to him, "So, you are the baby of the family, aren't you?" It was Jim's intention in this composition to go down the line, from eldest to youngest, and describe each of his siblings, but he did not go that far. He did tell about "Big Brother" John, known to the family as Buddy. Buddy had attended Johns Hopkins University and worked in Baltimore; sometimes he came home for the weekend. When he arrived he would ask his kid brother to take his suitcase upstairs. Jim obliged, but he did not like doing so. He explains why he couldn't refuse: it would be the same as telling your teacher you don't want to do your assignment. In both cases, you would be "laid out." All he says about Big Sister is that she's "a little worse than Big Brother." He moves on to the brother four years older than he—Willard Goldsmith Rouse, Jr,—Bill. Jim says, he's "last of all but far from the least." That's because Bill's "always hitting you or toughing you up as he calls it." Also, he teases all the time. "Lastly, is his everlasting Ideas which you have to carry." [That last word in Jim's text may actually be another word. Jim's handwriting is often hard to decipher; here "carry" seems to be the best guess.] Years later, with the Rouse Company, Bill Rouse was to be Jim's trusted lieutenant. But Bill was still engaged in toughening up Jim, trying to trim his idealism and make him pay more attention to the bottom line. The teacher's comment on "Being the Smallest" is of a kind that Jim probably elicited from most of his teachers: "Your paper is very interesting. If it were written more carefully, how good it would be!"

In late March of 1927, a soon-to-be thirteen-year-old Jim turned in a pile of compositions to his English teacher. In those days, the school year in Eastern Shore counties came to an end in April. One of Jim's compositions called "That's Me" tells about his after-school routine. It is a routine that is heavy on play and light on preparation for the next day at school. After unloading his books at home, Jim is gone until about a quarter after six, often later. When he returns home, the family is already at supper and he is told never to be late again. But "the next day I am later." After supper, for three quarters of an hour, he devotes himself to Algebra, which he hates. He says of the teachers: "If either Mr. Egbertin or Mr. Carpenter would meet me I could shoot him." After Algebra, he sticks to Latin as long as he can. It gets to be a quarter to nine, and he is too sleepy to keep going. He goes upstairs, undresses, and "kicks off" for the night. But he hasn't done his English homework. Oh, that's all right. He'll do the English in the morning. Probably he turned in the pile of compositions all at once at the end of March, because leaving them till morning of the day they were due was a plan that didn't work out too well.

Many of these compositions, including "My Ancestors" and "That's Me," the first and last chapters, are intended to be parts of an autobiography he has been assigned to write. Chapter II is "My Earliest Recollection." True to form, young Jim doesn't try to make himself look good. He tells of being with his mother at the "annual church lawn fete." His mother had volunteered to serve ice cream, no doubt making sure that her Jimmy did not get any until everyone else had been served. The branches of a tree are hanging down over the ice-cream stand, and Jim can't resist seeing whether he can climb to the top. He gets to the top all right, but then he slips and comes tumbling down. He catches a limb, and is saved from breaking a bone or two. He concludes this earliest recollection by saying, "I hope I have learned better by now."

According to two other chapters, ages four and five had their terrors. At age four, Jim experienced his "Narrowest Escape." That occurred when he was sick, and a local doctor said he might have one of three terrible diseases. It turned out that he did have one: infantile paralysis. He was taken to Johns Hopkins

Hospital in Baltimore, where he found himself in a crib with no one around. He wanted his mother and burst out crying. A stern nurse warned the four-year-old that if he didn't stop screaming she would close the door. "I still cried," he wrote, "so she came and closed the door. But I cried all the louder and she got my mother." However, this didn't help much, because Mother was not allowed inside the room. Surely, that constipated nurse would not have lasted very long in any modern hospital. In any event, pre-school Jim ended up spending three months in the hospital. He was learning to deal with adversity and not let it faze him.

When he left the hospital, he had to learn to walk again. "At first I couldn't walk a foot," but he persisted and by walking a few steps more each day he did learn to walk again. Most of the recovery took place in Ocean City, a resort town on the Atlantic, which even today most Marylanders think of as Paradise-by-the Sea. When Jim thinks of how many people are left disfigured by disease, he realizes how lucky he was to be completely cured.

In "My First Day at School," Jim tells of another traumatic experience. After a year of being schooled at home, he was taken by his mother to the public school, "the little building on the corner." His mother insisted on placing him in the second grade, but Jim wanted to go into the first grade with his friend, "practically the only boy I knew at that time." So what did Jim do? "I cried and cried" to be in first grade with Mark. But his mother insisted on second grade, and "I am glad she made me." His consolation was that he was "put in a double seat with another boy and remained there the whole year."

No impairment resulted from these traumas. When he was thirteen, he was mature and composed enough to be aware of the presence of beauty. "Moonlight on the Peach Blossom" is the title of another composition. "Coming over the trees, making a long single shadow of the woods," moonlight on Peach Blossom Creek, Jim says, is one of the most beautiful scenes he has ever experienced. He says further that if you will stand still for a moment, you will feel "a slight wind blowing down the creek making a steady ripple." If a sailboat is on the water, the scene is even more beautiful. In closing, Jim says, "If you have never been then go there some time soon." Here certainly we see the love of nature that was to be expressed in the planning for the city of Columbia.

The love of boats and sailing stayed with Jim all his life. As a boy, he also had exposure to golf and the country club. Caddying, he wrote in "One Way of Earning Money," is a better way for a boy to earn money than working in a store or a factory. On a bright, clear day, he'll get up, "pack my lunch and start off to the country club," stopping on the way at "the five corners" to meet several other boys. When they get to the country club they have to hang around for a while before they are hired. As each car comes up to the club, it is "showered with boys jumping on the running board and yelling, 'Caddy, Caddy Mister'" But half the time a man will step out of the car with a tennis racquet and say, "No thank you son."

The course is nine holes and, Jim explains, "it takes the average player about an hour and a half to go around. Every body gives us at least thirty five cents, most of them, fifty, and some seventy five." Most of the boys will eat their lunches together, and by then will have earned enough "to get a glass of lemonade from the caterer." Jim concludes by stating that on a good day he could make about a dollar. "Last summer, I made about seventy five dollars, and I hope to do the same this summer." Summer work and summer savings. Who could doubt their role in building a strong work ethic?

In another chapter of the assigned autobiography, Jim writes about his strange hobby. His hobby "is to go to college." This was written at a time when other school boys would not think that going on to college was anything like a natural, commonplace progression. His father and his eldest brother have gone to college, and from what Jim hears them say "college life must be wonderful." They have both gone to Johns Hopkins, and while in prep school that is what Jim hoped to do. In the composition, however, he says he wants to go to Princeton. He explains that he wants to go to college for "several big reasons." First, he wants to get an education "which fits me for my later vocation." Also, he wants to meet young men who "may have influence or great importance on me in later life." And "still another is to play the games and sports which are played at college." He is so determined to go to college that if necessary "I will work my way thru."

Of all the sports, Jim likes football best. While some people think football is "unreasonably rough," Jim writes in "On the Gridiron," compared to lacrosse, water polo, or field hockey football is "comparatively mild." But whether football is roughest or not is beside the point. What young Jim appreciates about football is that it requires "wonderfully consistent team work." No touchdowns are scored without teamwork. He also thinks football, at least the college version, is played with "positive fairness." And he concludes, "The fairness and the teamwork aid you thru your life and it's a wonderful college sport." Fairness is important to Jim; if he is to admire a boy, the boy must practice fairness. In another composition, Jim says he has no use for boys who are conceited, loud, spoiled, or "yellow." He likes boys who play all games and sports and are "perfectly fair." Also, a boy shouldn't be afraid and run from others.

In April of 1929, Jim, a junior, is Editor-in-Chief of the high school publication called *The Belfry Bat*. As Editor-in-Chief, he needs to make sure the work of the magazine's contributors makes it to the printer. He's got to organize the whole project and make sure the writers do not procrastinate too long. He's getting practice for being a CEO. But Jim is also a writer. He produces two pieces that clearly reveal the writer and businessman he is to become—"Banking" and "Soft Money."

Here's "Banking."

> The school bank has been far from the success it should be in Easton High School, and its failure is entirely due to the pupils. The bankers have been very efficient and are quite worthy of commendation, but the pupils have been negligent in depositing. There's scarcely a week that you fail to indulge in some luxury such as candy or soft drinks; think how much more sensible it is to

deposit your change and use it for a more extensive education or something really worth while. Think it over and make a deposit next week.

While "Soft Money" also has an economics theme, it is not an exhortation. It is an allegory. The story is about the effects of poverty. All of it is presented below, because it shows its fifteen-year-old author's great empathy and compassion. The young Jim Rouse went on to become an employer and a multi-millionaire, but there was not much change in the sensibility that imagined this story. Also, it should be noted that the story was imagined within six months of the crash that began the Great Depression, when thousands upon thousands of families would find themselves in situations comparable to the one depicted in the story.

SOFT MONEY

Joe Gordie strode easily down Gay Street up the brick walk to his mother's home. He reached the front door and almost automatically inserted his hand in the mail box to secure what ever mail might be there. But mostly he desired the want ad column in the daily paper. His mother, a woman well in the sixties, met him at the door and greeted the 18 year old boy with the same genial smile she had welcomed him with every day for the past few years. "Any luck today, Joey?" She asked with fervent hope spread across her face.

"No, mom, I'm afraid Donovan's succeeded in blacklisting me. I went to Charlie's today but he said he had no use for a kid who argued with his boss. Of course I tried to explain how Don kept cutting my pay but it weren't no use—"

"Joey, repeat that last sentence," his mother demanded.

"But it wasn't any use. That better mom? Well anyway I tried to explain but he just motioned me to the door. Things are looking pretty bad mom, I've just got to get a job."

"Yes, Joey," she agreed, "things are looking pretty black."

"Sammie Fenton said he wanted to see me tonight: he's in the same boat I am. Guess I'll step down there for a while after supper." In a few minutes Joey had finished his light repast so he strolled out the front door and whistled his way to Sammie Fenton's. Sammie greeted him very cordially and invited him inside. Joey accepted and the two young men were very soon enwrapped in a rather serious conversation.

"I don't know what I'm gonna' do Joey," Sammie was saying. "I'm up to my neck in debts and I haven't gotta' cent."

"Mom and I are eating but I don't know for how long," Joey responded.

"We're each getting five a week from the fire company but that just buys me food and cigarettes," said Sammie. "I'm almost tempted to rob."

"Sammie, that's just what I came to see you about. We could pull the bank job and get a coupla' grand apiece. As soon as we finished we could quit and no one would be the wiser."

"I'll think it over and let you know in the morning, Joe," said Sammie. In a minute Joey rose and went home.

The loud moaning of a siren woke the residents of Morristown and in a moment the whole sky looked ablaze. The people ran like mad to the burning building and crowded and pushed and fought their way until there were several hundred people assembled in a noisy mob.

But at the other end of town two very young men were seen climbing through the broken window of the third national bank with a revolver in the right hand of each. The two boys had just gotten successfully inside when a commanding voice at the window hollered.

"Come out now Buddy or get drug out later. Come easy and I'll take you easy; resist and I'll give you the works."

The two boys simultaneously dropped to the floor.

"Come now or I'll shoot," commanded the voice.

"1-2-3." Bang! Bang! Bang! The cop fired; bang! He fired again. A second later the lights flashed on and the cop was standing over two twitching bodies. One turned over and said,

"Tell—mom—I had to—try something. Tell her not to forget—dad had my life—insured before he died and tell her—to get a coupla' grand—outa' that." The face drew up, turned perfectly white and Joey Gordie dropped to the floor dead. Sammie couldn't stir."

The following year, as a senior, Jim produced for his English class an outstanding 1,000-word theme entitled "Censorship." Journalism was a career he occasionally thought about, and so censorship was a topic that interested him. A good portion of this paper consists of an exposition of the history of censorship in France as opposed to the relative freedom of the press in England. Here's a crucial paragraph:

> At the same time in England the existing situation was not nearly so bad. The church courts still existed and they could punish laymen for not attending church, for heresy, and for certain immoral acts. But their powers were little exercised compared with the clergy on the continent. Moreover one who published a book or pamphlet did not have to obtain the permission of the Government, as in France. In fact, nowhere was there such unrestrained discussion of Scientific and Religious matters, at this period, as in England. Now, it can readily be seen why England made such advancements in science at this time for all other Nations were burdening under the severe censorship of the Clergy and Court.

And here's the paragraph with which Jim concludes:

> "Will there ever be free speech or free press? NO! not as long as 84% of all the news printed is publicity, not as long as every politician has a publicity agent, and not as long as these unnecessary boards of censors continue to dictate what is fit to satisfy our desires."

Jim's writing here is strong. In other pieces, he shows himself as a boy with keen senses of humor and irony. While the censorship paper received an A, the grade in English for the year was B, probably due to a lack of interest in being a proofreader.

The big Rouse home had a two-acre garden, and Jim and big brother Bill were required to work it, planting, weeding, and finally harvesting. On summer mornings they would be up early to pick radishes, beets, and string beans to sell to the nearby grocer. Sometimes they would sell the very vegetables their mother was counting on for dinner, and she would have to go out and buy them back from the grocer. At the Talbot Country Club, he earned enough money caddying so that he could buy himself a bicycle. When he was thirteen he and Bill took summer jobs in a cannery. They were there from seven in the morning until six at night and hated the work. Jim worked at a corn-husking machine, and to fight boredom "I used to stand there making political speeches," the content of which he learned from his father.[4]

When he wasn't working he sailed, fished, played in ballgames on the home's large front lawn, and sometimes read under a big oak tree. At Easton High, in addition to editing and writing for *The Belfry Bat*, he was on the basketball and track teams. That he also was elected president of his class, the student council, and the athletic association testifies to how popular a boy he was. This was an outgoing, cheerful, energetic, independent boy, an athlete and a scholar, with a great zest for life.

As the youngest child, Jim might have received even more love from his parents than their other children did. They supplied him with everything he might want or need, and abundance of freedom. The Easton community had the highest regard for the Rouse family. Something about the father, though, made the family somewhat less than perfect. Family lore has it that Willard G. Rouse drank to excess and was a drug abuser. According to Jim Rouse's son Winstead "Ted" Rouse, his grandfather had to resort to heroin to ease the pain of an injury suffered during his service in World War I. Ted has said that his father told him that Willard frequently nodded off during dinner. Ted has speculated that his exposure to Willard's heroin use had a great effect on his father and made him particularly sympathetic to others who got caught up in drug addiction. There are stories about men having to be sent across the bay to Baltimore to bring Willard home after a drinking binge.[5] When the adult Jim tells about finding his father downstairs in the morning after reading through the night, one might ask whether the night was spent with a book or a bottle—or both.

Jim Rouse remembered his mother as a spirited, active woman who presided over a household that, in Jim's words, "was a house party an awful lot of the time." He described life in that household as "big living in a small-town way." But Jim had his mother for only fifteen years. Lydia Rouse died on February 17, 1930. In its front-page obituary, *The Star Democrat*, the Talbot County weekly, said,

> Her appealing personality made her an outstanding favorite; and her home became noted for its genuine hospitality and for the emphasis it placed upon those duties and phases of life that create higher values. . . . It is difficult to think of anyone whose loss would be more keenly felt.

His father had been in Baltimore's Union Memorial Hospital for nine months when he died on August 31, 1930. About Willard G. Rouse, *The Star Democrat*'s obituary said,

> He was an unusual combination of determination, forcefulness and gentleness. A man of unfailing integrity and of outstanding mental alertness and ability, he was a leader in any group or gathering in which he found himself. He truly possessed personal charm. . . . He truly possessed great public spirit, displayed keen interest in all affairs affecting the County, the State and the Nation: and cheerfully and wholeheartedly contributed the ability that he possessed to the solving of every civic problem that confronted the community.

Sixteen-year-old Jim had not had either of his beloved parents involved in his life for the better part of a year. After Jim graduated from high school in April, he lived without family in a boarding house. And there was so little money. His married older siblings helped—but not much. His half-brother, John Goldsmith Rouse, nineteen years older than he, got married in May, between the deaths of the parents. In those days there was no health insurance. When an office visit was made or when the doctor came to the house, the custom was to hand him his fee. The hospital and medical bills Willard and Lydia ran up must have been considerable. Willard was the breadwinner, and he had not able to conduct his business. It fell to brother Bill to provide for Jim. But in those early Depression years, Bill, who had started college at Johns Hopkins and then had to drop out for lack of money, was having a hard time keeping himself afloat.

Not long before his own death, Jim Rouse looked back and wrote about this period. His reaction to the deaths of his parents was different from what might have been expected. "I was not torn apart," he said, "by sorrow or feelings of desertion." His parents had been sick and home had been different for so long that he felt ready for whatever might happen. "I can remember," he said, "feeling 'This is good for me, a honing for life.' I had been put on my own at a very early age, but I had been prepared by a loving and caring family. I knew I could make it."[6]

Chapter 3 Jim at School

1. Autob, 2.
2. Jim's academic record at Easton High School, his scores on the examinations of the College Entrance Examination Board, and his record at The Tome School are at CA in the boxes with personal materials.
3. JWR letter to Daniel L. Bratton, 21 November 1988.
4. Autob, 3.
5. Ted's remarks about his grandfather are in the obituary for JWR in *The Sun,* April 10, 1996.
6. Autob, 5-6.

Chapter 4
A Poor Relation

Brother Bill, only four years older, became Jim's surrogate father. Bill wanted to do the right thing by Jim, but times were tough. Bill was fortunate to have a job, with the Easton branch of a Baltimore investment-banking firm. He had gotten the job in 1928 and managed to keep it through the immediate aftermath of the stock market crash of October 1929. But in 1931 the firm went out of business. At a time when the country was in the Depression free fall, Bill decided to start his own insurance business. He earned enough to hold on, but there were severe limits on what he could do for his kid brother.

When Jim graduated, his high school record was completely lacking in distinction. He had completed twenty-four year-long units. For thirteen of those units he received a grade of C. While he made three Ds in Latin and French, for three years he made Bs in English. He had seven Bs altogether but there is not a single A on the transcript. In mid-June he took the exams of the College Entrance Examination Board. The scores were mediocre.

The mediocre academic record posed a big problem. Bill was determined that Jim go to college at Johns Hopkins. Because he was a year ahead and because his high school grades were not good enough for Hopkins, it was decided that Jim would go to prep school and then apply to Hopkins. The Tome School in Port Deposit, Maryland, a town on the Susquehanna River, was the place for Jim. Students who were there for two years went on to Yale, Princeton, Dartmouth, Michigan, Virginia, and other top schools. At Tome, during the school year of 1930-31, Jim's school pattern remained the same: mediocre in the classroom, excellent in extra-curricular activities. At Tome, Jim's classmates were wealthier than the more mixed group at Easton High, but Jim had no difficulty getting along. He was on the track, soccer, basketball, and debating teams and worked on the school newspaper and yearbook. Bi-weekly reports of

Jim's grades were sent to Bill. On one was the notation, "Out of room after lights—10 demerits." On another, "Inattentive and disorderly in mathematics class—5 demerits."

Jim was on Tome's track team, and the team made it to the Penn Relays in Philadelphia. There a memorable event occurred.

> After running the one-mile relay [Jim wrote years later] four of us were full of sweat and dirt and headed for the locker room to get a shower. But when we stepped into the shower, there were four black athletes already there. We had never been in that situation and were not prepared for it. Without any discussion or thought, the four of us got dressed and went on.[1]

Jim and his teammates acted as they thought they were supposed to. Obviously, the incident had an impact on Jim; he still remembered it after fifty years. In all probability he remembered it on numerous occasions during those years. His growing empathy for blacks suggests that he came to understand how the black athletes at the Relays must have felt to have whites refuse to shower where they had.

During his stay at Tome, Jim "was very aware of not having the money that everyone else had." He didn't even have the money to buy his track shoes; his sister Dia in Chicago sent him money for the shoes. He later claimed that he didn't feel ashamed of not having money but missed not being able to take advantage of the opportunities that money brought.[2] Bill had undertaken to pay Jim's tuition and other expenses at Tome. But Bill was strapped. He had great difficulty keeping up with Jim's bills. In May of 1931, Bill, in Easton, received a letter from the school's director: "I note there is still a balance of $122.33 on James' account. I must ask you to let us have a check for this before the end of the week in order that he may finish out his year. We cannot let tuition arrears run beyond June 1st."[3] Bill responded with a check for $50.

In the worst way, Bill wanted Jim to get a second year at Tome. The school's director, too, wanted him back. But Bill's financial situation did not allow it. Bill then hoped that the one year at Tome would make Jim look better to Hopkins. A few days after receiving the dunning letter, Bill wrote to the director and asked him to send a letter of recommendation for Jim to Hopkins, "as I am trying to get him a Trustee's Grant."[4] Bill also wrote to Jim, trying to make him appreciate all that was at stake.

> I hope that you won't allow your outside interests to take more of your time than they should. I know it is awfully hard not to, particularly in the spring. The way things look now I would plan to take the College Boards [again], if you desire not to later OK. But, don't let up any on your studying particularly French. Best of luck to you in the race on Saturday and in your studies for this last term, please don't slack up any.[5]

Money for college was not available. But Jim found a way. If he could get to Hawaii and live with his sister Mary Day, who was married to a Navy lieutenant based at Pearl Harbor, then, as a Navy dependent, he could attend the University of Hawaii for a minimal tuition. In early summer Jim hooked up with two friends of brother Bill, Wink Marshall and Al Holland, who had a car and were driving to San Diego. They went by way of Bristol (Virginia), New Orleans, Corpus Christi, and El Paso. In a long letter from Hawaii written to his oldest sibling, half-brother Buddy (John Goldsmith Rouse II), Jim described the lark of a trip. About the stop in New Orleans, he says: "We spent three days in New Orleans and had a swell time went to a lot of 5 cents a dance halls; drove all over the city; visited the French quarters; and saw the Levy [sic] etc."[6] When they left, they drove continuously for forty-five hours, "stopping in El Paso with a broken radiator and other miner [sic] injuries to the car." Once started again, they made it to San Diego "in the next 24 hours." Jim then hitchhiked to San Francisco, where he boarded the Matson Line's *Sonoma,* bound for Honolulu. To his surprise the *Sonoma* went down the coast to Los Angeles, where he could have boarded without going to San Francisco had he known the ship's itinerary.

On the *Sonoma,* for his $60 ticket, he was assigned to steerage. For meals one drinking glass was provided for twenty people. All twenty steerage passengers ate at one table, and each meal was exactly the same, "some kind of meat covered with a black gravy." The bathroom was "a three-hole non-flushing john that was flushed only by the action of the ship bringing on water and taking it away." On the first day he found his bunk loaded with bedbugs, and for eleven nights slept on a coil of rope on deck. The trip was "a humbling experience."[7]

By October 27th, Jim was enrolled at the University of Hawaii. In the letter of that date to Buddy, he says, "The college is pretty good out here," and "I have arranged my course as nearly as possible to coincide with the Freshmen [sic] year requirements at Hopkins." He has been doing "a lot of writing on the side such as book reviews and a few essays and I intend to write a Short Story very soon." He soon was on the staff of the school paper and wrote a weekly sports column called "The Day's Dope." The column deals with mainland sports, and is surprisingly mature for a seventeen-year-old. With his tone of casual sophistication, Jim sounds a lot like *The New Yorker's* Roger Angell.

The year is 1931, Joe Louis is not yet on the scene, and the heavyweight boxing champion is Germany's Max Schmeling, who has just contracted to fight Jack Sharkey. Sportswriter James W. Rouse doesn't think much of this match-up.

> Schmeling will be too good for Sharkey—that's my guess. The German may not be a popular champion but even his critics have to admit he is good. He flashed real form against Stribling in the Cleveland fight and Stribling wasn't any push-over then. He licked Stribling on his stamina and aggressiveness. Sharkey is very little better than Stribling. The Gob is 34 now with his best fighting days behind him.
>
> The German is fast, clever and aggressive; he will force the fight the whole way and will pile up a winning margin in the last few rounds when the

old in and outer Sharkey is badly battered. He may not win by a knockout but the decision will be decisive.⁸

With this succinct, knowing style, the young Rouse also sounded a lot like the young Ernest Hemingway, whose short stories often featuring boxers or other tough characters might have been read by Jim.

Later in the school year our sports pundit also had an opinion on the heavyweight champion of baseball.

> Speaking of the Yankees there is the perpetual question of Babe Ruth's contract. Everyone knows that Ruth will be in the Yankee lineup this year and every year until he is so old and feeble that the fans stop going to see him perform. Jacob Rupert [Yankee owner] isn't going to let any other team grab his biggest star and drawing card. But all this discussion over his contract makes good publicity. It keeps the "Babe's" name before the fans and makes larger crowds come through the turnstiles in April and May.⁹

Had Jim Rouse seriously gone after a job in journalism, he undoubtedly would have risen to the top of the profession.

By the time the first semester at Hawaii was over, Jim was thinking about possibilities in journalism. He wrote a letter to Bill pleading to be allowed to take the spring semester off because it was such a hardship on Bill to support him. He reminded Bill that a "Mr. Shehan once said he could get me a job on the Balto Sun as long as Mark Watson and John Owens were editors of the Sunday and daily papers. I write good articles and I know I could do something on a paper." The immediate problem is that Jim needs $34 to enroll for the second semester, and he knows Bill can't afford it. So he proposes to Bill that he take the semester off and work. He says he could "probably make enough in 6 months to go a long way towards the money necessary for next year at Hopkins." He knows Bill won't accede. "Of course you immediately say, No! No! Never!" Jim then pleads to be heard out: "But just follow me." He goes on to rebut all the arguments he thinks Bill will make against dropping out for the semester.¹⁰ In the end, Bill must have come up with the money, because Jim did stay in school.

It was in the second semester that Jim produced an outstanding term paper on New York's Boss Tweed. The power of the paper, submitted on June 5, 1932, is well conveyed by the first and last paragraphs.

> Standing out as the most vivid and at the same time most grotesque example of that strange creature of our political system, the "Boss,"' is William Marcy Tweed. Probably there has never been in the history of our country a demagogue with power so great, control so complete or range of activity so extended. At one time he completely dominated the entire government of the State of New York—the executive, legislative and judicial. His word was law—his disapproval a veto.

There is real outrage in this paper, even more so at the end, after Tweed's career has been described. "Tweed never intentionally made a move for the benefit of anyone but Tweed." That's something Rouse might have offered about Donald Trump if he'd been asked for an opinion. Tweed, he goes on,

> never did a good deed without counterbalancing it with something wicked and nefarious. He was a great man in the measurement of his power and a genius in his abilities as a politician but the only good which came from his reign was a temporary horror of corrupt politicians with which the voters were inspired. A thief—a low, mean, groveling thief, was William Marcy Tweed—May his death be a long one.

After exams, on June 20th, Jim wrote home to sister Margaret.[11] With the completion of the school year, his plans were uncertain. He and a friend—"a boy named MacDonald from Nutley, N.J."—have been trying to get jobs on a ship so they can start on a journey around the world. But the competition with real seamen who are unemployed is too much, so they've given up on that idea. Now Jim has set another goal: to get a job on a ship that will get him back to the mainland, for he has been spending hours dreaming of being back in Maryland. "I'll get back if I have to swim—even then I'd have to walk the continent," he says. Bill had been sending him occasional checks while school was on, but there's no money for transportation home. Still, Jim is undaunted and looks back on a good year: "After all in every bunch of roses there's a thorn or two and this past year certainly has been like one Gargantuan bunch of roses for me. It really is the most marvelous year I have ever spent." He's found Hawaii to be "a land of transcendental beauty . . . a paradise—a taste of heaven."

But there's more to Hawaii than its beauty. "It is probably the most cosmopolitan town in the world," Jim's letter goes on. "It's a great thing to go to school with Hawaiians, Orientals, Hindus, (I walked to school every morning with two princes from India), Portugese [sic] and sprinklings of many other nationalities, Races, and religions." Later, he said of the Hawaii experience,

> Making friends with Hawaiians, Japanese, Chinese and students of other nationalities made the divisions in the world seem aimless to me. On campus there seemed to be little separation or division between people based on race or nationality nor was there much, if any, in the social life of the island.[12]

In the Columbia Archives is the draft of a Rouse essay that, unfortunately, is not dated. But it is filed with other material from the years Jim was in college and it sounds like a college essay. In the essay, Jim describes two men who are sick and near death. One is a friend in his seventies hospitalized with heart trouble; the other is his dying father. On a visit to the former, Jim is turned off by the man's attitude. To Jim that attitude came across most clearly after he reported that a friend of the sick man missed him. The response given Jim was a whining, "What good does that do me!" Jim says, "As I left his room I could not help but think, 'Therein lies the Curse of Selfishness'. . . . The direction of his thinking was so fundamentally in terms of self that when that self met difficult circumstances which could not apparently be corrected his world collapsed."

On the other hand, there is Jim's father, whom Jim recalls visiting about six months into his long, last hospitalization. Willard, in the hospital with a terminal illness, made business plans and took an interest in world affairs. "He did not consider life worthless," Jim says. "His world had not collapsed. His world involved something more than self." Jim is quite sure about what these two encounters mean: "Sooner or later selfishness must bring unhappiness in overwhelming proportion to any temporary pleasures which it may provide. And this is true not because of any mystic visitation or design of fate. It is true because of the nature of man." There are the selfish and there are the unselfish, and seventeen-year-old Jim Rouse has decided he does not like being in the presence of the selfish.

Jim managed to find a spot on a Navy transport bound for the East Coast by way of the Panama Canal. He must have had very little money with him, because Mary Day's husband anticipated he could get stuck somewhere with no money. William Lee Pryor, a lieutenant (jg) in the Navy wrote a "To Whom It May Concern" note for Jim to carry with him.

> This is to certify that James Wilson Rouse, my brother-in-law, is of sound mind, honest and capable, and that any reasonable and necessary expenses incurred by him in an emergency will be borne by me. Anyone wishing to verify his identity can communicate with me or with Willard G. Rouse of Easton, Maryland, his brother.[13]

It was the summer of 1932, and the Olympics were taking place in Los Angeles. During his ship's ten-day layover in Los Angeles, Jim managed to get a job with someone doing business inside LA's Coliseum. He managed to see almost all the Olympic events. In the fall, he was able to continue college, now at the University of Virginia, because his sister Margaret's husband, William Balch, in politics and having lots of contacts, helped him get a scholarship for tuition. He got a job serving meals at a student boarding house, and Bill sent him $10 a week for his room rent. In the classroom, he took the same six courses through the fall, winter, and spring quarters. Two of the courses were in Government, "Principles and Problems" and "European Governments." For the fall quarter he received a grade of 97 in both; for the rest of the year, the Government grades continued in the 90s. He took Greek during all three quarters, and the grades were in the 80s. His grades were so good overall that he was on the Dean's List for the second and third terms.

On January 20, 1933, Bill, on a letterhead of the United States Guarantee Company, wrote to Jim, care of Mrs. Pilkenton on Madison Lane, in Charlottesville. Enclosed is a check for $15. Bill apologizes for being late with the check but explains that "I did not realize that you were back in your rent." Some bad feeling has slipped into the relationship between Bill and Jim, and Bill puts the blame on his own procrastination, "one of my most prominent faults." Jim apparently again had been expressing reservations about continuing in school while there was so little money. But Bill insists he wants no change in course.

> I regret that you thought my last letter extremely formal and very curt. I was probably taking the privilege of an older brother in writing you when I had something else on my mind. We did *not* make a great mistake and you are exactly where you should be; at school working your fool head off and getting the best possible grades.

Bill wrote again on March 4th. This letter has a much broader context. For one, this was the day on which Franklin Delano Roosevelt was inaugurated for his first term as President; the 20th Amendment moving Inauguration Day up to January 20th had just been passed but would not go into effect until after the next inauguration. Secondly, Bill alludes to the banking crisis that is gripping the country, with various states finding ingenious ways to allow banks not to open. Bill tells Jim, who has been expecting a check for his room rent: "I will not be able to send you any money until the banks open, if then, as they may only pay us a part of our deposits." This letter, which is on the letterhead of The Union Central Life Insurance Company, says further, "We are still selling insurance and expect to continue to. If money is so tight that people can not pay us it just means that the companies will have to wait." About Jim's immediate need, Bill explains: "I can send you a check to pay your room rent, if your landlady would care to hold it, but it will be no good to her and would merely act as a promise to pay."

When the spring quarter ended, Jim left for Baltimore. He had had it with being dependent on Bill's checks. He had had enough with being poor. He had done his time in steerage. Or, to look at it another way, for eleven days on that voyage to Hawaii he had lived in a floating slum, and he hated it. He was determined to do whatever he had to do to never again be without money. But that did not mean he would chase after all the money he possibly could. That did not mean he would have nothing to do with people who weren't as well equipped as he was to pursue money. He wanted to make money, but he would not bring on himself the curse of selfishness.

He wanted to make money, but he also wanted to continue his education. He decided night law school was the answer. He could attend classes at night and work during the day. He could get into law school because in those days law schools required only two years of college. He was confident he could see his plan through, but finding work wouldn't be easy. "When I arrived in Baltimore that summer to look for work," Jim wrote later, "twenty-five percent of the workers in America were unemployed and thirty-five percent of the dwellings were in foreclosure." In that year, 1933, he remembered, more houses burned than were built.[14]

After walking the streets for days, Jim finally found a job parking cars at a garage on St. Paul Street. He didn't know how to drive but succeeded in persuading the manager to teach him. Looking back, Jim attributed his good fortune in finding work to one of FDR's pieces of New Deal legislation. The National Recovery Act encouraged businesses to reduce employees' workweeks and raise their wages. If they did that, they could display a blue eagle in their windows, and people were encouraged to do business only with places displaying the eagle. St. Paul Garage reduced its workweek from sixty-five to fifty-four hours and raised its pay to $13.50 a week. That created two more jobs, and Jim got one of them.[15]

When he went over to the University of Maryland Law School on Baltimore's west side, the dean, Roger Howell, did not like his plan. Jim was told it would be better to work and save and get established than to frantically work and study. But again Jim was persuasive. He said that if he followed the dean's plan he doubted he could maintain the discipline school required. If he didn't start law school right away, he never would. Then there was the matter of the tuition. The dean offered this deal: pay $100 down and pay off the rest at $5 a week.[16] Jim crossed the bay and went to see the president of the Easton National Bank, who was a family friend. Now nineteen, he was not old enough to legally sign a promissory note, but he got the $100 loan anyway. "That was the kind of thing a small-town independent bank could do. It made a big difference to my future."[17]

In his second semester of law school Jim found he still needed Bill's help. In answer to a request from Jim, Bill wrote that he wanted to make Jim eligible to borrow money from banks. On March 10, 1934, Bill sent Jim a check for $25, but he also sent a bank note form "to cover this loan." Bill says he will discount the note at the Easton National Bank, to which Jim should send his payments. Of course, Bill will make the payments if Jim cannot. Bill explains that "it is excellent business for a young man to borrow money by this means, when he can take care of his obligations as they come due." And indeed when in 1936 Jim applied to the Easton bank for another loan of $100, the bank was happy to oblige.

After his first few months at St. Paul Garage, Jim's job was changed from parking cars to auditing the account books. Then the regular auditor left and Jim began to work two shifts, from midnight through to 4 pm. For seven months, he worked more than 100 hours a week and still made his law school classes on three evenings. He would get to the classroom, close his eyes, and fall into a deep sleep for five minutes. He worked hard but he had no complaints. He had discovered how much endurance he had and how much he was capable of. The one negative consequence of the double-shift work and study routine was that he became a life-long workaholic.

After a little over a year at the garage, Jim found another job, as a result of persuading his Eastern Shore congressman to go to bat for him. He became a legal clerk in the Baltimore office of the Federal Housing Administration, which only recently had been created by New Deal legislation. One of the purposes of

.the FHA was to prevent foreclosures. In this time of high unemployment and economic slack, many families, like the Rouse family, had lost their homes or were in danger of losing them. The FHA provided an opportunity to refinance. It also would guarantee loans that qualified applicants made for the purchase of a new home or repair of an existing one. Jim Rouse moved up quickly in the Baltimore office of the FHA, becoming the senior clerk in just three months. He saw a bottleneck in the process that led from FHA application to the actual granting of a loan by a lender. As he went from banker to banker trying to persuade them to make loans that would be guaranteed by the federal government, he met almost automatic resistance. But when he had the opportunity to walk bankers through the FHA process, they would usually loosen. More loans were made by the banks, and the local FHA office was able to help more people. Jim Rouse was building a reputation among bankers and within the FHA.[18] When, after he had been with the Baltimore office for sixteen months, the agency needed a representative on the Eastern Shore, Jim got the assignment. He would spend Tuesdays and Thursdays in Salisbury helping with the paperwork and getting banks to approve loans. Jim Rouse was on his way to a career as a mortgage and a housing specialist.

Despite working full-time, Jim did well as a law student. The dean invited him to be a founding member of the Order of Coif, law schools' equivalent of Phi Beta Kappa. Late in 1937, he took and passed the state bar examination. The road had not been easy. Left to his own devices, he would have dropped out of school and tried to support himself. That would not necessarily have been a bad decision. Regardless of the extent of his formal education, someone with the personality, character, values, ambition, and power of persuasion of Jim Rouse—a young man bursting with exuberance—would have found ways to do things valuable both to himself and to mankind. But brother Bill kept cajoling and kept those checks coming, and Jim established good bank credit and he became a lawyer.

Jim Rouse never was admitted to Johns Hopkins University; instead, he got admitted to the FHA. In 1971, Hopkins' vice president for university affairs, pleased to be able to refer to James W. Rouse as Jim, sent him a copy of a book just published by the Johns Hopkins Press, *Open Land for Urban America*. He proudly told Jim the book had a section on Columbia, the city he had built. The irony got even sweeter in 1978 when Rouse was invited to be a member of the Hopkins board of trustees. And sweeter still in 1985, when Hopkins gave Rouse the honorary degree *Doctor of Humane Letters*, and Rouse gave the commencement address.

Looking back after he had made millions, Rouse said his life between 1930 and 1937 simply evolved, with one step leading to the next. He wanted to make the point that there was no dramatic transformation: "This was no Paul on the road to Damascus kind of thing. . . . It was just a natural growth of the road that I was on. . . . I was conditioned in a way that accounted for my life." There really was no such inevitability. True enough, the deaths of his parents had prepared him for further adversity. But the road he was on would have been a very different one if it weren't for the help of Bill. The road might also have been different if he didn't have the example of Bill earning his living by dealing with money.

Chapter 4 A Poor Relation

1. Autob, 5.
2. Autob, 6.
3. Letter from Murray P. Brush to Willard Rouse, May 25, 1931, in box with JWR's personal correspondence.
4. Letter from Willard Rouse to Murray P. Brush, May 28, 1931.
5. Letter from Willard Rouse to JWR, May 31, 1931.
6. JWR letter to John Goldsmith Rouse II, October 27, 1931.
7. Autob, 7.
8. "The Day's Dope," February 18, 1932.
9. "The Day's Dope," March 19, 1932.
10. JWR letter to Willard Rouse, January 16, 1932.
11. She is married at this point, and her full name is Margaret Robinson Rouse Balch.
12. Autob, 7.
13. Written for JWR at Pearl Harbor, July 16, 1932.
14. Autob, 8.
15. Autob, 8.
16. Autob, 9.
17. Autob, 9.
18. Autob, 10.

Chapter 5
The Ace

Working for the FHA made Jim feel connected to the whole New Deal. He was proud to be a Democrat. The Democrats in Washington were making over the country, and as an FHA employee he was a member of the team. His work for the FHA had thoroughly familiarized him with the mortgage business—with borrowing large amounts of money and paying back in small parts. "There was a real business here," he thought.[1] This was an outlet for Jim's exuberance.

In March 1936 he went to see a man who was a family friend from Easton. Guy T.O. Hollyday was on the board of the Title Guarantee and Trust Company. Guy Hollyday listened to Jim Rouse's proposal that Title Guarantee start a mortgage department that would specialize in making FHA loans. Later that spring Jim, at twenty-two, was hired to head Title Guarantee's new mortgage department. He was paid $3,000 a year.[2] As a newly minted lawyer he would have earned about $1,200. But the attraction of the mortgage business was more than money. He loved working with the people. Most of his clientele were working-class families for whom a house would be the centerpiece of their lives. He would take mortgage applications out to their homes and sit with them at the kitchen table. He found what he was doing enormously gratifying. He was helping people get into a home of their own.[3]

And as always he had the knack for finding a way to go one better in achieving his goal. He brought in insurance companies to buy the mortgages made by Title Guarantee. Title Guarantee became mortgage correspondents for Security Life of New York, National Life of Vermont, and others. They bought mortgages, and the money received was used for new mortgages. He had been with Title Guarantee less than a year when he met Hunter Moss, who had been working in commercial real estate, financing stores and office and apartment buildings. In the spring of 1939, with $20,000 put up mostly by Moss's sister, the two started their own mortgage banking business.[4]

Jim Rouse was in business. But his attitude was different from what would have been the attitude of most young men in his place. While he certainly wanted the business to be profitable, he saw the business as also having a higher purpose. He thought of the individual business as holding a license from society to pursue profit only to the extent that the pursuit also satisfied real human needs. He saw profit as the reward a business receives for providing a useful product or an important service. "The way to find new opportunities in business is to discover the needs and yearnings of people. The way to prosper in business is to do that extremely well."[5]

Within two years Moss-Rouse was servicing more than $8 million of mortgages, mostly FHA guaranteed. Given that most banks at the time did not care to get involved with the FHA, this was quite an accomplishment. Also, relationships had been established with two more large insurance companies, Continental American Life and Connecticut General. Churchill G. Carey came to Baltimore as the area representative for Connecticut General. He became friends with both Moss and Rouse, and in 1941 he was persuaded to join their company. But before leaving his old company, Carey recommended to an associate, Paul Swett, that Moss-Rouse become a correspondent for Connecticut General. Over the years Connecticut General was to become Rouse's primary lender.

With December 7, 1941, America entered World War II. Two months later, Rouse applied for a commission in the U. S. Naval Reserve. One of his recommendations was written by Edward L. Palmer, Jr., president of Title Guarantee. Among other things, Palmer wrote

> Mr. Rouse is a young man who has achieved a very remarkable success solely by virtue of his own efforts, industry and tireless application, coupled with keen intelligence and strength of character.... He maintains a breadth of outlook, reads widely, is interested in and familiar with public events, particularly those affecting international trends. Socially, he has a pleasing manner and personality and makes friends readily and receives their cooperation.[6]

When Rouse was accepted as an officer in the Naval Reserve as an Aviation Volunteer Specialist, a newly created military occupation specialty, the main concern at Moss-Rouse became very simple: keeping the company alive and functioning through the war years. Along with both Rouse and Moss, most of the company's men would soon be in the service. The previous May, Rouse had married Elizabeth Jameson Winstead, whom he had met three years before while parking cars at St. Paul Garage. On July 4, 1942, their daughter Lydia Robinson, later called Robin, was born. Before leaving in August for his training, Rouse drew up papers arranging for the survival of the company if either he or Hunter Moss was killed or if both were killed. In a letter to Moss, which he asked Moss also to sign, he says that in the event of the death of either of them, the balance in their business account would go to the other, with the stipulation that the widow of the deceased would receive half of the balance. In a letter to Elizabeth, he lays out what he wants her to do if Moss was to die first and he was to die subsequently. If that was to happen, Elizabeth would find herself in control of their company. Rouse expresses the wish that the Moss-Rouse Company be continued because of the obligation he feels to the people employed by the company. If both partners were to be killed in the war, Harry Batchelor, the middle-aged executive hired to keep the company running, would be left in charge of the company. In that event, Rouse asks his wife to confer with Mr. Batchelor and the other employees before disposing of her stock or liquidating the company. He writes, "I am particularly anxious that you give Mr. Batchelor every opportunity to make arrangements for the purchase of the stock himself in the event you decide to offer it for sale and if the price which he is willing and able to pay equals that which you can obtain elsewhere." In these letters we see the workings of the lawyer's mind, his concern that his wife be properly provided for, and the responsibility that he feels for the people who work for him.[7]

After training at naval bases at Quonset Point, Rhode Island, and Jacksonville, Florida, Rouse was shipped to Hawaii. To kill time on the ten-day voyage to Hawaii, Rouse and his fellow officers played a lot of cards. Rouse played in 25-cent poker games and penny-a-point bridge. He was reluctant to get into the bridge games because he didn't have much money. But the officer who invited him to play said he didn't have to worry: "It doesn't matter. I've been watching you play. You'll win."

On the ship Rouse and his friends played bridge every night until two or three in the morning. By the time the ship arrived in Hawaii, Rouse had won over $700—about the price of a new car then. Six months or so after arriving in Hawaii, Rouse was made personnel officer of Fleet Air Wing II and soon after became the manager for all enlisted personnel in Naval Air throughout the Pacific. He was transferred to Ford Island in the middle of Pearl Harbor and lived in Quarters 114 with men he called the best and the brightest in AVS. In Quarters 114, off-duty card playing was routine. Jim Rouse joined the nightly games and won and won and won. During the whole of his two-year tour of duty in Hawaii he did not draw his pay once. His winnings more than covered all his expenses; he put two years' worth of Navy officer's pay into savings.[8] That Rouse could win continually was extraordinary. His winning was not mostly a matter of luck. Jim Rouse had extraordinary abilities. Even experienced card players have difficulty staying focused, counting cards, remembering every play, but Jim Rouse did not have that difficulty. In addition, he had great intuition about what was happening with others; he could tell when an opponent's raise was justified and when it was a bluff. He calculated with ease and could feel The pretty sure of what was in an opponent's hand. He had confidence in his reading of people's motives. He won every night because he played better than anyone else.

Near the end of 1944 Rouse was transferred to Pensacola, Florida, where he was put in charge of personnel for the Naval Air Training Command. Back in the States, he was able to have Libby and two-year-old Robin join him. They set up housekeeping in a bungalow whose mortgage was FHA-insured and which was part of a development financed by Connecticut General Life Insurance. But before he departed Ford Island and Quarters 114, his fellow officers celebrated Jim Rouse in a poem, parts of which go like this.

> You've heard of Beau Brummel, Cellini, Don Juan,
> But have you ever heard of them wrapped into one?
> Have you ever heard of a man who requires no sleep,
> And never, no never, has had to count sheep?
> Have you heard of a man who goes on 'till it's sunny,
> Fleecing lamb after lamb by playing gin rummy?
> . . . .
> Yes, Jim's quite a boy, there's really none like him,
> And life on Oahu will be dim without him,
> But PENSACOLA will now really hum,
> And Putnam will now again play 'till the sun,
> And poor old Summie will again know that sting
> Of defeat at the table—of cards Rouse is KING![9]

These verses are a celebration of Jim Rouse's exuberance.

After the war, Rouse was given the Bronze Star for his work in Hawaii. The glowing citation was written by Admiral J. H. Towers, the man who founded the Aviation Volunteer Specialists. The citation conveys the extent of Rouse's managerial duties and the skill with which he performed them, despite the long nights at the card table.

> He planned and directed the distribution of enlisted personnel within the type command; analyzed proposals for revisions of compliments [sic] of Pacific Fleet aviation units; and exercised direct supervision over the highly complex functions of the Type Commander relating to rotation of duty, transfers, leave and transportation of air force, Pacific Fleet casual personnel to and from the Hawaiian Area. These highly valuable services contributed immeasurably to the efficient administration of the command. His conduct and devotion to duty were in keeping with the highest traditions of the United States Naval Service.[10]

Lieutenant Commander James W. Rouse was at Pensacola until late September 1945, almost a year. Not long after he left, Rouse was awarded the Legion of Merit for his management of enlisted personnel. "By the energetic use of his brilliant creative ability," he moved enlisted personnel from their places of naval air training to sea duty and maintained an even flow of replacements for combat veterans.

> By his establishment of a new operating allowance system he made possible very substantial savings in personnel and the more efficient use of the personnel assigned to the commands. His untiring efforts to bring about an economical distribution and utilization of personnel contributed materially to the achievements of the Naval Air Training Commands and were over and beyond the call of duty.[11]

The medal and the citation arrived when Rouse was back at Moss-Rouse. Both partners had survived, and in their absence Harry Batchelor had brought in a small profit. At first, the company continued with its specialty in residential mortgages, making most of them with the help of the FHA. But soon the company moved into commercial real estate and found funding for apartment houses and shopping centers. Rouse had already decided he did not want to be a practicing lawyer, but now he realized that by confining himself to being a mortgage maker and giver of advice he was basically doing the same kinds of things lawyers did. He was playing a supporting role. He wanted to be out front; he wanted to be more of a player.

> I was becoming frustrated with the limitations of the mortgage banking business. We were creating deals for developers, who would make a lot of money, and we would get paid a fee for arranging the financing. We had little influence over the purpose, the utility, the design, or the quality of the projects. To do so would require becoming the developer, not just the financial enabler.[12]

Shopping patterns changed after the war, and strip shopping centers were sprouting up both in cities and in their new suburbs. Rouse saw shopping centers as the way to go.

Chapter 5 The Ace

   1. Autob, 10.
   2. Autob, 10.
   3. Autob, 11.
   4. Autob, 12.
   5. Autob, 13.
   6. Edward L. Palmer Jr. to Naval Aviation Selection Board, February 24, 1942. A copy of Palmer's letter is in the file containing JWR's personal records.
   7. JWR letters to Hunter Moss of August 15, 1942, and to Libby Rouse August 15, 1942.
   8. Autob, 18-19.
   9. A copy of "Lament" is with JWR's personal records. It is undated and unsigned. It has the following subtitle: "Being a demure expression of the 114 community feelings upon the permanent departure of inmate JAMES W. ROUSE–A-V(S), USNR."
   10. A copy of Admiral J. H. Towers' citation of February 1947 is with JWR's personal records.
   11. C. A. Pownall, Chief of Naval Air Training, to Secretary of the Navy, November 29, 1945. A copy is with JWR's personal records.
   12. Autob, 21.

Chapter 6
The Fights Against Blight and War

When Jim Rouse returned from the Navy late in 1945, his social conscience had been strengthened. He wanted to make the world a better place. He wanted action taken against the human misery he found in Baltimore and also against the even greater misery caused by war. Not long after he was back in Baltimore, he joined the Citizens Planning and Housing Association, an organization devoted to improving the miserable conditions in the city's black slums. The group had high hopes, because the city official most directly involved had the same goal. G. Yates Cook had recently been put in charge of the Health Department's section dealing with housing; he was responsible for the "hygiene of housing," and he was seeking the support of the white community. Jim Rouse credits Cook for getting him more directly involved in wanting to do something about housing for the poor. Later Rouse was to say about this time: "Relating to the public sector appeared as both an opportunity and a responsibility."[1]

In his daily forays into slum streets, Cook would be overcome with disgust. Black people lived in the city's oldest neighborhoods, in blocks of ramshackle houses over 100 years old where an indoor toilet was a rarity. Cook decided that the best way to get white support was to subject whites to tours similar to the ones he took, which is what he did with a group from the CPHA. One CPHA member, Hans Froelicher, remembered his tour this way:

> For the first time I *sensed* a slum. I had been there before, but I had traveled them with passing glance. This time my senses took them in. I must have touched something, because I wanted nothing except to take a bath and burn my clothes. I could not bear the thought of food because I had seen and smelled a rotting mass in a filthy, faulty outside hopper. . . . Never was there a greater call for doing good.[2]

A magazine writer taken on a Cook tour reported,

> I went walking with Cook through some of his 'rock-bottom' slums for as long as I could stand it. He led me through so-called 'squeeze-gut' alleys—three feet wide—that were deep with excrement, muck and garbage. Hordes of persistent flies settled on us. I beat the air with a handkerchief in a not very successful effort to keep them off my face.[3]

Jim Rouse took similar tours.

The owners of these hovels were white businessmen who never walked these streets. They sent underlings to collect the rents due but otherwise totally neglected their properties. Many of the black people for whom these streets were home had come up from the South hoping to find work in the steel mill or auto plant or on the docks. While outside their houses, the yards and alleys were filled with garbage, junk, and excrement, inside there often was no heat or hot water, and ceilings, floors, and walls had gaping holes. The electrical wiring and the staircases were unsafe. The houses were great for flies, rats, and other vermin. For human beings, they were totally degrading.

With certain exceptions, Baltimore's white citizens were indifferent. If blacks did not like the conditions in which they lived, it was up to them to show some initiative and fix things up. The problem was that most people living in these slums did not have the money to buy tools and materials. But more than that, it was the responsibility of the landlords to fix up and maintain their property.

Yates Cook wanted his white supporters, including Jim Rouse and his sympathetic business friend Guy Hollyday of Guarantee Title, to join his work and help him as he focused on a single slum block. He was determined to get the block cleaned up by seeing to it that all housing code standards were enforced and violations corrected. According to Rouse, Cook felt "that if he could succeed on one block, he could demonstrate to skeptics that entire slum neighborhoods could be rehabilitated."[4] In his last years, Rouse employed a similar strategy as he worked to get an entire Baltimore neighborhood rehabilitated in hopes that it would become a model to be emulated in other cities.

Cook chose a block in South Baltimore that was to be called Block One. Made up of rowhouses with wooden fences and privies out back, the block was home to 450 people, and as many as eighteen people lived in a single house—with one outdoor toilet. He mustered a team of inspectors and volunteer workers. They called on landlords to correct violations. They collected enough refuse, debris, and junk to make up forty-six truckloads. They killed about 500 rats. They tore down dilapidated fences, and the privies were replaced with indoor toilets. Block One was rehabilitated.[5]

Cook's next venture was to go at twenty-seven slum blocks just to the north of Johns Hopkins Hospital, an area that came to be known as the Pilot Area. Working through the schools and the churches, Cook organized an effort designed to get residents to do whatever was within their capabilities and to get landlords to correct code violations. But what were they to do about residents who owned the places in which they lived but did not have the money to do repairs? Rouse was instrumental in creating the Fight Blight Fund, a nonprofit corporation that raised money to help such people. Mostly, the Fund helped homeowners by putting them in touch with lenders who would re-finance mortgages in order to provide fixing-up cash. Another innovation that resulted from this effort was the creation of a special housing court.

The attacks on blight in Baltimore came to be known nationally as the Baltimore Plan. Many cities from across the country sent delegations to observe what was being done. Nicholas Dagen Bloom quotes a Baltimore slumlord as saying, "When the Baltimore Plan descended on me, it was a bitter pill to swallow, for it was going to cost me five hundred dollars apiece to fix up my places. . . . It's been the best thing that ever happened to me."[6] But Bloom is skeptical. He thinks the for-profit participants are fooling themselves if they think "a comparatively low-cost program had the power to 'remake a city' without extensive state action or spending."[7] The Socialist mayor of Milwaukee, Frank Zeidler, a strong advocate of public housing, according to Bloom, disliked what he saw happening in Baltimore. Zeidler's response was carried in the newspaper of the American Federation of Labor:

> It is the realtors' story, garnished with deluding superlatives into a Utopian fairy tale of rainbows' gold, that is being told throughout the land to lull into oblivion the dreamers, plotters, and planners who would tear down the fetid barricades and bring to even the lowest of slum dwellers high standards of living. . . .[8]

And even Rouse himself had doubts.

> As the public housing fight grew, [he said,] real estate interests in a zeal to substitute alternatives grabbed at straws wherever they could find them. They grabbed at rehabilitation programs such as the Baltimore Plan which were hopeful, and they stated that they were panaceas.[9]

Meanwhile, Rouse was active in the Mortgage Bankers Association, of which Guy Hollyday was president. Rouse became chairman of the association's legislative affairs committee and in that capacity testified before a number of Congressional committees In so doing he gained national recognition as an advocate of urban redevelopment. Throughout his connection with Baltimore's anti-blight programs, Rouse believed that it was better to rehabilitate than to raze and that public housing was not a good alternative to private housing. Public housing, he believed, did not produce better living environments, because "it segregates people into lower-income groups and advertises their less privileged economic condition."[10]

In 1951, the mayor of Baltimore was Thomas D'Alesandro, Jr., the father of Nancy Pelosi, who, in 2007, was to become the first woman to become Speaker of the United States House of Representatives. D'Alesandro appointed Rouse, who at the time was chairman of the Citizen's Advisory Committee on the Baltimore Plan, to be chairman of the Mayor's Advisory Council on the new Housing Bureau. The Housing Bureau was set up within the Health Department. The Housing Bureau and the Housing Court, which was D'Alesandro's idea, had gained renown across the country as the Baltimore Plan. After two years Rouse was convinced The Baltimore Plan was not working, or at least not up to the level of his expectations. It was only the Housing Bureau that had the authority to post "unfit-for-human-habitation" notices. Everything had to go through the Housing Bureau and the Health Department and always there were roadblocks. Dr. Huntington Williams, who was Commissioner of Health, came to be known as Mr. Roadblock. That slum owners could get away with violations got under Rouse's skin. It made him very angry that white landlords could blatantly neglect their properties in slum areas and not be punished. Then he did something very uncharacteristic. He quit.[11]

In March 1952, the Advisory Council had recommended to the mayor that an independent agency be set up to handle enforcement. It took the mayor almost a year to respond. When he did respond, he said he had rejected the idea. Rouse then wrote a five-page letter of resignation. He again asserted that an independent agency with powers of enforcement was absolutely necessary. He said he knew of code violations that had still not been corrected two years after notice was given. The present system was "ineffective and inefficient . . . cumbersome and exhausting. . . . It is time we recognize that the Baltimore Plan in its present structure cannot grow and develop into the kind of a program the city desperately needs."[12] Since he thought it futile to pretend that something was being accomplished, he felt compelled to try to get legislation passed in the state's General Assembly that would enable the city to do the job as it needed to be done.

The resignation angered Mayor D'Alesandro.

> I appointed Mr. James Rouse, [he said,] as chairman of the advisory committee on the Baltimore Plan. He has not given advice but has attempted to dictate to the Mayor and to the city administration. . . . If this is the way Mr. Rouse intends to advise then it is proper that he resign and I accept his resignation.[13]

Rouse had the last word in this dispute. He wanted a more intensive effort that would have a wider and deeper effect. That what had been done was effective was born out in a December 1954 report of the U. S. Public Health Service. The Public Health Service conducted a house-to-house survey of housing conditions in the Pilot Area. Despite all the indifference and bureaucratic roadblocks, significant progress had been made. The report said:

> The data indicate that the enforcement effort resulted in significant improvement of the quality of housing in the Pilot Area without untoward effect on the residents. As a matter of fact, the improved dwellings are healthier and safer places in which to live. Furthermore, the improvement in

maintenance scores alone should insure that the useful life of these dwellings will be significantly extended.

This was the result of constant pressure on landlords to eliminate violations. When he was asked to comment on the report, Mayor D'Alesandro had nothing to say.

Rouse had much preferred Baltimore's previous mayor, Theodore R. McKeldin, even though he was a Republican. When Rouse spoke about McKeldin, who served two non-contiguous terms as mayor and who also was Governor of Maryland between 1951 and 1959, he made McKeldin seem like a man he would gladly emulate. In a 1976 oral history interview with Barry A. Lanman, Rouse said of McKeldin,

> He was a man of remarkable humanity. He wasn't profound, ingenious, or inventive. . . . He wasn't a master manager but he cared for people. He was a liberal, an open man, a compassionate man. He was a Christian and a preacher. He preached in black churches. He was comfortable with all people. He didn't look down on anyone. . . . He created an environment for a sense of equality.[14]

Rouse stated further in the interview that it was what he saw as he worked in the Baltimore slums in the 1950s that really began his concern with the problems of blacks. He had gone through his adolescence in Easton without having such a concern. It was only when he was at the University of Hawaii that he began to think about minorities at all, for in Hawaii whites were a minority. But the experience in the slums had a powerful impact.

The fight against blight was getting Jim Rouse known beyond Baltimore. Even the White House had taken note. In September of 1953, Rouse had to be pleasantly surprised to receive a letter from President Dwight D. Eisenhower, then in his eighth month in office. The president asked him to serve on his advisory committee to review the federal government's housing programs. Ike also wanted Rouse to serve, with four others, on the group's executive committee.

For a while in the late 40s and early 50s, Democrats as well as Republicans thought Eisenhower was one of their own. Leaders of both parties thought Eisenhower would be a terrific candidate for president in the 1952 election. Eisenhower, mostly because he believed it important to break the Democratic hold on the presidency, ultimately went with the Republicans and succeeded in winning the nomination over Senator Robert A. Taft. Jim Rouse had always been a Democrat, although in 1940 he had gone door-to-door in South Baltimore on behalf of FDR's opponent, Wendell Wilkie.[15] The Democratic Party's nominee for President in 1952 was Adlai Stevenson, a man who had made a strong favorable impression on Rouse. Rouse, however, thought Eisenhower would be better for the country. Just two weeks before the election, Rouse wrote a letter to a Navy friend, Harry Hollins, in which he carefully set down his reasons for supporting Eisenhower.

Eisenhower, he says, "represents an extraordinary opportunity for the American people." To Rouse, the most important consideration in the election was the extent to which each candidate was likely, in a world divided by the Cold War and with the U S. fighting in Korea, to bring about a climate favorable to maintaining peace. Eisenhower "has probably had the most far-reaching experience in the day-to-day problems of achieving unity among nations of any American in our history."[16] Rouse recognizes that many of his friends who also regard peace as their highest concern think Eisenhower is nothing more than a tool of the extremist wing of the Republican Party. Rouse doesn't think that is the case. He thinks Eisenhower will make the extremist wing less extreme. He thinks the internationalists in the party will become much more important with Eisenhower leading the way. Rouse detests the nationalists among the Republicans and sees Eisenhower having a mellowing effect upon them:

> Eisenhower, without ever embracing their methods, and while expressing clear disapproval of their methods, and of any methods which convict or injure the innocent, has, by emphasizing his points of agreement with them, withdrawn much of the fuel upon which they depend for survival. The election of Eisenhower will constitute, I believe, a crushing blow to bigotry, intolerance and to isolationism in this country.

In foreseeing an aggressive use of honey as a tool, Rouse is engaging in a good bit of wishful thinking, projecting onto Eisenhower attitudes and methods for conflict resolution that were more characteristic of James Rouse (the conflict with Mayor D'Alesandro excepted).

But then an event occurred that made Rouse step back from his carefully reasoned, whole-hearted endorsement. Republican Senator Joseph J. McCarthy engaged in still another act of slander, too outrageous to overlook. On October 27th McCarthy gave a speech in which he viciously attacked Adlai Stevenson with innuendo. He accused Stevenson of aiding the cause of the Communists by associating with Communist sympathizers. He also pretended to confuse the name Adlai with Alger, the latter being an obvious reference to Alger Hiss, the former Sate Department official who stood accused of carrying out espionage for the Soviet Union and who at the time was imprisoned for perjury. The next morning Rouse sent a telegram to Eisenhower in New York:

> Thousands of your supporters are sickened by McCarthy's outrageous speech. Common justice demands that you disassociate yourself from it, but more important is the frightful possibility that your candidacy might be allowed to benefit from it. As a strong supporter I implore that you speak out against this demonstration of McCarthy's methods.[17]

Eisenhower chose not to do so. A few days later, Eisenhower was elected president.

In any case, Ike invited Rouse to join his Housing Advisory Committee, a mixed group of bankers, realtors, and housing experts.[18] He was made chairman of the sub-committee dealing with problems of urban housing. He then led the sub-committee in shifting the emphasis from bulldozing slum blocks to slum prevention and neighborhood rehabilitation. While he was not the first to use it, his use popularized the term "urban renewal."[19] His work with the committee is reflected in two documents: The President's Special Message to the Congress on Housing, dated January 25, 1954, and the Housing Act of 1954, which was the product of the various recommendations made by the advisory committee (The U. S. Department of Housing and Urban Development was not created until 1965; its sub-department-level predecessor was the Housing and Home Finance Administration).

In the message to Congress, Eisenhower highlighted the problem of slum rehabilitation. His language and focus clearly show the influence of Rouse:

> Millions of our people live in slums. Millions live in run-down declining neighborhoods. The national interest demands the elimination of slum conditions and the rehabilitation of declining neighborhoods. Many of our local communities make good progress in this work and are eager to make further substantial improvements but are unable to find the needed resources.

The message called for strict enforcement of housing codes and the number of people allowed to live in housing units. It also called for attention to urban matters that were at the heart of Rouse's concerns. He wanted more rehabilitation of slum areas that were worth saving. In those areas he wanted rehabilitation facilitated and streets and traffic reconfigured to benefit the residents. He also wanted residents to have parks and playgrounds. To achieve those goals, the Congress would have to broaden the Housing Act of 1949, so that much more money would be available in grants and loans for work in salvable areas.

Rouse had worked for the FHA, and he knew how difficult it sometimes was for property owners to get loans to improve their homes. Changes were called for that would make that easier and also make it easier for low-income people whose homes were bulldozed to get insured long-term loans with which they could buy another house. A paragraph in which Ike called for equal opportunity for minorities to get mortgages undoubtedly had its origins with Rouse, for Rouse was very aware of how decidedly unequal the opportunities were for blacks to get mortgages. The scholar of urban problems M. Carter McFarland says,

> With conviction, force of personality, and sheer eloquence, Rouse persuaded the Advisory Committee to accept his sound modifications of the Urban Renewal Program. He also personally drafted the portions of the committee's final report expressing his vision of what urban renewal ought to be. . . . He emphatically demonstrated his special qualities of mind and personality at a time when the very future of urban renewal was at stake.[20]

The work of Rouse and the advisory committee was fed into the Housing Act of 1954. Here too Rouse's voice can be heard. The requirements stated in the section entitled "Slum Clearance and Urban Renewal" had to come from Rouse. A special urban renewal fund is created. In deciding whether to offer financial assistance to a local government, the Housing and Home Finance administrator is required to consider the extent of code enforcement within the jurisdiction. The HHF administrator also must require, as a condition of financial assistance, that localities present

> an official plan of action for effectively dealing with the problem of urban slums and blight within the community and for the establishment and preservation of a well-planned community with well-organized residential neighborhoods of decent homes and suitable living environment for adequate family life.

In the recommendations of the committee and in the legislation, we see Jim Rouse's basic attitudes toward urban housing. Bad housing must not be tolerated. If a house is so far gone that it would be futile to try to bring it up to code, then clear it away. If, however, a house is structurally sound, every effort must be made to save it. Every effort also must be made to save neighborhoods. Neighborhoods must have amenities: places for people to shop, nearby schools and houses of worship, recreational facilities. They must have parks and playgrounds and be pleasing to the eye. They must be areas where family life can thrive. Rouse takes it for granted that government must play a major role in keeping neighborhoods viable and helping to make decent housing available to everyone—that is *everyone*, without regard to race, religion, or nation of origin. It may be an acceptable practice under the tenets of free enterprise, but Rouse is well aware that the unhampered pursuit of profit by absentee property owners has been a primary factor in the creation of slums. Local governments must not allow them to get away with code violations. He wants private lending institutions to be more liberal in making loans to low-income homeowners so that they will have the means with which to keep their property in good repair.

Bloom looks at this period and argues that not enough was done to generate more public housing. He points out that Rouse had tempered his opposition to public housing but that he had not gone far enough. Rouse, Bloom says critically, came to accept public housing only as a stop-over location for poor people while they acquired the means to buy on the private market.[21] Bloom laments that Congress could not see the "humanitarian justifications for social housing." Instead, "Congress identified all public housing supporters as un-American. The Cold War, he says, played "an important role in defeating social welfare initiatives."[22]

Jim Rouse was an unrepentant believer in the potential of human beings to be rational, to make important decisions on the basis of reason. In Rouse's view the most irrational decision men make is the decision to go to war. There has to be an alternative to the destructiveness of war. In the early years after World War II, as he was building his business and waging his fight against blight, Rouse also committed himself to the struggle to find an alternative to war.

By 1948 the confrontation between the Communist world and the free world had intensified into the Cold War. Rouse worried that World War III might not be far off. On June 30, 1950, war broke out in Korea, and American soldiers were in battle against the army of North Korea, a newly made country that was a puppet of the Soviet Union. In November, when American forces broke through and approached the Yalu River in northern North Korea, the army of the People's Republic of China crossed the river and took on the Americans. Soldiers of two of the world's great powers were fighting one another. Soon the Chinese had pushed American forces back across the 38th parallel, the border between the two Koreas.

At the same time, late 1950-early 1951, there was great fear that the Soviet Union would launch an attack on western Europe. In Congress there was much debate about what the United States should do. Isolationist Republicans advocated a "policy of retreat"; they wanted to make the United States "the Gibraltar of Western Civilization." Senator Styles Bridges of New Hampshire asserted that we were already in World War III—and losing. He urged breaking off diplomatic relations with the Soviet Union. He called for an American-supported invasion of Communist China by the forces of the Chinese Nationalist leader Chiang Kai-shek. At home, he wanted a full-scale industrial mobilization. General George C. Marshall, who had been called out of retirement to be President Truman's secretary of defense, called for a draft of eighteen-year-olds. General Eisenhower took a leave of absence from the presidency of Columbia University to become supreme commander of the Allied Powers in Europe. He toured Western Europe to ascertain its willingness and readiness to go to war. He addressed a joint session of Congress and said that Western Europe was ready to defend itself but the United States must make a major contribution of equipment.

The longed-for sustained period of peace following World War II did not happen. For people with vivid memories of World War II, especially scenes of the atomic bomb aftermaths in Hiroshima and Nagasaki, it was a frightening time. In their minds drastic steps had to be taken to make another world war less likely. A peaceful world would be more likely if there were cooperation among nations rather than competition. Hopes had been high that the United Nations would be the means through which conflicts would be resolved and war prevented. But to some American intellectuals it was clear that more than the UN was needed; more national sovereignty had to be surrendered than was required by membership in the UN. They wanted to see progress toward "one world," a world government, a world federal system. Such goals were what reason said was the only way out.

Jim Rouse was among those seekers. He looked for other such seekers in the national business community. In January 1951, Rouse attended a meeting of the Mortgage Bankers Association in Chicago. At one of its sessions he listened to a speech by John Nuveen, the well-known Chicago financier and philanthropist. When Rouse got back to Baltimore, he wrote to Nuveen praising him for his talk on the international situation. "It was very inspiring to hear your talk on the need for a positive, aggressive political offensive by the United States if we are to provide leadership for the free world." While Rouse favors disarmament—"foolproof disarmament"—and less sensitivity on matters of sovereignty, he wants the United States to take a more aggressive peaceful stance regarding the Soviet Union. He tells Nuveen, "We should be talking about how we will dissipate the communist gains, unite the non-communist world and free the millions of unwilling victims of communist aggression."[23]

At the end of his letter he puts four questions to Nuveen, the most revealing of which is this one: "Must not this positive program include a basis for ending war and the threat of war and must not that basis involve a vigorous advocacy by the United States of universal disarmament under enforceable law as the essential condition for peace?"

In 1951 Rouse was a member of the United World Federalists. The UWF was formed in 1947, with a four-point program: to achieve permanent peace through universal disarmament enforced by law; to use the resources going into armaments for human needs; to promote freedom among all peoples; to aid the development of all peoples according to their own customs and culture.[24] Rouse was chairman of the Executive Council and of the Policy Committee of the Maryland branch.

On February 18, 1951 a gala fundraiser was held at Baltimore's Lyric Theatre. Among the fifty-five patrons of the event listed on the invitation were some of the leading figures in Baltimore's business world. Following the dinner, there was "a stage presentation" called *The Myth That Threatens the World*, directed by Oscar Hammerstein II. Among those participating on stage were such well-known personages as the actor Ralph Bellamy; the producer and playwright Russel Crouse; the playwright and screenwriter Robert E. Sherwood; the novelist Rex Stout; Congressman Christian A. Herter of Massachusetts, later to be U.S. Secretary of State; Alan Cranston, president of United World Federalists and future U.S. senator; Duncan M. Spencer, Chairman of the Board of the Fiduciary Trust Company; and Telford Taylor, who had been the chief prosecutor at the Nuremberg trials of Nazi war criminals. The theme of the evening was that the United States must take the lead in putting disarmament on the table for negotiation. The whole event was organized by James W. Rouse.

In 1949 as the post-World War II Red-scare was building, the Maryland General Assembly passed the Ober Law. Under the Ober Law, the state attorney general appointed a special assistant to coordinate anti-subversive activities within the state. One such anti-subversive activity was the appearance at the Lyric fundraiser of a note-taking anti-subversive agent. When this became known, a hue and cry went up that reached the Governor. In response Governor

McKeldin wrote a gracious letter to the president of the UWF Maryland branch, Daniel B. Dugan:

> There is no reason to suspect your organization of disloyalty or to single it out for special investigation. The members of the United World Federalists of Maryland are patriotic, loyal citizens. Their aim, like the aim of most of us, is the abolition of war.... It would be a shame... if any official action were to discourage those who now belong to the organization, those who want to belong, or those who merely want to hear the theories of the group....[25]

Within days of the Lyric event, Rouse wrote a single-spaced three-page letter to Alan Cranston (It is an inference that the letter without the recipient's full name or address on it but with the salutation "Dear Alan" was to UWF president Alan Cranston). Apparently Rouse was moved to write because Maryland UWF now had the receipts of the big fundraiser. It is a letter in which Rouse says he is putting down considerations about their organization that he finds troubling. He is troubled that the UWF's objective of eliminating war "through disarmament under enforceable law" has not been made clear "in places and among people who count." He also is troubled that "we have failed to relate these objectives to the security and self-interest of the United States and the American people."[26] The latter objective is very typical of Rouse. Many of his goals were also the goals of idealists, but Rouse thought of himself as a pragmatist and did not support causes for any reason other than the probability they could have a practical effect for good within a relatively short time.

Rouse thought there was a great misconception among the American public about who World Federalists are. Most people seem to look upon them "as a group of sincere idealists with great dedication to a fine ideal." He himself finds among some UWF members "an atmosphere of a 'cult' or a 'religion' or a 'movement.'" Although this atmosphere may attract and hold many people, he says, "it repels many others." And that includes James W. Rouse. Flaunting idealistic statements for the sake of being considered an idealist is not for him. He thinks the foreign policy of the United States is in a period of crisis and the times are dangerous. He wants to separate himself from "the more doctrinaire Federalists." He wants to be a participant in the making of American foreign policy, not an idealistic spectator. He wants the UWF to be involved "in a course of action which bears directly on the present foreign policy debate." The money he helped raise for UWF in Maryland should be put to use in regard to the current crisis. He is concerned that "unless some positive and worthwhile program for its use is immediately evolved the money will gradually be dissipated and the UWF will slowly desiccate."

Throughout his adult life and his continued participation in good causes, Rouse worried that glittering rhetoric could be self-flattering and would lull people into being pleased with themselves and make action seem unnecessary. At the end of his active life, as head of the Enterprise Foundation, Rouse cautioned his successors about falling into complacency. Just having a sense of doing good is not enough. "That is not our purpose. It is not enough. We must be real about our mission. And as we are we will lift our own expectancy and that of the cities and neighborhoods where we work."[27]

The Executive Council of the Maryland UWF met in June. A lengthy resolution about UWF goals was passed unanimously. The resolution contains Rouse's views on what the goals of the UWF should be. The resolution begins,

> Our goal, and the hope of most other U.S. citizens, is to abolish war. The special role of UWF is to show the United States that this requires disarmament by all nations under protection of a world federal government, and that the determined and sincere advocacy by our government NOW will give purpose, unity and new strength to American foreign policy.

Acknowledging that the "forward motion" of the organization has not been commensurate with the depth of the crises the country faces, the resolution promises that UWF will again move forward vigorously. This will be accomplished by focusing on both "brass" (high-ranking officials) and "grass" (as in grass roots). On the one hand, there will be a stronger attempt to make the organization known and win support for it on the grass roots level. On the other hand, there will be an attempt to familiarize the leadership of the country with the UWF program.

It is this "action" aspect of the resolution that most represents Rouse. He wants to gain support from "leaders in Congress and the State Department, in labor, business and professional groups and in membership organizations throughout the country." With such support there will be a direct effect on the formation of national policy. Getting into the minds of policy makers on all levels the idea that through a world federal government secure disarmament is possible is the key step in moving toward a world without war. Talking up the idea and getting reputable leaders to accept it and spread it—that's the action Rouse wanted to see.

Chapter 6 The Fights Against Blight and War

1. Autob, 57.
2. Olsen, 32-33.
3. "These Slumlords Got Smart," *Saturday Evening Post,* January 21, 1953, 62.
4. Autob, 57.
5. "These Slumlords," 62.
6. Bloom, 65.
7. Bloom, 67.
8. Quoted by Bloom, 69
9. Quoted by Bloom, 71.
10. Olsen, 31.
11. "Rouse Resigns," Baltimore *News American,* March 25, 1953, 38.
12. "Rouse Resigns," 38.
13. "Rouse Resigns," 2.
14. Available at the Maryland Historical Society in Baltimore.
15. Autob, 60.
16. JWR letter to Harry Hollins, October 24, 1952.
17. A copy of the Western Union telegram is available at CA.
18. Letter of President Dwight D. Eisenhower to JWR, September 12, 1953.
19. Bloom, 72.
20. *The Federal Government and Urban Problems,* (Boulder: Westview Press, 1978).
21. Bloom, 74.
22. Bloom, 78.
23. JWR letter to John Nuveen, January 29, 1951, with JWR's personal records.
24. www.indiana.edu/uwrldfed.html. Accessed in March 2004.
25. *The Sun,* May, 17, 1953.
26. JWR letter to Alan Cranston, February 27, 1951.
27. JWR memo to Bart Harvey and Paul Brophy, April 15, 1991.

Chapter 7
Stepping Stones

If you discover you're unbeatable at the card table, it's only natural to think you might be unbeatable at other things. You'd think big and quickly see opportunities. And if you can get the calculations right, remain flexible, maintain your energy and pleasing personality, and turn on your persuasiveness at the most opportune moment, you're going to make those opportunities pay off. In the 1950s Jim Rouse seized opportunities in the new and rapidly changing shopping center business—and they paid off.

Let's begin with the smallest and most conventional. Early in 1953 Rouse moved to build the Waverly Tower Shopping Center, a conventional in-city shopping center in a working-class neighborhood. He did this at the same time he was moving to build Mondawmin Mall, a very different kind of shopping center, to be discussed later in this chapter. The Waverly Realty Corporation was to be the shopping center's owner, and Rouse put on the corporation's board his brother Bill and an experienced local developer, Jack Meyerhoff. Set back from Greenmount Avenue, one of Baltimore's main north-south arteries, between 28th and 29th Streets, Waverly Tower was part of a redevelopment project in the Waverly neighborhood. A mortgage of $650,000 from the Mutual Benefit Life Insurance Company provided Rouse with a big chunk of the financing he needed; the city offered him the land on lease. The center was L-shaped, and in the middle of the 450-car parking lot stood the transmission tower for radio station WWIN. The center opened on October 30, 1957, and among the seventeen tenants were Food Fair, Sun Ray Drugs, Western Auto, and a White Tower burger joint—all stores that would provide things needed by the blue-collar people of the neighborhood.

Another piece of Waverly's redevelopment was the apartment buildings being put up by the Waverly Redevelopment Corporation, owned by Harry Bart and his brother-in-law Albert Stark. Bart and Stark had a long history as developers of houses, apartments, and commercial properties. With Waverly Redevelopment, they were doing the first private enterprise slum clearance project in Baltimore. In fact, according to Rouse, it was "the first redevelopment project in the U. S. developed by a private builder through the mortgage insurance facilities of the Federal Housing Administration."[1] Fifty years later, the neighborhood was close to being blighted again. The still-active but grungy shopping center again could stand a lot of redevelopment.

Jack Meyerhoff was Waverly Realty's chairman of the board, and he was to be chairman of all Rouse's corporate boards until he retired in 1973, when he was named chairman emeritus. Harry Bart and Albert Stark also were to be constant presences on Rouse's boards. Meyerhoff, who was Jewish and born in Russia, came to Baltimore as a child. He attended the prestigious City College High School but did not finish. Instead, he went to work in the homebuilding industry and soon started his own business, the Columbia Construction Company. At the time Rouse planned the Waverly shopping center, Meyerhoff, with his brother Joseph, already had built Baltimore's Edmondson Village Shopping Center, one of the country's first planned centers. Opened in 1947, Edmondson was built in the style of Colonial Williamsburg, with red-brick facades and dormer windows. It had twenty-nine stores, including a branch of one of Baltimore's leading department stores, Hochschild, Kohn. It also had a clubroom, a movie theater, and a bowling alley. Lots of trees and shrubbery surrounded the stores. Out front, between the buildings and Edmondson Avenue was an 800-car sunken parking lot.[2]

Thus, the Meyerhoff brothers already had done on a larger scale what Rouse was planning for Waverly. Rouse could not have made a better decision than to get Jack Meyerhoff on his team. It was an interesting alliance—between the Eastern Shore WASP and the Russian-born Jew. In Jack and Joseph Meyerhoff, Rouse saw a pair of young developers who were moving from rags to riches via shopping centers. In 1956, the Meyerhoffs went on to develop the Eastpoint Shopping Center. This time they had *two* anchor department stores, the best from downtown—Hochschild, Kohn once more and Hutzler's, the most successful Baltimore retailer. Jim Rouse was not yet an innovator; he saw what the Meyerhoffs had done and he was striving to emulate them.

Jack Meyerhoff was a Rouse business associate for a quarter century. Upon his death in 1983, Mathias J. DeVito, the then president of the Rouse Company, described Meyerhoff as "a pioneer" who had been of great importance to the company. Jack and Joseph, who in Baltimore is the far better known brother mainly for having put up the money for the city's beautiful symphony hall, had an unfortunate falling out. This may be the reason why Jim was very careful in his dealings with his own brother. It may explain why everything he wanted to communicate to Bill about business was typed up in a formal memo, although Bill's desk was usually close to where Jim worked. Jim had great admiration for Joseph Meyerhoff. Looking back years later, he said of Joseph:

He meant a lot to me. We had a very close relationship when we were just emerging from the Great Depression in 1934. I was a young man in the first FHA office in Baltimore, and he was a home builder coming out of the Depression's dark days. We worked together. He taught me much that I needed to learn, and he was a warm friend. He never forgot those days and always reminded me of them when we were together.[3]

In October 1954 Rouse incorporated the Talbottown Shopping Center. Talbottown was to be built a few blocks from the center of his hometown of Easton, the center of business in Talbot County on the Eastern Shore. On this board too were Bill Rouse and Jack Meyerhoff. Rouse also included the builder Harry Bart and a financial whiz who remained in the company's employ until he retired, Albert (Bob) Keidel, Jr. Although at first the design was modernistic, the L-shaped shopping center that finally went up was basically the same as Waverly Tower. It had a 450-car parking lot and fourteen stores. Among the stores were Food Fair, Lee's Pharmacy, a local bakery, laundry, and cleaners, and a Hecht's department store. Talbottown opened before Waverly Tower, on March 14, 1957.

In 1950, the Moss-Rouse Company had set up a research department called Metropolitan Research and Development. It sought all kinds of data that would be relevant in the evaluation of real estate and in obtaining financing for new projects. Information about local populations was garnered from studying the latest censuses. The research also produced data on disposable income, the number of building permits, the unsold inventory of new housing, market prices of houses, characteristics of new homes, the number of VA and FHA mortgage applications, department store sales figures, corporate bond yields, and the results of land-use studies locally and nationally. The company even bought its own traffic-counting machine. Site selection for new projects was crucial. Metropolitan's research gave Moss-Rouse a competitive edge over other mortgage bankers.[4]

Across the country, strip shopping centers were springing up by the hundreds. Developers competed for new, more attractive sites. The most spectacular new shopping center was to be on Long Island, where work was proceeding on the site of a former airfield. The Roosevelt Field Shopping Center, with William Zeckendorf as developer, opened in 1956. It had Macy's largest suburban store in the East, it had 11,000 parking spaces, and it cost $35 million. Designed by architect I. M. Pei, it offered more than shopping. It included an ice-skating rink, a 400-seat community theater, an art gallery, and space for car and boat exhibitions. On the grounds of Roosevelt Field were also industrial areas, restaurants, bowling alleys, a hotel, and a medical building. By the end of 1956, 300 acres had been developed.[5] But Roosevelt Field was not enclosed, and thus it was soon to lose its avant-garde status.

When, in June 1949, Jim Rouse read that Alexander Brown had died at age 90, he must have felt the same excitement as when he pulled four aces. Alexander Brown had been a Baltimore icon, a grandson of the founder of the first investment bank in the United States in 1800. The deceased lived in a mansion on a 46-acre estate not more than three miles from Baltimore's central business district. The heir to the estate was Alexander Brown Griswold, who did not want to live on it but wasn't sure what to do with it. Jim Rouse took the initiative. He knew Griswold would be swamped with offers from developers. He wrote to Griswold and told him that the value of the property would depend on how potential buyers intended to use it. Rouse asked Griswold to keep the property off the market until he could have research done to determine whether housing or a major regional shopping center would be the most profitable use.[6] Griswold agreed.

Rouse, with a retainer from Griswold, commissioned a study by the marketing analyst Sidney Hollander, Jr., who used public sources to gather facts about the people living within the potential market area. The results, put together in a book with maps and lots of charts, showed that a regional shopping center would be the logical use. Rouse also commissioned studies by two well-known consultants, Miles L. Colean, the former head of the Rental Housing Division of the FHA, and Seward H. Mott, land-use specialist and director of the Urban Land Institute. The property had been given the name Mondawmin by the poet Henry Wadsworth Longfellow, who, after a visit to the estate, suggested that it be named after the legendary Indian spirit of the cornfields who wrestled with Hiawatha. Both consultants, after inspecting the property and looking at Hollander's analysis, agreed that a regional shopping center would be more profitable than any other use. Rouse asked Griswold to keep the property off the market and let him "lay out a program by which this use might be best achieved."[7]

In his report, Colean gave a major reason why housing on the property would not be a good investment. He said the area "faces encroachment from an advancing Negro settlement. . . ." That advance "may be expected to absorb all the blocks to the east of Reisterstown Road immediately adjoining the Mondawmin tract [the estate]."[8] In his subsequent letter to Griswold, Rouse objectively presented the Negro advance as a factor "mitigating against" a regional shopping center, but he then offered a "partial rebuttal." The negative argument, he said, emphasized "the rapid movement of negro population towards Mondawmin from the South and Southeast [of Baltimore] and the possibility that this movement might engulf it." But weighing against that point was this:

> The Negro population to the south is among the highest-income Negro groups in the city. These families have moved into the area within the past two years. They are largely home owners who have paid from $7500 to $15,000 and up for their houses. The noticeable improvement in recent years in the living

habits of the higher-income Negroes and the strong trend against racial segregation may make this part of the walk-in market more acceptable than normally would be anticipated.[9]

Rouse does not voice any anxiety about the "advancing Negro settlement."

He was not going to let the racial situation deter him from going ahead with plans for a shopping center. This was Baltimore in the 1950s, and segregation still ruled; there was not, at least not yet, a "strong trend against racial segregation." Baltimore, after all, was the principal city of a border state with strong Southern sympathies. Segregation was the long-accepted custom in movie theaters, ballparks, eating places, trolleys, trains, buses. In department stores, the custom was that black people could not try on clothes, not even hats or gloves. Whites and blacks at local high schools and colleges did not play on the same teams. Baltimore's attitude toward integration is perhaps best illustrated by the experience of Jackie Robinson and his wife Rachel when Robinson came through in 1946 as a player for the Brooklyn Dodgers' top farm team, the Montreal Royals. At the time both the Montreal Royals and the Baltimore Orioles were in the International League. The Royals came to Baltimore for a weekend series in April. The team had been warned that "the people are up in arms in Baltimore" about Robinson's playing with and against whites. When Jackie came to bat, Rachel sitting in the stands would hear such things as, "Here comes the nigger son of a bitch." Throughout the three-game series Jackie and Rachel Robinson had to endure torrents of vicious verbal abuse.[10] Just a few years later Rouse was counting on the success of a shopping center in which whites and blacks would shop together, use the same dressing rooms and bathrooms, eat and drink at the same counters. According to Libby Rouse, her husband at that time never discussed with her the racial situation; he considered himself "color-blind and inclusive" and thought everyone else should be too.[11] In going ahead with this project, Rouse was casting a very loud vote for integration and an end to segregation.

His first step in building Mondawmin was engineering the formation of the Mondawmin Corporation. Alexander Brown Griswold took 45% of the ownership, the builders Harry Bart and Albert Stark took 45%, and Moss-Rouse, which was soon to become James W. Rouse & Company, took 10%. Harry Bart, who was on the boards of Waverly Tower and Talbottown, became the president of the corporation; his approval was needed for all expenditures. In April 1952, Moss-Rouse officially became the "owner's representative." For fees to be worked out with Bart, it would engage consultants for the design of the center, obtain financing, arrange the leasing, set up management, and in general "represent the best interests of the project with all the ingenuity and resourcefulness we can command."[12] That, typically, was the role of the developer. Once a shopping center was in operation, the developer usually sold it off. Rouse, though, usually combined development with continuing ownership.

In May 1951, Rouse won the needed zoning change, with the City Planning Commission retaining complete jurisdiction over the development of the property, a stipulation that never became a problem. Rouse then created a Board of Design, made up of leading practitioners from all over the country on matters related to the planning of a shopping center. Among them were Pietro Belluschi, dean of architecture at M.I.T., and Kenneth C. Welch, a specialist in shopping center architecture and an enthusiast of the two-level structure. Welch also brought to the planning process what was called "Reilly's Law of Retail Gravitation," which made use of calculations of time, distance, and size to determine the drawing power a particular shopping center would have in relation to other nearby centers. Seward Mott was the operations consultant, and Moss-Rouse would provide economic analysis and research. The Board of Design met every three weeks over a period of seven months and discussed every aspect of the relationship between people and merchandise. "We very seriously considered an enclosed center," Rouse says, "but we lost our nerve."[13]

Mondawmin went up as a two-story rectangular building with overheads that protected shoppers on the walkways from rain, but it did not have a roof over its central atrium. While a Sears was among the sixty original stores, Rouse had wanted a major local department store. But none was willing to come to Mondawmin; the reason given was that the site was too close to the flagship store downtown. A spiral staircase over a fountain linked the first-level main court with the second. Access to the stores on the upper level was from a gallery that ran along the stores' fronts. There was a forty-foot ornamental pool. A large room was set aside for community use. No neon or flashing signs were allowed. "But Mondawmin's greatest design asset," Rouse said, "was its overall plan and scale. It was built for the pedestrian, not the automobile," although on the outside 4,000 parking spaces were provided.[14]

Because it would draw both white and black customers, it was not easy for Rouse and his brother Bill, who was Moss-Rouse's vice president for leasing, to get tenants. "White merchants, like most other whites in those days," Rouse wrote later, "were unprepared for racial integration." When Mondawmin opened in 1956, it had a coffee shop with the unfortunate name of White Coffee Pot—and it refused to serve black people. But picketing and Rouse persuasion got the owner to change his mind. Black customers soon sat at the same counters as whites, and life went on.[15]

Mondawmin was an immediate success. Shoppers came from as far as the Eastern Shore. In a letter written in January 1968, Rouse brags about the good behavior of the young people who come to the mall. Even though almost all-black Frederick Douglass High School is right across the street, there is no problem with disorderly behavior: "A good relationship exists between Mondawmin, its guards, and the Negro youth who use it. There have been very few incidents, pilferage is at a very low level, and conditions are generally good."[16] But then the initial enthusiasm began to dwindle. Middle-class black families began moving northward to more stable neighborhoods, and the area around the mall became run down. Sears, the one anchor store, left in 1973, and soon more stores left. Finally, Rouse discontinued the association with Mondawmin.

Then in 1979, despite a 17% vacancy rate, the Rouse Company decided to re-engage. It bought Mondawmin Mall, gave it a renovation that included a roof, and began to bring back national chain stores. In addition, a concerted effort was made to bring more economic activity to the Mondawmin area. The Liberty Medical Center and Baltimore City Community College expanded their operations nearby. The state's Motor Vehicle Administration and the U.S. Social Security Administration located field offices in the neighborhood. A transit center was built with a stop for Baltimore's new subway line and nine city bus lines. Mondawmin became a good example of the kind of synergistic effect Rouse believed in: individual centers of desirable activity generating larger amounts of overall activity. But then most of the national chain stores again began to leave; in their place came stores whose clientele was entirely African American. When Jim Rouse died in 1996 the future of Mondawmin Mall was shaky. But slowly Mondawmin began to prosper again. By 2007, seventeen national chains had locations in the mall. The great majority of businesses were aimed at an African American clientele, but the mixture of African American and national chain stores finally seemed to be right. General Growth Properties, the new owner of the mall, began a $70 million expansion. Among others, GGP looked forward to having Target, Marshall's, and a national big box outlet.

Jim Rouse always wanted his malls to be centers of community life. Ironically, after his death, Mondawmin became more so then ever before. The Community Room became heavily used, baby showers among its leading uses. Most of the business of everyday life could be done at the mall. Bank of America was there, and the U.S. Postal Service. So were Rite Aid, H&R Block, a check-cashing service, a liquor store, and a cleaner's. Also, two health maintenance organizations, a Maryland Social Services office, and offices for training and rehabilitation. Groceries could be bought at Stop, Shop & Save. And there were plenty of benches on which old-timers could sit and chat in a safe and pleasant setting.

With the opening of Mondawmin in 1956, Jim Rouse found the nerve to take the next big step, developing an enclosed shopping center. He wasn't the first to do it. That contribution to American cultural history belongs to the Austrian-born architect Victor Gruen. In 1952 Dayton's department store in Minneapolis owned 483 acres southwest of the city. Victor Gruen was hired to design a shopping center on eighty-four of those acres. But he wanted to do something much bigger. He not only would design a shopping center but a whole community, which would include single-family homes, apartment buildings, a medical center, a park, a lake, highways, and schools. The department store's executives went along with the idea. But it was not to be. Dayton's found itself in need of cash and began to sell off the undeveloped parts of its holding. Gruen's enclosed Southdale shopping center, in Edina,

Minnesota, opened in the same month as Rouse's Mondawmin, October 1956. Southdale was America's first enclosed shopping center. But not by much.[17]

Jim Rouse had got up the nerve to develop one. He chose a site in Harundale, a neighborhood in the working-class suburb of Glen Burnie, about nine miles south of Baltimore on State Route 2. Rouse then had a hard time borrowing the $4.5 million he thought it would take to do the project. One reason is that merchants were very skeptical about having their front doors face inward toward the central court rather than outward toward the parking lot.[18] Also, Rouse had discovered that most insurance companies were reluctant to make loans for more than one million. His proposals to borrow $4.5 million were turned down twenty-seven times. He then thought he would try to get financing from several insurance companies in packages of under one million. In the end, he worked out a deal with Connecticut General in which the land was sold to the insurance company and then leased back.[19] In a memo to his top staff regarding the financing, Rouse remarked, "The work we are doing with Harundale is difficult but extremely educational. I believe it puts us in a position to make our future projects meet the conditions of the market."[20]

Harundale had its origin in an approach to Rouse by Hochschild, Kohn, the downtown department store, which wanted to put a branch in a suburb south of the city. After he had Sidney Hollander, Jr., conduct the requisite market research, Rouse decided to go ahead. Hochschild, Kohn would be an anchor, and at the other end would be a Food Fair supermarket. Running down the center of the main court, indoors, would be the Sidewalk Café. When completed, there were fifty-two tenants in 364,000 square feet. Outside were 3,300 parking spaces. Among the other tenants who came were two banks, two drug stores, a bakery, a laundry, a barber shop, a Kresge five-and-ten, and an office of the Household Finance Company. If all the stores had been aligned side by side, in the manner of a strip shopping center, they would have stretched for a mile and a half.

Although the numbers at Gruen's Southdale were greater in every category, for the Baltimore area and the whole East Coast Harundale was a big deal. Even during the winter coming soon after opening there would be warmth. Shoppers would be able to sit at the sidewalk café and stroll leisurely in the garden courts amidst oleander, orchids, and cactus. They would hear the chattering of tropical birds and above them would be leaves of various kinds of palm trees.[21] There was much debate about what Harundale's official name should be. Rouse favored Harundale *Haass*. Haass was an acronym he made up for heated and air-conditioned shopping street, a coinage Rouse thought would quickly catch on. He was persuaded by others in the company that his word did not have the right sound. Instead they picked up on a word that was being used in the name of a shopping center in northern New Jersey.[22] The Bergen Mall, which was not enclosed, had lawns between its buildings that were called malls. And so Harundale Mall became Rouse's first heated and air conditioned shopping street. And across America, "mall" became the word for an enclosed shopping center.

At the opening, on October 1, 1958, a lot of excitement was generated by the presence of Senator John. F. Kennedy of Massachusetts, two years before his run for the presidency and already adulated. For Jim Rouse, the more important presence was that of Victor Gruen, whose staff had designed the Hochschild, Kohn department store. According to Rouse's vice president for promotions, Ned Daniels, Rouse was ecstatic that the "master" would see the mall.[23] But Rouse was flabbergasted when the master did not approve. The landscaping, the birds, and the sidewalk cafe were things Gruen had done at Southdale.[24] The most noticeable features at Harundale, recalled Daniels, were all the palm trees and the fountain. As Rouse and Gruen walked along, with Rouse proudly pointing out the features of his building, Gruen listened without saying a word. When Rouse was done, he asked, "Well, Victor, what do you think?" Without hesitating, Victor responded, "Jimmy, it's *atrocious!*"[25] Aesthetically, Gruen thought the place was tacky; pragmatically, he thought all the flora hid too much of the merchandise.

At about the same time Harundale opened, so did Westview, a strip shopping center on the western edge of Baltimore. Its developers had been able to get as a tenant the city's most successful department store, Hutzler's. But a survey done after six months found that shoppers preferred the enclosed Harundale Mall to Westview. This bore out Rouse's belief that the heyday of the strip shopping center was over.[26]

Rouse was well aware of the special mark Victor Gruen had been making as a shopping center architect. With his partner and wife, Elsie Krummeck, Gruen had been asked by *Architectural Forum* in 1943 to design a shopping center that would set a standard for the post-war period; the project was called 194X. Gruen and his partner were determined to avoid designing anything resembling a strip. They put their stores between two highways and had the storefronts face one another with a plaza between. What was especially different was that among the stores were placed community facilities—thirteen public places among twenty-eight stores. The public places included a nursery school, a post office, a library, a theater, a game room, a clubhouse, an auditorium, and an exhibition hall. Gruen and his wife-partner saw post-war shopping centers serving as "the center of cultural activities and recreation."[27] But they also would induce shoppers to spend more time in the centers and do more buying.

In 1950, Gruen was hired by developer Russel Nix to design for the city of Houston the largest shopping center in the world. He anchored the Montclair Shopping Center with two department stores and between them he placed 109 stores. Recognizing the discomfort caused by Houston's humidity, Gruen planned to enclose his shopping street and install air conditioning. The project never got off the drawing boards as Nix was unable to raise the required $12 million. In June 1952, Gruen's design appeared in *Progressive Architecture* to illustrate the way a new generation of shopping centers would look. The text of the accompanying article, written by Gruen and Larry Smith, the shopping center consultant, pointed out that the shopping center as a public space was not a new idea but went all the way back to the agora of the ancient Greeks.[28] Gruen had become the star of shopping center architecture. And this was confirmed when he was invited to speak on "Design of Urban Centers" at the Harvard Urban Design Conference in April 1957.

In the planning for Harundale, Rouse tried to incorporate some of Gruen's ideas. Harundale included a 350-person auditorium and a good-sized meeting room. It was not long before the auditorium was used by church and civic groups and the meeting room for classes such as bridge, tap and ballet dancing, first aid, baton, and Girl Scout Leadership

One of Harundale's tenants was the United Church of Christ. In 1967 the church was having trouble paying the monthly rent. It proposed giving its space over to a church youth group, perhaps at a lower rent. This raised for Rouse and his company the whole issue of the extent to which it should deviate from its basic retail mission and get more involved in community affairs. The company commissioned a study by Barry Schuttler, a public opinion expert, on the question of what its role in the community should be. Schuttler's completed report called "The Harundale Study" was submitted on July 10, 1968. One of Schuttler's main points was that the company could expect more and more competition from other malls focused exclusively on selling. Getting deeply involved in community affairs would be a way of setting the company off from the others. While Schuttler's recommendations were based on what was learned about the effects of the Harundale Mall, the report's intention was to offer a comprehensive and systematic development plan that could be used for any new mall or mixed-use development. The heart of the report was the proposal that each future development be regarded as a "community life center."

To start with, Schuttler advocated market analyses that would include "a broader interpretation of need than a market survey alone would reveal." The growth of the suburbs meant that former city dwellers who moved to the suburbs had left behind the kinds of institutions that contribute to the good life: libraries, theaters, colleges, hospitals, concert halls—pretty much what Victor Gruen said in his 1960 book *Shopping Town USA*. In Harundale, Schuttler said, high rates of crime, alcoholism, divorce, and high school dropping out are indicative of community-wide boredom and disappointment. The apathy and neglect found in many suburban communities are reflected in a community's negative or indifferent reactions to bond issues, tax-supported facilities, crime and delinquency, education, economic growth, and zoning. Community erosion takes place without resistance. The mall can be the neutral ground for private-public sector cooperation for community improvement. In suburban communities, shopping centers can be the new focal point. About what the company was already doing, Schuttler said,

> The changes we have observed in the teenagers' outlooks and behavior to our limited offerings clearly indicate that any process which is honest about present failings, democratic in resolving conflicts, positive in proposing new solutions

and is capable of providing personal growth for future goals is a workable formula for most people.

His conclusion: "We feel a private developer can be the catalyst to accelerate the institutional development of suburbia."

Rouse liked these ideas. He already had decided to set aside the church's space for a youth center, which provided drop-in recreation and crisis intervention. But Schuttler's recommendations were not implemented for Harundale. The youth center, though, brought positive results. The company received reports of a decrease in vandalism and shoplifting. It also learned of the beneficial effect the center was having on individual lives. The Anne Arundel County Council, the county's governing body, was very supportive. In 1971, Jim Rouse wrote to the Council and thanked it for its support. "The Youth Center," he said, "has been an important experience for us and, we hope, for the County. We believe it has extended a helping hand to many young people at a time of need in a way that may prove to be critical in their growth."[29] One mother thought the youth center was responsible for a great change for the better in her son. In 1972, she wrote that the staff "made my son feel that he could trust them and gave him confidence so that he completely turned around from a course toward serious trouble to where he is deciding what kind of life he wants to lead and taking the steps to insure just that."[30] That letter had to make Rouse very happy. While he always cared about profits, learning so directly that his actions could produce positive effects on an individual life had to be especially heartwarming. Schuttler's conclusions made a lot of sense to Rouse, but to implement them he would have to overcome constraints that it was not always possible to overcome.

In succeeding years, the Youth Center began to see more and more young people with serious problems. The state and Anne Arundel County began to provide funding, and the center was licensed by the state Department of Juvenile Justice. Although Rouse by then had retired, in 1994 the company donated more space so that rooms could be set up for individual counseling. Over the next few years, however, Harundale Mall declined rapidly. Marley Station, a newer, bigger mall, had been opened only a mile down the road. It had Hecht's, JCPenney, Sears, and Macy's. Harundale Mall, which once had led the way in offering a distinctive retailing environment, was obsolete. In 1997 the building was sold. The Youth Center moved to the nearby town of Severna Park, where it became known as Robert A. Pascal Youth and Family Services, Inc.

The mall building was renovated and eventually all of it became a Value City discount department store. The ceiling of the main floor was lowered and in orderly lines a thousand fluorescent lamps were installed. No café, no gardens, no tropical birds. If Victor Gruen thought the original mall was atrocious, what would he say about its successor?

To drive south from Baltimore on State Route 2, is to be back in the 1950s. The highway is lined with used car lots, auto repair shops, fast-food places, and chain stores specializing in mattresses and junk furniture. Nine miles out, you get to the site of what had been the Harundale Mall—and on the site in addition to Value City there is a strip mall. Those nine miles contain just the kind of unplanned suburban sprawl Jim Rouse hated.

Chapter 7 Stepping Stones

1. In *Prospectus for Community Research and Development*.
2. www.baltimorestyle.com/ma03issue/timeline-ma03.html. Accessed in March 2004.
3. JWR letter to Joseph's son Harvey, July 1,1988.
4. Autob, 22.
5. www.newsday.com/extras/lihistory/8/hs803a.htm. Accessed March 2004.
6. In Companies/Development files, JWR letter to Alexander B. Griswold, December 6, 1949.
7. JWR letter to Alexander B. Griswold, October 2 1950.
8. Colean's report is dated February 6, 1950.
9. JWR letter to Alexander B. Griswold, February 10, 1950.
10. Jules Tygiel, ed., *The Jackie Robinson Reader* (New York: Dutton, 1997), 114-15.
11. Libby Rouse in phone conversation with author, September 29. 2003.
12. JWR letter to Harry Bart, April 7, 1952.
13. Autob, 27.
14. Autob, 28.
15. Autob, 29.
16. JWR memo to William P. Fulton, January 16, 1968.
17. M. Jeffrey Hardwick, *Mall Maker: Victor Gruen, Architect of an American Dream* (Philadelphia: University of Pennsylvania Press, 2004), 142-44.
18. Autob, 38.
19. Autob, 38.
20. JWR memo to "All Directors," November 8, 1957.
21. Autob, 39.
22. Autob, 40.
23. Olsen, 99.
24. All the information about Southdale is from Hardwick, 142-48.
25. Jim Holechek, *Two Cross Keys Villages* (New York: iUniverse, 2003), 95.
26. Autob, 39.
27. Hardwick, 79-80.
28. Hardwick, 113-14, 119.
29. JWR letter to Anne Arundel County Council, September 10, 1971.
30. Letter from June M. Lewis to Robert Harmon, Harundale Mall manager, November 1,1972.

Chapter 8
The Company and the City

Jim Rouse had gotten Mondawmin built in a changing city neighborhood. With Harundale he had his first enclosed suburban mall. Mondawmin would help foster racial integration. Harundale would provide a new kind of shopping experience as well as services to the community. Ignoring warnings that he was taking on too much, Rouse did not want to put his business on hold, to wait for unequivocal proof of success. Expanding the business and raking in money was something an energetic, optimistic man who had gone through some very tough years in his youth just had to get on with.

The plunge into shopping center development put a strain on Rouse's partnership with Hunter Moss. Rouse was going at a pace that Hunter did not want to even try to keep up with. When the war ended, Moss was a Marine Corps officer in San Diego. In a generally friendly letter to Jim of August 25, 1945, Hunter let it be known that he had no intention of returning to the hectic pre-war business pace that had been set by Jim: "Our previous operation left much to be desired in my opinion." What Moss was saying was that he had been forced into a tandem with a workaholic, and he wanted that to change.

> Financially we were successful as has been borne out in these war years. But we paid the usual price for this success in the form of long hours, little vacation, business at home and on Sundays, and a concentration and pressure that left little time or space for other things that to me constitute living. . . . So maybe you can understand when I say that our past operation is not my pattern for the future.

To put it simply, Hunter Moss's level of exuberance did not come close to Jim Rouse's.

The partnership ended in 1954. Looking back years later, Moss said about Rouse that he "always had 15 balloons up in the air at the same time. He would run over and tap one up, then run over and tap another up."[1] It was a pace that was not for him.

Other friends also told Rouse that between business and his civic work he was doing too much, tapping too many balloons. Moss's departure began a string of changes that ultimately led to the creation of the formidable Rouse Company. The loss of Moss, however, was not a signal to Rouse to slow down. Twenty years later, that frenetic pace was to contribute to the end of his marriage. With Moss gone, Rouse put even more balloons in the air, expanding his business and trying to help cities.

Rouse bought Moss's 50% share in the company, and formed James W. Rouse & Company. He divided the other 50% into five portions of 10% each. Ten percent shares were given to two top Moss-Rouse executives, Lawrence P. Naylor and Tink Carey. Another 10% share was given to Albert (Bob) Keidel, who had been working for Piper & Hill, the mortgage banking house Hunter Moss worked for when he first came to Baltimore. Keidel joined Rouse's company because Jim bought out Piper & Hill in order to get Keidel into his company. Later Keidel was to become the Rouse Company's Chief Financial Officer. Another 10% share was given to brother Bill; as an officer of the company, his focus was to be on leasing tenants for new shopping centers.[2] The remaining 10% was divided up among lower-level executives. Rouse refused to make his own share a controlling 51%. To have done that, he said to those who advised it, "would mean to the others that I am afraid I cannot persuade even one of them to be with me if a conflict arises. . . . It would be an insult to my friends and partners and would reveal something fearful about my attitude toward the deal." Later, he explained further: "I felt that if I insisted on majority control, it would have made them feel less than full partners and the whole plan wouldn't have worked. To me, it was an essential element in building the kind of company we all wanted."[3]

Once committed to shopping center development, Rouse, in 1956, decided to form a subsidiary called Community Research and Development (CRD), which was to be publicly owned, with James W. Rouse & Company remaining privately owned. The prospectus for CRD tells of the accomplishments of James W. Rouse & Company. Among them are representing eighteen life insurance companies and twenty-four savings banks, and having provided the financing for thirty-three shopping centers. The company was servicing more than $150 million in mortgages.

Through the sale of 6% debentures, $3 million was raised for CRD. Major purchasers were Jack Meyerhoff and the partners Harry Bart and Albert Stark, who also had invested in Mondawmin and Harundale. Work for both Waverly Realty and Talbottown was farmed out to CRD, which contracted to be paid 5% of rentals collected for its property management services and another 5% for doing corporate management. But in 1960 and 1961, first Talbottown and then

Waverly Realty were merged into Harundale Mall, Inc. Rouse's purpose was to get mortgage refinancing for the two smaller centers and to generate a better cash flow for CRD.[4]

The 1957 prospectus for CRD was much more than the usual corporate promotion statement.[5] In it Rouse reveals a lot about his business philosophy and intentions. He sees great opportunities for a network of Rouse-style shopping centers, for few, in his opinion, among the current 3,000 have been planned and designed well: "There are not a half dozen well planned centers in the East, nor half that many in the South." Without mentioning Mondawmin, Rouse brags about the coming of the two-level shopping center: "The dramatics of design are increased, the visual pull enlarged; the carnival atmosphere emphasized." Harundale is not yet ready, but Rouse makes it clear that the enclosed shopping center is the coming thing, and will make shopping "a huge bazaar, gay, festive and extremely convenient." The centers to come "will not only have a sharp competitive advantage in relation to old fashioned business districts but also in relation to many new so-called shopping centers which are poorly located or poorly planned or both." The cost of taking advantage of the opportunities for these centers—developing and maintaining ownership—"substantially exceeds the present organization of Rouse & Company and the capital resources of Meyerhoff and Bart and Stark." Thus, going public with CRD was an opportunity to raise money and to provide the framework for going ahead in "community development based on sound research and good planning."

It is often said that the proliferation of Rouse's suburban malls is partly responsible for the decline of central business districts. Isn't it hypocritical for Rouse to lament the fate of those districts and cities when his malls were helping to lure families out of cities? Rouse didn't think so. He thought he was making a much-needed contribution to suburban life.

In the 1950s, Rouse had difficulty appreciating the difference between an in-city shopping center in an outlying neighborhood and a new-style mall in a suburban town. He was aware that shopping centers could have an adverse effect on downtown shopping areas. He argued that they wouldn't. He saw the outlying shopping center and downtown both benefiting. The outlying shopping centers, he said, represented consolidation, not decentralization. In the CRD prospectus, he used Talbottown on the Eastern Shore as an example. He said Talbottown would be "tightly related" to the existing shopping district in the couple of blocks around Easton's centrally located courthouse. Because of the greater amount and variety of merchandise in the combined area, shoppers would come to Easton from greater distances than they had formerly. Rouse acknowledged that in the short run there might be "some initial adjustment for some Easton merchants," but he insisted that in the long run "Easton will be strengthened by Talbottown and Talbottown will be strengthened by Easton." He saw this notion of mutual benefit as a concept that could be applied in numerous smaller cities, especially in the South, where there were as yet relatively few shopping centers. It would seem, though, that Easton, a town of only 6,500 at the time, was a special case; for Talbottown was only a brief walk from the courthouse.

In any case, in the CRD prospectus Rouse foresaw "enormous growth of our cities." He is trying to sell the idea of taking advantage of that growth by placing shopping centers in outlying neighborhoods of small and medium-sized cities, doing more of what was being done with Waverly Tower Shopping Center and especially with what had been done in Jack and Joseph Meyerhoff's Edmondson Village, just within Baltimore's western city limit. Rouse wanted to offer within the city an alternative to downtown shopping. Listen to this paean to the shopping center in outlying neighborhoods:

> The old business districts are not only congested and inconvenient, they are also ugly, grim, formal and impersonal. The well-planned, well-managed new shopping center is a pageant by comparison. The stores front along landscaped malls ["malls" is being used in the older sense]. There are flowers, benches and music in the air . . . literally. There is unity in the design and organization of the stores, signs are controlled and subdued; there are shows, displays, and special events of many kinds. There are children everywhere. Entire families shop together. The air is fresher. The sidewalks are cleaner. People are smiling. There is a gay carnival atmosphere. This is no overstatement. It is one of the aspects about the new well-planned center that is most striking to shoppers and merchants alike. It is a condition with which the old business districts find it almost impossible to compete

If the old business districts can't meet their new competition—tough! But once Harundale in suburban Glen Burnie was up and running, the point about consolidation became moot. Rouse became an enthusiast of enclosed shopping centers in the suburbs—malls. His interest in downtown redevelopment remained very much alive, but it would be quite a while before a Rouse retail development was placed downtown.

Rouse was confident about how to make shopping centers profitable, and the concept carried over into the period of the enclosed mall. After all the relevant research is done and a site is selected, rents have to be determined; the arithmetic is all done before one spade is put into the ground. The amount of rent coming in must be guaranteed; it is the product of careful and thorough research. This is what Rouse called "Guaranteed Minimum Rents," and the total must provide a substantial margin above debt service and operating costs. His rule of thumb was that debt service and operating costs should not be more than 70-80% of the minimum rents. Then on top of the minimum rents, the developer should be able to count on *overage* rents, which are written into leases. The overage is based on a store's gross sales. The percentage paid to the company varies with the type of store, whether or not the store is a desirable tenant, and other such factors. He gives the example of Edmondson Village, where overage rents are more than 100% of the guaranteed minimum rents.

From its origin in 1954 James W. Rouse & Company had been making its shopping center money as "owner's representative." It had been doing market analyses; coordinating planning, engineering, and architecture; and handling leasing, financing, promotion, and management. Now, Community Research and Development (CRD) will build, own, and operate. At the same time, the prospectus says, the company "plans active participation in the nation's growing Urban Renewal Program," and will "follow closely local and federal urban renewal programs for profitable opportunities for residential and commercial redevelopment at the center of American cities." Most of the company's operations, though, were to be far out, not close in.

CRD was formed at a special time in America's history. The country was prosperous: "Our families are making more money and working shorter hours. This means a yearning for space, gardens and recreation of all kinds. It has meant an explosion of our cities into a scatteration of residential communities flowing into the farm lands in all directions."[6] The movement of people to the suburbs has led to increasing sprawl, a hodge-podge that the word "scatteration" aptly conveys. But this movement also has created new retail markets and thus new opportunities for shopping centers: "Massive forces . . . are now at work in the reorganization of the American city." Often Rouse speaks of the *city* when he means the metropolitan area, lumping together city and suburbs. But that is misleading, because while the suburbs are prospering the cities are hurting. Sometimes he acknowledges he is not talking about a win-win situation. Here is what he says in the same document in which he can barely contain his excitement about opportunities in suburbia:

> The upheaval in our cities has not been painless. It has accelerated the deterioration of the inner-city and underscored the problems of the central business district, the economic heart of most major cities. To get rid of the resulting slums and blight; to create decent communities for families of all income levels; to stabilize the inner-city, huge governmental programs have emerged through which billions of dollars will be invested in the renewal and redevelopment of vast areas of the inner city.

In other words, the movement to suburbia has created great opportunities in suburbia at the expense of inner cities, but the consequent deterioration of the inner city itself will present other great opportunities.

CRD's first annual report, dated October 31, 1957, was actually a report made after only four months of operation, so that its fiscal year would correspond to those of the subsidiary shopping center corporations. The report is all of two pages, but James W. Rouse, president, is anxious to tell what has been accomplished. Market studies have been done in thirteen cities, and in a number of them sites are being chosen and negotiations are taking place. He is proud of the work CRD is doing in market research. There are only a few organizations equipped to do what CRD does in analyzing market areas, planning, leasing, financing, and development of shopping centers.

But Rouse also wants it known that "the company has maintained interest in the renewal and redevelopment of the inner core of the older cities." The header in one of the company's publications reads, "The biggest industry in America is the development of the American City." He confidently asserts that

> as this program gathers momentum around the country there will be increasing opportunities to perform important research and development roles and to develop new commercial projects in the heart of the cities. We are equipped to render valuable service in this field and will be alert for appropriate opportunities.

But the company's building projects were not in the hearts of cities. True, Charlottetown, opened in October 1959, was only ten blocks from downtown Charlotte, but North Star Mall, opened in September 1960, is on the northern edge of San Antonio. Cherry Hill, opened in October 1961, is in the heart of South Jersey suburbia. Neither of the next projects—Louisville Mall and Northway Mall (Pittsburgh) is anywhere near the heart of the city. Hamilton Mall, a project that did not work out because no department store was interested, was to be near Cincinnati, not in it.

In 1966, the parent James W. Rouse & Company was acquired by CRD, and the merged firm's name was changed to the Rouse Company. James W. Rouse & Company continued its operations in mortgage banking as a wholly-owned subsidiary of the Rouse Company. All the outstanding stock of James W. Rouse & Company was acquired by CRD.

In the years immediately after the split with Hunter Moss, Rouse, without a partner, pursued new mortgage business, fulfilled the role of President Eisenhower's expert on urban renewal, carried on a study of slum housing in Washington, D. C., and became one of the leaders of the American Council To Improve Our Neighborhoods (ACTION). He was the driving force behind the founding of the Greater Baltimore Committee (GBC), an organization of corporate and civic leaders committed to finding solutions to the region's problems—but mostly the city's. And he also was one of the founders of Baltimore Neighborhoods, Inc., a local group devoted to fighting white flight from city neighborhoods. Jim Rouse's plate was overflowing.

While he spoke frequently on the national slum problem through ACTION, as chairman of GBC's sub-committee on urban renewal Rouse had a platform from which to focus on Baltimore's renewal problems. ACTION, an advisory body on urban renewal, was authorized by the Housing Act of 1954. The work of ACTION fell into three parts: fact-finding and research, which Rouse knew well from the work of his own Metropolitan Research; public information and education, which Rouse did through his frequent speeches; and field service, which Rouse was eager for, because that was *doing* rather than talking. From its beginning Rouse was a member of ACTION's board. In 1958, he succeeded Guy Hollyday, his former boss at Guarantee Title, as president of ACTION. At

ACTION's 1959 conference in Newark, he could not refer to a single American city in which renewal was keeping pace with the rate of deterioration, although the means for renewal were readily available. In both slum and not-yet slum, Rouse said, he wanted to see neighborhoods that were an indignity to their inhabitants broken up. He wanted everyone to be able to live "in an environment where people can not only walk and shop but also rest and smile and breathe fresh air." The city should be brought back to a human scale, so that "it would honor and uplift the people who live in it instead of oppressing and degrading them."[7]

The Greater Baltimore Committee was formally established on January 5, 1955. In December 1955, Jim Rouse circulated his urban renewal subcommittee's report, which certainly must have been written by him. The report said while Baltimore was ahead of most other cities, it was distressing that there was "no plan, program or organization with a potential remedy remotely approaching the problem we face." Rouse had a vision of what the city should be. What needed to be done was, first, stop the downward spiral of the inner city and then breathe new life into it. With much forcefulness the report goes on to say that the purpose of urban renewal is "to clear away rock bottom slums—to rehabilitate dwellings worth saving—to create parks, playgrounds, green areas—to replan the inner city into a community of healthy neighborhoods where people can be proud and happy to live and raise families." This vision could not be realized so long as the planners involved acted separately; there must be a comprehensive plan. Brought up is the example of what Pittsburgh had done with its Golden Triangle. In contrast, in Baltimore, "a cautious, piece-meal few blocks at a time approach, could never have created the values which Pittsburgh has uncovered in its Golden Triangle." In Pittsburgh, the fulfillment of a comprehensive plan had increased tax revenues by $1 million per year.

For a "full scale urban renewal effort," authority and responsibility must be consolidated, not scattered in various bureaus and agencies. In Baltimore, there is "no sharp pinpointing of responsibility, no clear-cut lines of authority." Rouse wants a renewal plan for the entire inner city, and he wants to see movement at a much faster pace. Also, in 1955 Rouse and Nathaniel Keith, a former director of the federal Slum Clearance and Urban Redevelopment program, were asked by the Commissioners of Washington, D.C., to come up with a slum clearance plan for that city, and they did—*No Slums in 10 Years*. Rouse and Keith found "that it is economic and feasible to do the total job; that it is largely a matter of organization and determination to do it." As result of the plan 25,000 people were relocated to public housing in the Northeast and Southeast parts of the city. But not much else happened. Bloom quotes Harry Jaffee and Tom Sherwood, Washington journalists, as saying, "the housing projects were allowed to deteriorate and the surrounding neighborhoods took a turn for the worse."[8] Now Rouse urged Baltimore to plan for the elimination of slums in a fixed number of years. These were to be recurrent themes in Rouse's speeches about cities.

Rehabilitation must be comprehensive and must move along on a fixed, relatively short schedule.

By 1959, thanks to prodding by the GBC—primarily by Jim Rouse—Baltimore had a plan for renewal comparable to Pittsburgh's. In the heart of the central business district, most of the older buildings on twenty-two acres would be demolished. With great exuberance, Rouse, in a speech at a conference in Los Angeles, told about Baltimore's plans for Charles Center.[9] There would be nine new office buildings, new stores, a new hotel, a civic auditorium, underground parking for 4,000 cars, and "several Rockefeller Center-type parks connecting the various elements of the center and tying them in with the city around it." Rouse insisted that the arithmetic of a renewal project would demonstrate its feasibility. In the case of Charles Center the increase in the assessable base of the real estate, he said, would more than make up for what the city would invest in the project. In less than twenty years, the assessable base of the central business district would be increased by over $50 million. The Charles Center project will be completely self-sustaining, and "it will change the entire personality of the central city." It was during the Charles Center planning phase that Rouse made his famous statement about big dreams and great vision: "We have got to have big dreams. We have got to have great vision. We have got to fire people up and get them excited. You've got to enlarge the boundaries. . . . To be large enough to have an impact but small enough to have some immediate success."

Rouse's vision is for all American cities. His hope is that every older city will be remade

> into a slumless, beautiful, efficient city, of healthy neighborhoods and workable business areas. . . . Just as Pittsburgh's Golden Triangle and Baltimore's Charles Center are little demonstrations of what can be done, so will some city in America . . . do the total job that will make itself totally livable. Once it happens there will be an irresistible tide running throughout America.

Still, there was the on-going battle to make livable the slums that weren't going to be wiped away. In 1959, Rouse was still fighting City Hall to get a comprehensive, enforceable housing code. He got the membership of GBC to endorse his sub-committee's report and recommendations. The recommendations were then sent to the four affected city agencies: Urban Renewal and Housing, the Health Department, Fire Department, and the Bureau of Building Inspection of the Department of Public Works. Rouse notes the result: "A disappointing and temporizing report from this group followed shortly thereafter, indicating an unwillingness on the part of some officials to relinquish personal sovereignties in this field."[10]

A new problem reared its ugly head. White people were moving out of the city to the suburbs and being encouraged to do so by a large sector of the local real estate industry. Neighborhoods were rapidly changing from all white to all black. In 1959 a new civic group was organized to deal with the problem. Jim

Rouse, developer of suburban malls, was one of the founding members of Baltimore Neighborhoods, Inc., a mostly white group, founded to hold back panic and white flight, to lodge complaints against unethical realtors, and to carry on a campaign stressing the advantages of urban living. Put down with the label "integrationists," members took the fight against blockbusting as their main purpose. Blockbusting was what realtors did to create panic on a block by selling to one black family and then encouraging white families to sell cheaply so that the same homes could be sold to black families at jacked-up prices. Baltimore Neighborhoods also sought to keep city neighborhoods attractive so that new white buyers would settle there. They did not want to see the city become mostly black while nearby counties became even whiter. Along with Rouse, one of the founders was William Boucher III, then executive director of the Greater Baltimore Committee. The two of them saw to it that GBC provided the integrationists with space, clerical help, and a grant.[11]

Jim Rouse set the Greater Baltimore Committee on the course that led to major urban renewal downtown. GBC created The Planning Council and commissioned it to come up with a plan for the renewal of a "worn out" section of the central business district. It expeditiously formulated the plan for Charles Center. Accepted by the mayor, the plan still had to run the gauntlet of a half-dozen governmental agencies. As the approval process was nearing completion, Rouse was hard pressed to contain his enthusiasm. He wanted to be the developer. Although his company had not done a job of this kind, he was absolutely confident of his and the company's ability to get it done. Before the developer had been chosen, he took the bold step of sending off a proposal for financing to the vice president for real estate investment of the Connecticut General Life Insurance Company. He proposed that Connecticut General become a major partner in the project.

Beyond the likely return on its investment, Connecticut General would earn other rewards.

> We believe you may find some very stimulating collateral interest in this project [Rouse wrote]. Because it is the first project to attack the very heart of the central business district and because the plan deals with the problems so effectively, the project will attract wide interest and attention throughout the country. The fact that the plan itself has been produced by the business community and presented by it to the Mayor, also gives CHARLES CENTER a unique association with an outstanding example of private business initiative in the public interest. If Connecticut General could see its way clear to participate as an equity investor . . . it might open up an important avenue for insurance company activity in major urban development.[12]

It took more than a year for the remaining approval hurdles to be cleared. Only then did the city's Urban Renewal and Housing Agency choose the developer. Despite the fact that more than anyone else he had gotten the project started, put it on the rails, and pushed it forward, Rouse and his company were not chosen. This was one of the most bitter disappointments of his business life.

Still, he remained gracious. After being notified, he wrote a most admirable letter to J. Jefferson Miller, the general manager of the project for the Urban Renewal and Housing Agency:

> Of course, we are disappointed as this is a project which we would have much liked to do. However, no one can quarrel with the manner in which this selection has been made. You have been fair and efficient in handling the selection task and no one can honestly feel that there was a better presentation than the one you chose. . . . Congratulations to you and to Metropolitan Structures.[13]

Chapter 8 The Company and the City

1. Olsen, 48.
2. Olsen, 49-50.
3. Autob, 34.
4. JWR memo to Lawrence P. Naylor III, September 13 1961.
5. This prospectus, other CRD publications, and annual reports are available in CA.
6. In a special two-page blurb called "What is CRD?"
7. JWR speech to "Newark Conference on the ACTION Program for the American City," May 5, 1959.
8. Quoted by Bloom, 81.
9. "Conference on Family Happiness and Security," January 9, 1959.
10. GBC annual report for 1959.
11. Michael L. Mark, *But Not Next Door* (Baltimore: Baltimore Neighborhoods, Inc., 2002), passim.
12. JWR letter to Irving G. Bjork, February 20, 1959.
13. JWR letter to J. Jefferson Miller, May 5, 1960.

Chapter 9
Bad Mall, Good Mall

With Harundale Mall, the die had been cast. Enclosed shopping centers were the wave of the future. While there was big money to be made, not every project worked out. Almost exactly one year after Harundale opened, Rouse's second mall, the first in the South, opened on October 28, 1959, in Charlotte, North Carolina. It was a lot like Harundale but about a third smaller. Charlottetown had a succession of problems. And since space was limited, service to the community would be too.

For one thing, there were problems with Bon Marche, the anchor department store. The highly regarded local store Ivey's soon took its place. But Ivey's too didn't work out; it went bankrupt. A year after the opening, Rouse found himself in a major dispute with the company that had installed the heating and air conditioning systems. A side of Jim Rouse came out that was rarely seen; he could be combative. He thought the bill from Hicks & Ingle was greatly inflated, and he refused to pay. "We have been treated dishonestly and irresponsibly," he wrote the Rouse Company's Charlotte lawyer. Even though Rouse found "incredible discrepancies" between what was agreed to and the size of the bill, he eventually accepted the lawyer's advice and settled—but not for the amount Hicks & Ingle wanted.

> It is probable that Hicks & Ingle were motivated by the belief that we could not afford to be sued; that we could not permit a lien to be filed against the property; that they could prevent us from servicing the equipment and operating the Center; that they could prevent us from concluding any financing of the Center which we might be negotiating.[1]

Rouse told the lawyer, Robert Lassiter, Jr, he would settle only if Hicks & Ingle knocked $125,000 off their bill, charged no interest, and provided $10,000 in reimbursement for what the Rouse Company had to pay to maintain the equipment. Hicks & Ingle refused the offer.

It was only after Jack Meyerhoff became involved and lawyer Lassiter persuaded Rouse that at a trial his company's case would not look as clear-cut as Rouse thought it did and that indeed the only witness for the company would be "murderous" to the company's interest—it was only then, after months of letter-writing, that Rouse agreed to let Lassiter negotiate a settlement. When he was convinced he was right, Rouse could dig in his heels.

During the first two years of Charlottetown's operation there were numerous management problems. Jerome S. McDermott, the management director for all Rouse properties, did not have much enthusiasm for Charlottetown's management. There were problems with trash collection and with store hours. Some tenants did not want to be open evenings. Two of the most important tenants, Bon Marche and Western Auto, did not want to open before noon, as management thought they should. The mall's Merchants Association had difficulty working with the company's promotions manager, who "by nature or personality" was not a good choice. There were problems with the flora, seemingly because the air conditioning system put out a combination of dust and oil that left a harmful film on the plants. The lady who owned the city's best bookshop and who had moved it to Charlottetown complained bitterly about the low quality of the stores she had as her neighbors. Later on, when Ned Daniels came down from the home office, he found much of the mall filthy and desecrated with homemade signage.[2]

This was not the kind of operation with which Rouse wanted to be associated. Things did get better. But soon Charlottetown, which was renamed Madison Square, was in competition with newer malls. This mall was not a winner. The Rouse Company sold it off.

The experience with the Cherry Hill Mall in South Jersey was entirely different. Cherry Hill was Rouse's proudest achievement in the first phase of his career as a mall magnate. Eugene Mori was South Jersey's foremost developer. He had built subdivisions, apartment complexes, and the Garden State Race Track. He also had plans to develop a regional shopping center on farmland across the Delaware River and about ten miles to the northeast of Philadelphia. The piece of land was called Cherry Hill, and, in 1954, he obtained a commitment from the major Philadelphia department store Strawbridge & Clothier (S&C) to build a branch at his center. But Mori was unable to get the financing he needed, and by 1957 the project seemed dead.

Strawbridge & Clothier was determined to see the shopping center built. S&C sought the advice of Larry Smith, the well-known shopping center consultant and now a partner in Victor Gruen's architecture firm. In trying to help S&C find a new developer for the South Jersey site, Smith thought of Jim Rouse.[3] When Rouse was approached by Smith, he could not resist. He would be joining in a project with one of the country's leading department stores and with Victor Gruen, the country's top shopping center architect. It was testimony to Rouse's own growing reputation that he would be asked.

Gruen had designed Southdale and, before that, had gained fame for introducing the outdoor pedestrian mall at Northland, in suburban Detroit, which had a branch of the J. L. Hudson department store. Earlier, he had become known for the work he did designing individual storefronts. Victor Gruen was attractive to Rouse because like himself Gruen was a man of broad interests. As a young man in Vienna Gruen had lived the life of a bohemian. While he worked at a day job as a storefront designer, away from the office he was an actor, a cabaret impresario, and an active member of the Socialist Party. When the Nazis annexed Austria in 1938, because he was Jewish he had to flee. He quickly won design commissions in New York and soon was asked to design stores on the West Coast. He moved to Los Angeles and became the chief designer for the Grayson-Robinson chain stores. Victor Gruen came to America as a refugee. After only a few years, he was deeply involved in writing and speaking about the American way of life. Having started in America as a clothing store designer, he soon had a reputation as an astute commentator on the societal implications of commercial architecture.[4]

Jim Rouse and Victor Gruen were involved with retailing, but both cared about social consequences. At Cherry Hill two passionate, closely aligned sensibilities were brought together. Once Rouse was involved the project got moving. He was able to get Connecticut General to come through with the financing for the purchase of the land. He was able to get financing for construction from The First National Bank of Boston. From the beginning Rouse thought of Cherry Hill as a two department-store mall. Strawbridge & Clothier, though, had not thought that its branch would have a competitor just a hundred yards away. Rouse had a major task of persuasion to get G. Stockton Strawbridge, President of S&C, to accept his two-store concept, especially since Rouse wanted the second store to be Wanamaker's, S&C's chief competitor in Philadelphia. Rouse argued that a mall with two department stores would enlarge its drawing area. With his very persuasive letter to Strawbridge, Rouse included a list of twenty-two locations in various parts of the country where two department stores had a synergistic effect beneficial to both stores. Rouse's ingratiating concluding paragraph made it hard for Strawbridge to say no to this unusual developer: "We fully respect the sincerity and thoughtfulness with which you have approached this matter. We will accept ungrudgingly your decision whatever it may be and will work with undiminished enthusiasm to make Cherry Hill as great a Center as it ought to be."[5]

Strawbridge agreed to accept Wanamaker's. But Wanamaker's decided it wanted to locate at a different South Jersey site. Rouse was not stymied by the rejection. He sent his brother to New York to lure Macy's to Cherry Hill. The mission was successful, and by getting Macy's, under its New Jersey name of Bamberger's, Rouse won the love of Strawbridge and also his lenders. With later expansion, the mall added a third department store, JCPenney.

The mall would be "L"-shaped, with Bamberger's added to the shorter of the two shopping streets. At the juncture of the two streets, in front of S&C, would be the fountain court with its huge fountain. High up was the beginning of a long skylight, adding to the feeling of spaciousness on the two wide streets. Rouse carried out an experiment by making Community Research and Development the general contractor for the project. But having to work with all the separate tradesmen—the carpenters, the plasterers, the electricians, the plumbers—proved to be a big headache, and Rouse would not take on the job of general contractor again. Another headache was caused by a big oak tree on the property. Brother Bill wanted it taken down; Jim thought it worth the expense of working around it. Memos went back and forth. Jim had the last words:

> What bothers me is that we are so inflexible and unresourceful about taking advantage of natural assets that can give personality, warmth, appeal to the Center. If we were doing our job properly, we would find the way to make use of a tree such as this.[6]

Bill Rouse was in charge of getting tenants signed up. The challenge was to get shoppers away from the fountain area and to the far ends of the L. To help accomplish that, he leased to a movie theater and a large Woolworth's at one end and a supermarket at the other. He managed to get seventy-five smaller stores in between. Many of them specialized in foreign gift items. That led to the idea to get into the courts, as they were called, kiosks and pushcarts that also sold exotic items. As a result, the mall was able to advertise its International Bazaar.[7]

The enthusiasm of G. Stockton Strawbridge for Cherry Hill can, perhaps, be best conveyed by his desire, as opening day approached, to fly near the site the country's largest American flag. He wrote to Rouse in August 1961 that "The raising and lowering of the 'colors' of the country's largest flag could add character and appeal to the whole Cherry Hill enterprise in our judgment and provide a substantial conversation piece for all and sundry."[8] Rouse told his staff that Strawbridge deserved to have his ideas taken seriously and designated a staff person to find out where the country's largest flag at the time was. It was in Detroit, and it was so large that it required the work of a team of attendants. In the end, Strawbridge settled for the flying of a conventionally large flag.

The relationship with Victor Gruen and his firm did not work out too well. Rouse was not the kind of manager who always deferred to the professionals he contracted with. While he was not eager to take issue with specialists, he respected his own judgments and sometimes openly questioned theirs. That was especially true with architects, whom he suspected were too eager to turn their work into aesthetic statements at the expense of the overall good of the projects they were working on. "Victor Gruen Associates" was based in Beverly Hills, California. Karl Van Leuven, one of Gruen's associates, was the firm's Cherry Hill manager. Rouse took issue with Van Leuven's selection of colors and let him and Gruen know about it. The annoyed Van Leuven responded with, "We would like to heartily recommend that, please, they be left as they are."[9] Now Rouse was angry and wrote out a detailed criticism. He raised four points, of which the following is one:

> Inasmuch as we are using white brick, it seems to me that we should avoid the use of white paint anywhere on the exterior in order that there will not be a conspicuous contrast between the whiter white of the paint and duller white of the brick. Such a contrast, it seems to me, will only make the brick show up poorly and give it an impression of dirtiness. In this connection, I think the columns of the exterior entrance units should not be white. Also, the coping which runs around the entire building should not be white.[10]

The architects yielded.

Difficulties with the Gruen firm continued. One cause was that Strawbridge & Clothier went directly to the architects when they were unhappy about something that was within the developer's jurisdiction. Rouse had to remind both the store and the architect that the architect was working for him. The difficulties continued after Cherry Hill's official but partial opening. Rouse concluded that Van Leuven had an attitude problem. Van Leuven did not like the work being done by the company that the developer hired to do signs for smaller stores. He expressed his judgment in a letter filled with sarcasm. His closing sentence was, "With these small reservations, I hereby approve, with a shutter [sic] of revulsion, the store front as submitted including the sign."[11] Rouse called Van Leuven's letter "a real shocker," but he resisted the temptation to respond with sarcasm of his own directed at a professional who didn't know the difference between shutter and shudder. "Who is responsible to whom for what?" Rouse asked. He called for a meeting between Van Leuven, Victor Gruen, and himself to review their relationship.[12]

Despite the tensions that developed with Gruen, Rouse continued to use his firm. But in a few years, after 30 years in America, Gruen went back to Vienna. When Gruen turned 70, Rouse sent his greetings and told the architect of the influence he had had.

> Surely most lives that you have touched have been warmed and lifted by your own warmth and inspiration. . . . You touched me and my associates at an important point of time in our individual growth and in the growth of the company. You enabled us to move from the "provinces" to the "big time" when you opened the doors for us at Cherry Hill. . . . There is no space that we have produced that is as grand and floating as Cherry Court. I have always felt that you built it with your own hands.[13]

In memos and at meetings Strawbridge again and again expressed doubt that the developer could have Cherry Hill ready for an October opening, which the department store needed to fully capitalize on Christmas shopping. Rouse tried to reassure him, but such reassurances were to no avail. Strawbridge brought in experts who confidently asserted that an October opening was out of the question. But on October 11, 1961, a very grand opening was held. Built at a cost of $30 million, the Cherry Hill Mall was called by Rouse "our proudest venture." Scores of business associates of Rouse and Strawbridge, Governor Robert B. Meyner of New Jersey, and other public officials were invited to the festivities, which began with parties the night before. Nowhere east of the Mississippi was there a comparable shopping palace. Estimates of the number of people who passed through the mall that day ranged from 35,00 to 60,000. They browsed and bought in the seventy-six stores that were ready for opening day. In the part of the mall called Cherry Court, a twenty-foot high birdcage held Australian finches and toucans and mynas from the jungles of South America. There were gardens and a total of 14,000 trees, flowers, and shrubs. There was a stream. And clusters of benches invited visitors to sit and relax.[14]

Three months later, Rouse decided that one of the two courts was not generating enough emotional warmth in visitors. He wrote a memo to Bill Rouse suggesting some changes:

> It seems to me that the general environment at Market Court would be much improved if there were a few benches placed at the edge of the Court near the walkways which go around it in order that people could sit and relax in it. These might or might not have planters associated with them depending on the space involved. There is a feeling of coldness about Market Court that might be relieved by benches and people sitting on them.[15]

To further demonstrate the mall's role in the community, that first spring management invited the junior class of Cherry Hill High School West to hold its prom in Cherry Court.

The partnership between Jim Rouse and G. Stockton Strawbridge at Cherry Hill turned out to be a great success. The collaboration was extended. They reprised their roles with the development of the Echelon Mall, also in South Jersey, and three malls in Philadelphia suburbs in Pennsylvania. The Plymouth Meeting Mall, the first two-level mall in the East, was a Rouse-Strawbridge collaboration. Together they also did the Springfield, Neshaminy, and Exton Square malls. Then Strawbridge asked Rouse to do a mall in downtown Philadelphia. In 1977, at Ninth and Market Streets, the 125-shop Gallery opened, a suburban-type mall in the heart of the city. Strawbridge's enthusiasm for this project was perhaps excessive. On opening day, August 11th, he said that Jim Rouse's "imagination and vigor have changed the face of suburban retailing and now are doing the same for downtown Philadelphia."[16] A few years later, Willard G. Rouse III, Bill Rouse's son and Jim's nephew, developed buildings that produced an even greater change in downtown Philadelphia.

In April 1963, the Harvard Graduate School of Design held a conference that was focused on shopping centers. Jim Rouse was asked to speak on Cherry Hill Mall. The topic of the conference was "The Regional Shopping Center: Its Role in the Community It Serves." Rouse was enormously gratified by being invited and being named the conference chairman. One of Rouse's major points was that designers should create an environment that can be used "to serve the community—to become central to the community, so that the community will adopt it as its center and develop deep feelings of pride, enthusiasm and concern for it, and for its shops." With the arrival on the retailing scene of the big discount stores, Rouse asserted that for the shopping center "the surest route to achieving relative invulnerability to excessive competition in the retail field is to build a center of such quality and such importance to the community that it doesn't become readily assailable. . . ." There must be fewer promotional spectaculars "and more and more responsible serving of the community needs through art shows, music and displays and activities of all kinds that are useful and important to the community."

He spoke about some of the effects on the community of the Cherry Hill Mall. He had learned that the principal of the local high school remarked that behavior of students at the high school had improved as a result of the standards for behavior at the mall. The mall had given people in the area a sense of community that they had not had before. He had learned also that two department store managers considered the employees at their stores the best they had ever encountered. The high quality of the employees, the managers thought, was directly related to the high quality of the environment in which they worked. "These people didn't look upon working as a department store clerk in the Mall in the same spirit as in a department store downtown or in a strip mall." One of the stores, Rouse said, whose first year sales were double what was expected, attributed its success to two things: the design of the mall and the quality of the salespeople. "If design created an environment that produced salespeople that produced sales that produced increased rents, then this proves you can design for people and produce profits as a residual of that effort."[17]

But also heard at the conference were the voices of skeptics who believed more control should be exerted by local townships over private development. Raised also was the issue of the effects of such projects on nearby cities. Edmund Bacon, a University of Pennsylvania planner, stated that he decisively rejects "whatever vitiates the life of the central core" [Philadelphia is only a dozen miles from Cherry Hill]. Further, Bacon let it be known that he didn't think much of typical mall culture: "cub scout dens, fashion shows, and barber shop quartets."[18]

A decade later, the Camden County Economic Development Commission made a statement about what Rouse and his company had accomplished. They had

> revolutionized the retail structure of Camden County with the opening of the Cherry Hill Mall in 1961. Shopping patterns dramatically changed for thousands. The convenience of the all-weather mall and the variety of stores wrought a merchandising miracle in the Delaware Valley. While the architecture and the construction of The Rouse Company projects in Camden County have drawn national acclaim, the malls are recognized, too, as more

than shopping centers. Their generous contribution of space and facilities have added new dimensions to communal life. They're really the main street of suburbia...."

On the mall's fortieth anniversary, the local mayor, Susan Bass Levin, said the mall had brought national recognition to the area. "It put us on the map.... It changed our way of living and it pushed suburbia forward and showed that Cherry Hill was a place to live."[19]

Just inside the mall's main entrance is a boulder on which are inscribed the names of James W. Rouse and Victor Gruen as the persons responsible for the mall's development. Cherry Hill Mall was the proudest achievement of the first phase of Jim Rouse's business life. Nevertheless, the Rouse Company, founded by Jim Rouse, decided in April 2003 that the time had come to cut the tie. Seven years after the founder's death, Cherry Hill Mall was sold to the Pennsylvania Real Estate Investment Trust. It wasn't that the mall wasn't making money; it wasn't making enough. It was the kind of bottom-line decision Jim Rouse would have frowned upon.

Chapter 9 Bad Mall, Good Mall

1. JWR letter to Robert Lassiter, November 8, 1960.
2. "Report to Directors of Charlottetown," 1961.
3. Olsen, 99.
4. Hardwick, 48-49.
5. JWR letter to G. Stockton Strawbridge, December 30, 1960.
6. Quoted by Olsen, 106.
7. Olsen, 104.
8. G. Stockton Strawbridge letter to JWR, August 21, 1961.
9. Quoted by JWR in memo to J. Franklin Groff, August 15, 1961.
10. JWR memo to J. Franklin Groff, August 15, 1961.
11. Quoted by JWR in letter to Karl Van Leuven, January 30, 1962.
12. JWR letter to Van Leuven, January 30, 1962.
13. JWR letter to Victor Gruen, June 14, 1973.
14. Olsen, 103.
15. JWR memo to Bill Rouse, January 4, 1962.
16. Peter Binzen, "The Rouse family and Philadelphia go way back together," www.philly.com/business/columnists/peter_binzin/10991943.htm. Accessed January 2006.
17. JWR Harvard speech, April 26, 1963.
18. Bloom, 120-21.
19. Quoted by Thomas A. Bergbauer, "Cherry Hill Mall started a new era," www.southjerseynews.com. Accessed May 2004.

Chapter 10
The Summer of 1963

For Jim Rouse 1963 had several high points. Among them was the speech at Harvard in April. Another was the speech scheduled for Berkeley in September. Between April and September, the fantasy of a planned city between Baltimore and Washington looked more and more like an idea that could be carried off. Ideas were percolating; he was developing s sharp sense of what was good, not so good, or unacceptable. In August the European new towns that came under his eye in were sharply scrutinized. While the Harvard speech had been mostly devoted to the story of Cherry Hill Mall, Rouse began the speech with a celebration of developers and a putting down of architects. He was unhappy with architects because he thought they were more interested in self-expression than in function and service. He didn't think architects were really interested in the effects of their designs on the people who would have to live with them. He didn't think architects seriously considered whether their designs would elevate or degrade people. "Our cities are filled largely with tasteless, ugly, disordered products of the profit machine [built by other developers, the ones without a social conscience] or with cold, inhuman, unrelated monuments to architectural eminence."[1] In this, Rouse was echoing the ideas of Victor Gruen, who had spoken at this very conference a few years before.

But Gruen was an architect, and Rouse the developer was out to trump him. At a conference of architects a few years earlier Gruen had asked,

> Do we as representatives of a profession concerned with the shaping of the man-made environment, have a right to enjoy the luxury of discussing from Olympian heights the merits and demerits of styling certain aristocratic buildings—which stay away from the plebes?[2]

Rouse would never be so flip as to speak of "plebes." And the clashes they had had at Cherry Hill revealed an approach by Gruen and his firm that bespoke the 4architects' aristocratic superiority. In Gruen he had an ally, but what could Gruen accomplish beyond designing a few shopping centers? Gruen's tone is often belligerent and mocking; Rouse's almost never is. Gruen does not have an approach, or a profession, that could have an impact comparable to a developer's, that could produce a truly major accomplishment. Community-oriented shopping centers certainly are accomplishments. But Rouse the developer could build whole communities of which shopping centers are only a part. Hence the opening sentence of Rouse's Harvard speech: "This is a great day for us developers."

Despite the difference in approaches and the clashes on Cherry Hill, Rouse preferred Gruen to any other architect. He and Gruen continued to work together. They collaborated on the Plymouth Meeting Mall and also the Greengate Mall, near Pittsburgh. When Norfolk, Virginia, cleared out a large area in its central business district, Rouse and Gruen were brought in and together made plans for a mall and two 15-story office buildings, although the plan collapsed when they could not find a suitable department store willing to invest. They made plans for a downtown revitalization project in Paterson, New Jersey, but again they could not find a willing department store.

It was in the Harvard speech that Rouse expressed his opinion—shocking to architects— that "the greatest piece of urban design in the United States today is Disneyland." Disneyland, he said, shows a respect for people. "It fulfills all the functions it set out to accomplish unself-consciously, usefully and profitably to its owners." Good urban design avoids "the arrogance of self-conscious architecture and self-centered profit making." Good urban design is based on what "works best for people in a physical environment," gets "people to relate to one another successfully."

Rouse continues to think of suburbs as just extensions of the city; a metropolitan area is still a city. When people move to outlying areas, that is but a natural movement from the congestion caused by close-in growth and a natural preference for the new over the old. Population growth, the automobile, and "new informal ways of living" are responsible for the proliferation of regional shopping centers. When he talks about the regional shopping center, he acknowledges no white flight, no self-segregation based on income or race. He sees the regional shopping center as the "new downtown." With his own children in private schools, he seems unaware that a powerful force in the migration to the suburbs is the downward slide in the quality of city public schools. Court-ordered desegregation is taking place in city schools. White children are being bused out of comfortable white neighborhoods; black children are being bused in. And more and more white parents in the city are trying to decide whether it's private school for their children or a move to a suburb. On the inside of the city line, the public schools are becoming noticeably inferior; on the other side of the line is a suburban public school system with far fewer problems and safer schools.

The ideal regional center, Rouse said, does not yet exist. "We are continually discovering new vacuums, new gaps, unmet needs which, once discovered, can be tapped with profit and a real sense of service to the community." But there is a crucial difference that is already evident between the old collection of stores out on the highway and the newer regional centers: the quality of management. Once the older stores were rented, the landlord walked away and had an agent collect the rent. "That doesn't begin to resemble the role of management in a regional shopping center today." In contrast to the newly arrived discount stores, the successful regional shopping center must focus on quality, the quality of the whole mall experience, rather than on price. The design of the mall has to be such that the community it serves will "develop deep feelings of pride, enthusiasm, and concern for it, and for its shops." That's the surest way to beat off the discount store's challenge to malls.

Rouse's pride and joy was Cherry Hill. It had become an integral part of the community. It clearly had reinforced the idea that a good physical environment could do much to enhance the quality of people's lives. Yet, Rouse said,

> Some people think it absurd that we should consider moving into this field; that our job is to do the best possible job of retailing and not seek to take over from the churches and the schools many of the community functions that they can best perform.

At this point in time Rouse was not sure how far to go with service to the community. And despite speaking of the malls as new downtowns, he really wasn't at all sure about their effects on the old downtowns.

Near the end of the speech, he asks a series of questions about the effects of the regional shopping center and especially on the central city:

> What does it do to downtown? Is it a threat? Is it a reasonable threat? Is the battle to make downtown serve many of these needs the right answer? Are we breaking up the market in such a way that the central city can never really do the job that it ought to do?

If at this point Cherry Hill is the exemplar, the questions which Rouse should have asked are these: Did Cherry Hill hurt the city of Philadelphia? Did the great benefits to the Cherry Hill community outweigh the damage that might have been done to the city? In deference to the needs of Philadelphia, should Cherry Hill not have been built?

For two years, Community Research and Development, had owned the 68-acre parcel of land in northern Baltimore that was to be developed into the Village of Cross Keys. When the contract for the purchase of the land was signed in June of 1961, construction at Cherry Hill was in high gear. At first Rouse wasn't sure what he would do with this most desirable piece of land. Then the idea of a residential community settled in, and in a memo to "Everyone in the Company," he announced that this will be the largest, and potentially most important development in the history of Baltimore. We look upon it as a great opportunity to do an outstanding job in residential development. We hope that we can bring to the residential field some of the fresh thinking, good taste and high standards which we believe have marked our shopping center development.[3]

A year later, after his staff people had visited dozens of communities across the country to learn what they could, Rouse arrived at some conclusions about the type of community he wanted. He did not want it to be "out of scale" with the people who would be living there, "oppressively out of scale with a man, his wife and their family."

The terms of the land purchase required him to keep the seller, the Baltimore Country Club, informed of the company's plans. So he wrote to the chairman of the club's committee, on July 16, 1962, to describe his latest thinking.

> There is a real need [he said] for residential developments in which there is a strong sense of community; a need to feed into the city some of the atmosphere and pace of the small town and village; a need to create a community which can meet as many as possible of the needs of the people who live there; which can bring these people into natural contact with one another; which can produce out of these relationships a spirit and feeling of neighborliness and a rich sense of belonging to a community of which the man, wife and family are genuinely a part.[4]

He projected the eventual population of his Village of Cross Keys to be about 5,000. This, he thought, would be the right size for a village.

Through the rest of 1962 and into 1963, discussions were held and decisions on Cross Keys were made and unmade. As the summer of 1963 approached, Rouse broke the family's summer tradition. Instead of the annual trip to a remote wilderness spot, father, mother, and three children would go to Europe. None had been there before. They would be away for forty days, and for Jim it would be a *working* vacation. There was much to be done with regard to the Village of Cross Keys, but Rouse was now thinking of a project that would go way beyond that one. He was buying farm after farm for a huge new project: developing a completely new city.

It was just two days before departure, on July 23, 1963, that he wrote down and circulated his notions on new towns and villages for feedback from his top staff. He said he was uncomfortable with the discussion of professional basics that he was accustomed to hearing among planners and architects. They talk about space and scale and land use, but never get to the all-important question of the ultimate purpose of a community. He, though, is convinced that the ultimate purpose must be the improvement of mankind, but he is not sure about what constitutes improvement.

> Is the "advanced" civilization of New York truly superior to the "undeveloped" society represented by the swamp slums of San Juan when it develops hostility,

violence and delinquency in Puerto Rican immigrants who, although illiterate and underfed, were friendly people in their native land?

He hoped to find some answers by investigating the new towns that had sprung up in Europe. He hoped to gain insights from conversations with their planners and administrators.

Most of the vacation was spent in Great Britain. While in London he spent an afternoon with an important English developer, Sidney Mason of Hammerson Properties. Mason hoped to expand his operations to the United States. Rouse asked Mason what he aspired to achieve in the U.S. Mason's answer was simple and direct: he wanted the highest possible return for the lowest possible financial commitment. No talk of "ultimate purpose" from Mason. Rouse might just as well have been talking to Donald Trump. Mason wanted to know what kind of deal he would get if he put up money for a Rouse project. Rouse said that if Mason, as the capital partner, put up all the capital needed, he might get a 50% return at first but then the return would sharply decline. On the trip, Rouse used a company Dictaphone to record his observations and impressions. About the proposal he had made to Mason, he said, "This proposal did not stir him."[5]

Rouse had heard about the "Peckham Experiment" and asked the New Town people he met what had happened to it. Peckham had been a London health center in the 1930s that was very much like a comprehensive community center in America. It was founded by two physicians who believed in a preventative rather than a curative approach to health. More specifically, they believed that a person's social and physical environment had a decisive effect on health. One of their emphases was exposure to light, which, they believed, the English did not get enough of. For one shilling a week the 950 families who signed up were able to participate in exercise, games, workshops, and other recreational and educational activities, all in addition to health care. The center closed down in 1950, by which time the National Health Service had become the common person's main source of health care. Rouse was interested to find out whether there was confirmation of his own thinking about the effects of the physical environment on people's well being.[6]

He was impressed by the dance halls and bingo parlors he saw in new towns. Essentially these were community spaces. He asked in his notes, "Why couldn't such a dance hall be built and run commercially as a part of a total unit in a center the size of Cherry Hill?" He saw the multiple uses such places could have: "the total unit would include an auditorium, a dance hall, a teen-age club, a club for the elderly, a cocktail lounge club. . . . Here would be a real community center." Through its fees it would sustain itself and might even be profitable so that it would attract other profitable tenants adjacent to it. "How about trying it," he asks, "at the Food Fair end of Cherry Hill?"[7] In fact, later, on a much larger scale, the basic principle of providing amenities for a fee was put into effect with the Columbia Association.

Basildon New Town was authorized in 1949, to be built on 7,834 acres in Essex. When completed it was to have a population of 80,000 in both rental and individually owned homes. Rouse visited and spoke with the top staff. If he could do it over again, the manager told him, he would plan for neighborhoods of approximately 5,000 people. A neighborhood that size, he was convinced, has the most vitality. That's just what Rouse had been thinking. Rouse noticed that Basildon has everything except major retail stores and places of employment. He thought the neighborhoods would be strengthened if these facilities were located around the small central campus and each could benefit from the presence of the other. Some of the local officials agreed with him that this would be a big improvement. And later, of course, large retail stores and places of employment were to be included in Columbia.

Rouse was disappointed that the officials he had been speaking to had not considered the question of "ultimate purpose." For them, new towns served a very simple worthy purpose—to move people out of slums. They wanted their new towns to be reasonably economical and to have some aesthetic appeal, but that is as far as it went. Although they acknowledged that there was a growing problem with boredom, their horizons had not been raised sufficiently for them to be interested in fostering community involvement. There is a community center consisting of a main hall, a kitchen, and two smaller rooms. Rouse noted that it was "much like our community centers in the shopping centers" and implied that this was barely adequate.

In Sweden, he visited Farsta, the planned mixed-use community outside Stockholm. Farsta, built in the 1950s, is one of a number of Swedish planned suburbs that attempt to provide everything a community might need. Shops, medical buildings, libraries, and recreational facilities are at the center of the community along with several high-rise apartment buildings. Smaller buildings, row houses, and single-family homes are in surrounding areas. Each residential area has a day-care facility, a playground, and other recreational facilities. Woods and lakes are close at hand. Camping, swimming, boating, cycling, and walking are popular activities along the numerous public trails. Rouse was impressed, and, on a far larger scale, Columbia was to incorporate much of what Rouse saw in Farsta.[8]

August 28, 1963, was an important day in the United States, the day of the civil rights movement's March on Washington for Jobs and Freedom, the day on which Martin Luther King, Jr., delivered the famous "I Have a Dream" speech. The racial situation in America was a hot topic in Europe. In conversations with local people, Rouse refused to be defensive about American race relations. He spoke of the march as "a magnificent demonstration of the true resiliency of democracy." He thought it was wonderful that

> a minority racial group was winning its full rights through a use of the democratic process, and winning them because the white people were helping

them win. . . . This was not the shame of America—this was the pride of America. . . .

Earlier, he had got into a heavy conversation with the English student, a freshman at the University of Leicester, who was the family's guide in London. The student, to Rouse's dismay, did not like Americans. His attitude was the result of the tours he gave Americans. He found them to be "uncultured, unobjective, inarticulate, provincial, flagwaving, overanxious about Russia, oppressive to the Negro." As Rouse says in his New Towns notes, "all in all, an unpleasant picture." "The biggest disappointment," he went on, came in the form of the end-of-the-day compliment from the young guide. The student said that his conversation with Mr. Rouse was the first he had been able to have with an American on important issues that was worthwhile. The student said, according to Rouse that "always before, after a few thrusts, he had found that Americans were so opinionated, emotional, and provincial that it was impossible to carry on a conversation. Thus he withdrew from further attempts." Rouse felt a duty to try to tip the balance the other way. In his notes about another conversation, Rouse wrote down his position as this: "America should be proud of the freedoms which are being won by 20,000,000 former slaves through the stretch and dynamics of the democratic process."

Rouse got onto the subject of another minority group in a speech he made the following February at the banquet of the Baltimore Real Estate Board. He said he had detected "human renewal" in Baltimore, a new respect for the dignity of the individual, in particular a new attitude among his peers toward the Jewish people of Baltimore. "We're beginning to throw off in Baltimore," he said, "the intolerance that has shamed many of us for a long, long time, and that's the fearful segregation of our Jewish community within our City." He went on:

> Here we have among us 8% of the population that but for which Baltimore would be a hollow shell. Every major sports team in the City, every major cultural facility, every major charity drive, every major public interest effort in the City of Baltimore depends indispensably upon the strength and support of the Jewish community, and yet for generations these great people have felt the cold, hard thrust of the turned away cheek in the City of Baltimore, and I think that there are such wonderful signs that not yet gone, but gradually breaking down, is this particular form of human indignity.[9]

Jim Rouse and his family were back in Maryland on September 5th. When he put in his request for company reimbursement for expenses on the trip, Rouse explained that the purpose of the visits to new towns "was to gather information concerning site selection, design, construction, leasing, sales, management, and overall planning and development of these projects." The information was necessary for "the planning and development of 14,000 acres of land acquired in Howard County, Md" (Of the total cost of the trip, Rouse indicated that 20% was for business purposes, coming to $247.37). It is clear, though, that he was far less interested in gathering technical data than he was in hearing about the quality of life of the residents of the new towns.

On September 26, Rouse was in Berkeley to deliver a speech to a conference on The Metropolitan Future. He gave his speech the title "It Can Happen Here," a play on the title of the 1935 novel by Sinclair Lewis *It Can't Happen Here*. Lewis, of course is being ironic, for what he shows in the novel is that it certainly can happen here. It happens when a folksy and likable but ignorant man is elected president. He quickly succeeds in turning the United States into a tyranny along the lines of those of Nazi Germany and Fascist Italy. As Lewis intended to depict the very worst that could happen, Rouse was intent on depicting the very best that could happen here.

Rouse pegged his remarks on the assumption that within twenty years or so, by 1980, there would be a huge growth in the populations of America's major metropolitan areas. Given the sorry state of the planning and development process in the country, such growth is very bad news. In all but a few cases the problems of the city have not been successfully dealt with. American urban society is characterized by "slums, blight, disorder, congestion, ugliness, grimness, juvenile gangs, declining self-reliance, slipping morality, increasing neurosis, loneliness, bewilderment, lack of high purpose and principle." In speaking about the metropolitan future, now at Berkeley as at Harvard earlier, Rouse shows no awareness of the forces motivating people to move out of cities. He predicts that the populations of major cities would double by 1980. By the year 2000, however, many city populations had gone down by 20%.

Rouse complains once again that the professionals involved with cities fail to ask the important questions about purpose and needs, about what constitutes "the good environment." Rouse's main criteria for the successful community are now clear: "The most successful community would be that which contributed the most by its physical form, its institutions, and its operation to the growth of people." And what constitutes such growth? *The improvement of mankind.* That is the ultimate test. Does a civilization "uplift, inspire, stimulate, and develop the best in man?" What encourages such improvement? Rouse's answer is simple: behavior in accord with the first two of the Ten Commandments—loving God and loving one's neighbor. And he asks,

> If that were the target and the test of community planning; if we were really trying to create inspired, concerned, and loving people, might this not begin to influence the kind of plans we would unfold; and might it not point the way to answers we are not now perceiving?

In our planning for enlarged metropolitan areas, we need to plan "out from the real needs of people instead of inward from the preconceived notions of the designer." We need to ask what kinds of neighborhoods make people feel secure, comfortable, and important; what is the ideal size for getting people to take an interest in and to participate in community life; what degree of racial, ethnic, and economic mixing is desirable? And, perhaps picking up on his interest in the Peckham Experiment, Rouse asks whether community health and activity centers could help to discover medical and emotional problems at an early and more treatable age.

Anticipating some of the recommendations that soon would emerge from the Work Group helping to plan Columbia, Rouse again asserts his belief in the virtues of the small community—the small town or village. "I believe that a broader range of friendships and relationships occurs in a village or small town than in a city." In the small town or village, "There is a greater sense of responsibility for one's neighbor and also a greater sense of support by one's fellow man." Ideally, people also should be close to nature physically and be able to allow nature to infuse their spirit. They should be able "to fish and watch birds; find solitude; study nature in a natural environment; feel the spaces of nature—all as part of everyday life." The ideal he visualizes is a city of "small communities separated by topography, highways, public institutions, or greenbelts, and united by a center that provided cultural, educational, recreational facilities. . . ."

But Rouse is careful to say that there is no one right answer to the question of what is the best kind of environment. He does know that the professionals involved in planning must change their attitudes and become "people-centered." They "must find their excitement in what works for people." The architect, in particular, must think of himself less as an artist and more as a "social servant." A new attitude also is necessary among public officials. They must rid themselves of their negative expectations regarding the city.

"Well-organized, efficient, livable, beautiful cities are possible." Yes, it can happen here, and Rouse is determined to prove it. It's September 26, 1963. For two years he's been working on plans to make Cross Keys a model village; construction is under way. For a year he's been secretly accumulating land in rural Maryland; he's got over 13,000 acres. On September 30th, back in Maryland, he makes a public announcement of his intention. A planned city will be built between Baltimore and Washington.

Chapter 10 The Summer of 1963

1. JWR Harvard speech, April 26, 1963.
2. Quoted by Hardwick, 161.
3. JWR to Everyone in the Company, June 20, 1961.
4. JWR letter to Charles H. Buck, July 16, 1962.
5. Transcriptions of JWR's observations are in CA Series VII, subseries 3. JWR and Mason, August 7, 1963.
6. Information about Peckham can be found at www.open2,net/modernity3_6.htm. Accessed May 2004.
7. New Towns notes.
8. On Farsta, see www.auldenfire.com/contacts/directions/fs.shtml. Accessed April 2004.
9. JWR speech at the Baltimore Real Estate Board banquet, February 1, 1964.

Chapter 11
The Village of Cross Keys

In 1961, with the pressure of G. Stockton Strawbridge on him to have Cherry Hill ready for an October opening, Jim Rouse jumped into another big project. On June 16th, he had bought sixty-eight acres inside Baltimore from the Baltimore Country Club—at $25,000 an acre, at the time a large amount.

It all happened very quickly. Rouse had been hoping to do a residential project within Baltimore, but a suitable site had not been available. Suddenly a site was available. The Baltimore Country Club, located within the city, decided to build a new golf course outside the city and sell off the old one. The southern end of the old course would be taken by the city and used for two high schools; the northern sixty-eight acres were suddenly available to the right buyer. At the June meeting of the Community Research and Development board, the goal of building a residential community was reaffirmed. Later on that Wednesday, news broke about the availability of the golf course land. Before Rouse was heard from, several other potential buyers had expressed their interest. On Friday, June 16th, Rouse, having canvassed his board, submitted a signed contract in which he accepted the club's steep price. With the contract and covering letter, he enclosed a check for $100,000.[1]

In the letter he related his plans to build several elevator apartment buildings along with retail facilities and acknowledged he would have to have the approval of the club's Architectural Committee as well as the city's zoning board. Until then the focus of CRD had been on shopping centers. A few days after the purchase was announced, in a memo to "Everyone in the company," Rouse excitedly proclaimed that the new development "will be the largest, and potentially most important development in the history of Baltimore."[2] He said he hoped the company could bring to the residential field "some of the fresh thinking, good taste and high standards which we believe have marked our shopping center developments." Once a public announcement was made of the purchase, inquiries about buying shares of the project came in from other developers and real estate people. An inquiry even came from a representative of the Zeckendorf company.

Familiar with bad housing in Baltimore and Washington, Rouse now had an opportunity to demonstrate what housing within a city's borders could be like. He could be developer and landlord of a balanced residential community of good taste and high standards. He would avoid all the temptations to cut corners and hold services to a minimum. At the top of the organizational pyramid, Jim Rouse would make sure everything was first class.

In a report to CRD stockholders, Rouse explained the purchase of the country club property somewhat differently than he had to the staff. The emphasis in the report is more idealistic than it was earlier:

> There is a real need for residential development in which there is a strong sense of community; a need to feed into the city some of the atmosphere and pace of the small town and village; a need to create a community which can meet as many as possible of the needs of the people who live there; which can bring these people into natural contact with one another; which can produce out of these relationships a spirit and feeling of neighborliness and a rich sense of belonging to a community.

The property was just the right size to envision a village, "an urban Village," of approximately 5,000 residents.[3]

The new community would meet another Rouse criterion for a city neighborhood. It would be set off physically, making it "a virtual island in the North Baltimore area." It would be set off by an arterial road, Falls Road, on the east; by another arterial road, Belvedere Avenue, on the north; by an expressway on the west; and by the two high schools that would be going up on the south. This would allow for strong identification with the village by the residents. At the same time, Rouse said, "It is our sincere purpose to plan our development in such a way that we will not invade or overwhelm" the Roland Park community just up the hill.[4]

What's in a name? In the real estate and development business—a lot. Rouse did not want any cutesy name like Rolling Hills or Hidden Valley. He wanted a name that would have some resonance, preferably historical resonance. Near the southern end of the property there had been at the beginning of the twentieth century the Cross Keys Inn. The name of the inn was also the name of the immediately surrounding small community, which was made up mostly of descendants of slaves. That small community was known as Cross Keys Village. Rouse chose for the name of his new community The Village of Cross Keys.[5]

The property was zoned for apartment construction no higher than forty feet. Rouse wanted to go higher, and he also wanted commercial establishments on the property. He needed to persuade municipal authorities to approve a zoning change. In order to get that approval he thought he'd better have the approval of the homeowners in the adjacent upscale Roland Park community. If the homeowners who were most likely to be affected did not protest, then there should be no difficulty in getting the zoning change approved. Because plans called for offices and stores, which would generate additional traffic, everyone assumed Roland Park residents would protest. But Rouse said over and over again during this period, "We are dedicated to making this new development a fine addition to the Roland Park community."[6]

Rouse had to use some delicate footwork with the residents of Roland Park. Roland Park itself was a planned community, going back to 1891. The developer then, Edward Boulton, sold land only to white Christians. He recruited families from the city's social register, marketing the community as "restricted" and for "discriminating" people only. While there was nothing in writing barring Jews, the unwritten understanding was that Jews were not welcome in Roland Park. Even as late as the 1960s real estate agents would not show Roland Park properties to people they believed were Jewish. Covenants against the sale of properties to blacks were written into Roland Park deeds. Until the last three decades of the twentieth century, Jews felt they were confined to the western side of Falls Road.[7] All the while Jim Rouse sought support for his project from residents of Roland Park, he knew that he was going to have Cross Keys open to all people.

Roland Park was one of two or three enclaves within the city for Baltimore's most wealthy. In addition to the expansive homes, it had a small cluster of shops near its center. That group of shops is generally considered to be the very first shopping center in America. To win the support of the residents, Rouse's Roland Park strategy was that he and brother Bill would meet with small groups of the forty-six homeowners who would be closest to his village. At a typical meeting, there would be two plans of development for the Country Club property on an easel. The top plan showed what the usual developer would do with the property: extending streets coming out of Roland Park and flattening out the Club property's small hills and valleys, thus creating thoroughfares and taking away some of the beauty of the area. Before the Rouse presentation began, the homeowners studied the top plan and were not happy.

When the meeting began Jim or Bill would acknowledge that the plan on the easel was pretty awful. It would be damaging to Roland Park, wouldn't it? Then they would say that under existing zoning that is likely to be the result of any further development in the area. But that plan was not their plan. While their plan had a variety of townhouses and apartment buildings, a gatehouse, shops, offices, and an inn, it would not create any thoroughfares and it preserved the hills and valleys and other natural attractions of the former golf course. The Roland Park homeowners much preferred the Rouse plan. The Rouses concluded every session by saying they would not go ahead with development unless every single adjacent property owner felt comfortable with the plan. They wanted not 90% but 100% approval.[8]

All the meetings went well. The Roland Park homeowners were led to believe that the residents of the new community would be much like themselves in a setting whose beauty might even surpass their own. Indeed, when their own needs changed some of them might want to consider moving to a more suitable residence down the hill. When the necessary zoning changes were asked for, there was no opposition from Roland Park.[9]

Construction began in September 1963, only days before the announcement of the Howard County land acquisitions and two months after Rouse had circulated his "ultimate purpose" memo. In August, Rouse had investigated a number of new towns in Europe in which lived ordinary people, yet now Rouse had planned a community that very few ordinary people would be able to live in, because they would not be able to afford the rents. For the most part, the new community was going to be an extension of Roland Park, a community in which there was much inherited wealth. It might be that once the property was purchased there was no alternative than to have the new community be an extension of Roland Park. It does seem likely that in the ultimate purpose memo Rouse was looking beyond Cross Keys, to a project in which he would have a much freer hand.

Once the public announcement was made of the plans for Columbia, the workload on Rouse and his staff was huge. Workdays of at least twelve hours were the norm. As the much bigger venture, Columbia took precedence. Bill Finley, who had been brought in to manage the Cross Keys project, also became the development director for Columbia. As result, work for Cross Keys often was put on hold.

Jim Rouse slept only a few hours a night. When he traveled by air, Rouse worked, slept, worked, slept. The story is told that once just before he fell asleep at a stoplight he asked his passenger to wake him when the light changed. He had catnapped while on the double shifts at the St. Paul Garage. He had caught five minutes of sleep while waiting for his law school classes to begin.[10] Catnaps were all he needed. It was an exciting time. Big decisions had to be made. Why would he want to sleep?

Ned Daniels, the vice president for public relations and promotions, had a vivid image of Rouse during this period.

> In those days, with Jim Rouse at the midway point of building Cross Keys, his personal philosophy was "go for it." He exuded confidence. He had this reputation for imagination, doing things that never had been done before. Try things, fall on your face, get up and try again. He had enormous respect for himself.

But that did not include his outward appearance. Daniels saw Rouse as someone attired by Goodwill: "worn and tattered clothes, stained sweatband on his porkpie hat, madras coat buttoned at the wrong button, the lining hanging out—it was a disaster, but with his imagination and creativity, we'd follow him anywhere."[11]

In February 1964 the first townhouses at Cross Keys were ready for occupancy, but there were relatively few buyers. With the shopping centers, stores were usually under lease *before* construction began, but it wasn't working that way with the Cross Keys apartments and townhouses. Proposals to advertise were rejected. W. Scott Ditch, who had been hired by Rouse to be marketing director for Columbia, remembered a conversation with Bill Rouse in which he said that they must do some advertising. Bill Rouse, Ditch says, didn't like that idea: "Oh, no, it'll draw the wrong kind of people, and we don't want that."[12] Jim Rouse, however, conceded that advertising had become necessary.

But now Jim did not want the rentals at Cross Keys to be wide open. Despite the slowness with which apartments were being rented, he wanted to give residents of Roland Park and members of the Baltimore Country Club first crack. He wrote: "I think it is VERY IMPORTANT that we really not accept an application from anyone outside . . . until the priority date [November 1, 1964] has expired." He wanted to see the first ninety-eight units rented before rentals were opened to the general public. If that could be done, "we would have gone a long way toward establishing the ultimate atmosphere of the Village."[13]

Over the next four years, townhouses, garden apartments, a mid-rise apartment house, the stores in the village square, and the office complex went up and were readied for occupancy. The garden apartments were the least expensive, and that is where a potential problem lay. Roland Park up the hill not only was all white but was Southern in outlook and sentiments. But Rouse was committed to having his new community open to blacks and to anyone else who could afford to live there. Middle-class blacks could afford the rents for the garden apartments.

In a January 1966 memo to Rouse, Ned Daniels wondered how to proceed. He knew Rouse would never tolerate racial discrimination, but the local branch of the Congress of Racial Equality (CORE) was checking on them, making sure blacks would be allowed to live there. Daniels wanted to show them that was indeed the case. He saw two possible approaches. One was to let the whole matter take its natural course: "Just let it happen and possibly face a lot of publicity—spoken and printed—that makes our acceptance a 'major breakthrough'—possibly pictures, articles, etc." The other approach was "to quietly seek out a qualified Negro, thus trying to neutralize the publicity. . . . Will it happen with less disruption if we seek them? If we take this route, does the fact that we sought them work against us more than letting it happen."[14] Nothing was done, and so racial integration at Cross Keys just happened.

Another racial matter had to be faced by the company a couple of years later. This was in regard to the Vacation Cottage Program that Rouse had initiated. Among the company employees who were entitled to a free week at a company-rented seaside cottage were eight of the twelve black employees. But some of the cottages were located in places that did not have any integrated housing—Virginia Beach, Hilton Head, Stone Harbor in New Jersey. In 1967, the company had a policy of giving a $100 bonus to blacks who did not choose to take a vacation at the cottage in Delaware that was supposedly open to them. None of the six eligible blacks chose to go to Delaware. The director of personnel saw the problem this way:

[Our] policy can be criticized as being a dodge—insincere and inconsistent with Company philosophy; it might be looked at as reverse-discrimination by white employees. Eligible white employees, who, for some reason, chose not to take a cottage might, with some logic, ask for $100 instead.[15]

What to do for the vacation season coming up? Here again two approaches were proposed: Have the company ask real estate agents and owners to guarantee acceptance of *any* person assigned to a cottage. Or, for the 1968 season, continue the program as tentatively scheduled and limit the blacks' choices to "open" cottages while the company works to have all cottage choices open for succeeding years.[16] Although no documentation has been found, it is inconceivable that Rouse would have chosen any course but the former.

At Cross Keys the garden apartments were renting at a disappointing rate. Rouse was reluctant to advertise for fear of attracting the wrong type of people. The community was open, but Rouse did not want it too open; he was very sensitive to the possibility of offending the Roland Park people up the hill. To find out what was attracting people to the garden apartments and what was putting off people who came to look but did not sign leases, Rouse commissioned a survey by the Sidney Hollander, Jr., market research firm. The results were interpreted by the man in charge of promotions, Ned Daniels, as meaning that it was the *idea* of living in Cross Keys that was motivating people to rent the garden apartments; it was the appeal of being part of the whole village rather than any appeal of the apartments themselves.

"The townhouses set the tone of Cross Keys," Daniels said. Located somewhere else, the garden apartments would have no particular appeal. "It's quite a wonderful tightrope we have . . . successfully walked." Prominent people were inquiring about townhouses.

> The fact that they feel it would be acceptable to them combined with the fact that we have Negro families (probably not widely known) and accommodate a political rally one night, a debutant party the next; are the residence of a socially prominent poet [Ogden Nash] and a not so socially prominent nightclub and vending machine operator; that our beauty shop coifs every "important" jewish [sic] head along with some broken down gentile (and genteel) aristocrats; the widely divergent clientele of Octavia [an upscale women's clothing shop]–the Roland Park matching baggy tweed and madras set and Bar Mitzvah dress buyers; the combination of the Robert E. Lees and the Robert E. Nobodies is great to watch and it is a real tribute to Jim Rouse and the whole company. BUT let's not shake this rare combination by going to what I'll term the "Garden Apartment-Hi-rise Route" without at least a smattering of the "Townhouse-even better than we have-Route." Not just because it's nice to have classy units or to attract the wealthy, but for what they (the people) and they (the units) really do contribute to the appeal of Cross Keys.[17]

By 1970, the townhouses at Cross Keys had become among the most desirable places to live in the Baltimore area. But Rouse received a steady stream of complaining letters about defects in construction and insufficient service. Potential tenants had difficulty getting leases negotiated. Rouse complained to his staff:

> I don't know where the problem lies, but I have heard comments recently about very prominent people in Baltimore having difficulty getting a lease in connection with their rental of our most expensive townhouses. . . . We simply cannot afford to look sloppy, foolish, and inefficient. We should have the ability in our company to be clear-cut and positive in these kinds of dealings.[18]

The chairman of the board of the Equitable Trust Company had moved to VCK and was unhappy about a number of problems: a sticking door, a leaking exterior faucet, inefficient heating, "poor drainage in front of our garage," "the electric light receptacles which you cannot force a male plug into," etc. Rouse, the president of the company, was now receiving complaints similar to those he himself had made when, as a young married man, he took possession of a house and sent to the developer a list of 15 items he was unhappy with, including a leak in the cellar, incomplete window caulking, ceiling stains, missing doorbell, missing thermostat, missing light switch plate in upstairs hall, etc.[19]

It wasn't clear whether Cross Keys was making money for the company. Through 1970, every year showed an operating loss. It was thought that there were too many operating inefficiencies and problems related to construction; that the property was underdeveloped and administration too loose.[20] Scott Ditch, thought that the development process had taken too much time: "I suspect that the long gap between the opening of Townhouses One and the achievement of enough occupied units to justify the extras was about as unfavorable a pressure on the economics as could have been imagined." But Ditch was optimistic despite the disappointing numbers:

> The attention to design and to landscaping is worth it. . . . Now that the village has a few years on it, the value of the plantings, the good detail that is so much a part of the design surely give it the richness that underlies the acceptance in the market. . . . Some of the gardens and groves, and the spaces between the rows of townhouses, are as warm and attractive as any I've ever seen. In not too many more years, I suspect that Cross Keys will be the classic "country village in the city."[21]

And he was right. Despite the problems the reputation of the Village of Cross Keys continued to grow. The December 1973 number of *Baltimore* magazine had an article by Jeanne B. Sergeant with the title "The Ultimate Cachet." VCK was Baltimore's latest "in" place to live. The article referred to the variety of interesting people who lived there: "They are not a band of the idle rich." VCK residents are on the boards of all sorts of educational and cultural organizations. VCK people "are committed to their city, their convictions and their heritage." While nationally annual turnover in rental units is 20%, at Cross Keys the turnover is less than five per cent. Also, all the shops in the Village Square are enhanced by their location; they acquire "a certain gloss in the jewelbox setting of the Village Square."

The article goes on to note that "the only unfavorable publicity Cross Keys has received in the media came when the management changed the first ninety-eight townhouses, originally rental units, to condominiums." That was one way of dealing with the disappointing financial situation. Another was to develop more of the property. In November 1968, the company had won approval from the city's Zoning Board to proceed with an expansion of VCK that, in addition to enlarging the Village Square and constructing an inn, would include three fifteen-story apartment buildings. Originally the company had requested approval of four apartment buildings. In the end, only one fifteen-story building went up, and its apartments were sold as condominiums.

Harper House, named after Robert Goodloe Harper, a distinguished Marylander who owned the property before the Country Club did, was designed by Frank Gehry, who also did work in Columbia and came to be regarded as one of the world's preeminent architects. But not long after residents moved in, it was discovered that the building's construction was faulty. When it rained, water came in through the walls and window frames. The Rouse Company was sued by apartment owners, and the company sued the architect and the general contractor.[22]

The apartment owners suffered through much frustration and inconvenience. Residents had to live with boarded-up windows. To correct the problem, scaffolding had to be put up around the building, and the original brick had to be replaced. New windows were installed. A shuttle service was set up to transport residents to and from their parked cars. The reconstruction process began in April 1987 and took more than three years to complete. The ultimate cost to the company was about $15 million. It took time but eventually Harper House joined the townhouses as a prestigious Baltimore address.

By the time it did, Jim Rouse was no longer active in the company. The Village of Cross Keys had been a source of much grief to Rouse. But looking back at the project in his last years he saw only good things. "The lessons were valuable," he wrote. For one thing the venture proved that "a variety of uses could be developed in close proximity to one another that could strengthen rather than detract from their collective marketability." He saw positive results from the special considerations brought to the project: comprehensive planning, planning for a range of community needs, "respect for the givens [the natural landscape]—all paid dividends."[23] The lessons learned would benefit Columbia. But Cross Keys was a victim of Columbia, for Columbia was the priority concern.

Was Cross Keys worth doing? From Rouse's perspective the answer is quite simple. If he hadn't bought the property, some other developer would have. It's unlikely that another developer would have had as much respect for the "givens" or provided the lavish landscaping; it's not likely another developer would have produced a community as pleasant to live in as Cross Keys. But as a village within the city, Cross Keys has relatively little direct contact with the city. The

Cross Keys gatehouse guards a community that is fenced in. Few people other than those who come down the hill from Roland Park are likely to walk into the community for the sake of enjoying what is there. The busses that stop near the gatehouse bring to Cross Keys the city people who do all the community's menial work. As a community of society's privileged, it probably has even less to do directly with the city than does Roland Park. Still, its privileged residents live within the city. They pay taxes to the city, and their participation in the city's cultural and educational activities do contribute to the city's betterment. Cross Keys was not Jim Rouse's ideal community. Columbia was to be that.

Chapter 11 The Village of Cross Keys

1. Autob, 64-65; JWR letter to BCC committee, June 16 1961.
2. JWR memo, June 20, 1961.
3. Undated, unnumbered CRD report, probably in 1962.
4. JWR letter to BCC committee, July 6, 1962.
5. Holechek, 75-77.
6. JWR letter to Charles H. Buck, July 16, 1962.
7. Frank Langfitt, "Jewish congregation begins," *The Sun,* December 7, 2003, 1, 4B.
8. Autob, 66.
9. Autob, 66.
10. Holechek, 110.
11. Holechek, 123.
12. Holechek, 116-17.
13. Holechek, 137.
14. Ned Daniels memo to JWR, January 28, 1966.
15. George R. Hayman memo to JWR, October 31, 1967.
16. George R. Hayman memo to JWR, October 31, 1967.
17. Ned Daniels memo to William H. Winstead III, cc JWR, September 16, 1965.
18. JWR memo to Mathias J. DeVito, June 22, 1970.
19. JWR letter to Louis E. Rider, August 6, 1946.
20. Michael D. Spears memo to Mathias J. DeVito, cc JWR, February 17, 1971.
21. Scott Ditch memo to JWR, August 23, 1971.
22. Holechek, 147.
23. Autob, 67. 1; Autob, 64-65; JWR letter to BCC committee, June 16 1961.

Chapter 12
Columbia: The Dream, the Plans

The creation of Columbia was the greatest adventure of Jim Rouse's life. Columbia was the ultimate opportunity: the chance to embody his ideals in a whole new city, to demonstrate that it was possible to carry out the Biblical injunction to "love thy neighbor as thyself," regardless of differences in skin color, vocation, or income. It was a chance to demonstrate that communities could have orderly growth and avoid ugly unplanned sprawl, that nature could be made part of everyday life. It was a chance to take on "the ultimate test of civilization," to provide an environment that would contribute to the growth of people, making them better people. It was an opportunity to "generate a new, creative thrust" that would show that new communities rightly done can "release among the people in them the potential for the noblest civilization the world has ever known."

If you're Jim Rouse, you've been a mortgage banker, and you've done deals that had the opposite effect. You've made loans to businessmen who have desecrated the environment. You've felt grief at the way development usually occurs:

> A farm is sold and begins raising houses instead of potatoes—then another farm. Forests are cut, valleys are filled; streams are buried in storm sewers. Kids overflow the schools—a new school is built. Churches come up out of the basements. Traffic grows; roads are widened—front yards cut back. Service stations, tasty-freeze, hamburger stands, car dealers pockmark the old highway. Traffic is strangled; an expressway is hacked through the landscape. This brings clover leafs, shopping centers, office buildings, high-rise apartments.[1]

If you're Jim Rouse, you're disgusted with the growth you see. Unplanned, uncoordinated, ugly.

And the businessmen have taken it upon themselves to exclude whomever they feel like. You've heard the contemptuous remarks about black people. You've been a witness to white flight. You don't like it. You don't like any of it. You have memories of growing up in a house, neighborhood, and town that allowed you to flourish—in places and circumstances that seemed ideal.

Neighbors cared about you. School was within walking distance. Nature was close. You left that pleasant town and saw at first hand how bad things are in the slums of Baltimore and D.C., how more and more black people are squeezed into dilapidated row houses and cruddy apartments. You've seen how futile so much so-called redevelopment is.

> In the battle of the old city we were fighting the symptoms of a dehumanized urban environment—slums, crime, delinquency, neuroses, congestion, filth, disorder. We were acting as though we believed that if we could tear the city down and build it up again, just as it is, except with shiny new housing and good, rapid transit to everywhere, our urban problem would be solved and our civilization would flourish.[2]

How foolish. How shortsighted. Do those city planners know anything at all about what human beings need?

If you're Jim Rouse, you say to yourself, God, if I had the chance to plan an environment I could make others flourish, just as I flourished. I could make sure everyone had a decent place to rest in a neighborhood they could be proud of. If you're Jim Rouse, you say, I could build a brand-new city that would bring out the very best in people. Yes, I could. I've seen enough to know what it takes for a human being to flourish. *All* human beings, people of all colors. You say, Well, then, go for it! You say, I've got a track record with the moneymen. They trust me. Whatever I need to build a brand-new city, one way or another I can get it. *Build* a *whole new city*. Show how to do things right. Show how a better environment makes better people. Within a radius of fifty miles of the nation's capital, soon there'll be one million more people. They'll have to be housed. They'll want to feel proud of where they live. They'll have to be educated. They'll need responsive local government. They'll need health care and recreation. They'll need to shop. They'll need all kinds of places found in cities. I can get it done. With careful, long-range planning, with help from the profit motive, it can be done. Piece by piece, it *will* get done.

Find the land. Where is the land where a new city can be built? Rouse's first thought was Virginia. There was land to be had along the Potomac south of D.C. Mel Berman had heard what Rouse was thinking about. Berman was a member of Rouse's board and had seen a piece of land Jim might start with. On a blustery April day in 1962, Berman had Rouse and his brother Bill accompany him out into the Maryland countryside, out to the farmland of Howard County. There he showed Jim and Bill the big sign announcing 1,039 acres for sale by Security Realty Co.

Back at the office, with that property as the center, a circle was drawn that included within it about 18,000 acres. A number of existing subdivisions were within the circle; they could not be disturbed. But most of the land inside the circle was farmland. Offer the right price and farms could be bought. Rouse thought he could build his city with only 12,000 acres. And the land did not necessarily have to be altogether contiguous or symmetrical. Rouse and his staff did some calculations and decided the land they wanted could be bought for an average of about $1,500 per acre, making the initial total needed about $18 million. More would be needed later to put in the infrastructure. But for the land they'd need about $18 million.[3]

Find the money. Once the site was settled on, lenders had to be found. Rouse would start with his partner in previous projects, Connecticut General Life Insurance Company. He and his staff were invited to a meeting at company headquarters in Hartford. At the meeting were CG's top real estate and mortgage people and the company's chairman of the board, Frazar B. Wilde.

> We sat down at lunch and I had the opportunity to describe the proposal to Mr. Wilde. The others in the meeting asked all the questions that people in their position should be asking. They were negative and challenging, trying to determine if this thing really was really feasible. They would ask and I would answer. Then someone asked a question and Mr. Wilde answered it. When that happened I knew we were home. He was taking my side against his own people.[4]

That is the way Jim remembered that historic meeting. Wilde thought CG couldn't lose. The land that would be invested in not only would retain its value but would be worth more with every passing year. If Rouse's project didn't pan out, the land could always be sold—probably for a better price than what it cost.

CG wrote a contract and brought it to Baltimore. The contract included all kinds of stipulations and conditions. Rouse was upset. After he reviewed it, he told CG, "We don't need all these conditions. The contract should be on very basic terms. If at any time and for any reason CG feels that the project is not moving satisfactorily, we would both have the opportunity to pull out." CG decided to go along—and committed $18 million.[5]

The land for the new city would be owned by a subsidiary called Howard Research and Development Corporation. CG would own half of that corporation and Community Research and Development the other half. CRD would be responsible for the management of the acquired land and for preparing a master plan for development. The plan would have to be submitted for CG's approval by April 1, 1966. And money for infrastructure? CG put up some. Teachers Insurance and Annuity Association and the Chase Manhattan Bank put up the rest.

With CG's money available, the land purchases could proceed. Of the utmost importance was keeping the whole thing secret; otherwise, landowners would hold out and the price per acre would skyrocket. That meant deception, not letting on who the real buyer was or what the purpose of the purchase was. The first parcel bought was the 1,039 acres spotted by Mel Berman. Robert Moxley was the realtor who handled the transaction for the sellers. He couldn't tell what the buyers were up to, but he did see that they were interested in buying more land close to the first parcel. When Moxley quickly came up with another 2,000 acres for sale, he became the primary broker for the enterprise. In order to avoid any direct contact with the buyers, Rouse had hired John Martin Jones of the Baltimore law firm of Piper and Marbury. Jones set up a dummy corporation, and became the intermediary with whom Moxley would deal.[6]

Rouse instructed Jones to be flexible and try to accommodate the objectives of the landowner. With the CG money in the bank, the buyer could pay cash and could let the seller determine the settlement date. Word got around among farmers that if they were thinking of selling, now was the time to get a good price. With most potential sellers, Moxley did not have to push very hard. But some turned out to be tough.

Moxley had an interesting time with the Dasher family, who owned a critical parcel. After much discussion, Moxley had persuaded Mr. Dasher to sign a paper, written in longhand, in which he agreed to the sale of his 600-acre farm. A few days later Dasher informed Moxley that the family had changed their minds. When he met with the family again, Moxley told them they did not have to go ahead and sell the farm but they did have to pay the realtor his fee even if they did not go ahead. Since the fee was thousands of dollars, they changed their minds again and the sale was made.[7]

The climax of the land acquisition program came with the negotiations with the three Gs—Goldsmith, Gudelsky, and Gould. C. Oliver Goldsmith owned a racehorse breeding farm. Moxley saw Goldsmith a number of times and became a friend, but he could not get Goldsmith to seriously entertain the thought of selling. For Goldsmith, selling meant giving up his business, which he was much too young to do. Moxley decided that the only chance he had of getting Goldsmith to sell was to present him with an alternative site. He found one that seemed to fit Goldsmith's needs perfectly. Moxley was so certain he had found the solution to his problem that he bought the property himself and planned to sell it to Goldsmith at cost plus 10%. But Goldsmith, a slick horse trader, still would not sell his farm, or at least not most of it. He proposed to sell 100 acres outright but would lease the rest of it for ninety-nine years. This was not the kind of deal Rouse wanted but it was what he would have to take. By taking it, he at least would have the freedom to go ahead and develop the land.

Isadore Gudelsky and his family were in the sand and gravel business. They owned about 1,000 acres close to the center of the project. They too were not interested in selling; they usually bought. Moxley decided that the only chance he had of getting the needed land was to offer Gudelsky a swap. He got hold of 4,000 acres that included a country club and a golf course to the north. But then Gudelsky, because of his failing health, was advised not to make any deals that did not leave him with more liquidity. So instead of taking the 4,000 acres he asked for $3 million dollars for his 1,000 acres. Moxley agreed and produced a realtor's listing contract. Gudelsky wouldn't sign. He said his word was his bond and would only shake hands. To get his commission, Moxley needed a signed listing agreement. He also needed the OK of Rouse's lawyer, Jack Jones. Jones was booked to fly from Baltimore to New York to Europe. Moxley wanted to get something agreed to and signed before Jones was out of range. He took Gudelsky to meet with Jones at the Baltimore airport. Gudelsky softened. He agreed to sign a partially completed handwritten document that Moxley drew up on the spot. Thirty days after the purchase settlement Gudelsky died.[8]

Kingdon Gould, grandson of Jay Gould, the railroad magnate, had a large holding. On it he converted a stone house to a restaurant he called "King's Contrivance." Gould was a good friend of Bill Rouse, whom he had met at the Republican convention in 1952. As plans were unfolding to get him to sell his land, Gould called Bill to ask for help with the development of that very land. Bill, pledged to secrecy, said he couldn't help. Gould wanted to make an investment and needed cash. He had got involved with the formation of the Madison National Bank in Washington. Reluctantly, he decided to sell 800 acres of his 970-acre estate. Bill Rouse felt he owed Gould an explanation. Just before the public announcement of the purchase, he called Gould to let him know who the real buyer was.[9]

But not all the land that was wanted could be had. A family that operated an orchard loved their lifestyle and refused to sell. An elderly woman who had only a couple of acres and lived in an old stone house in the middle of the target area refused to sell. Armed with a rifle, she threatened anyone who came close to trespassing on her property. During the course of the buying period, farms were bought from three brothers. The first sold early and received about $2,000 an acre; the second, who sold a little later, got $4,000; and the third, who didn't sell until the buying was almost complete, got $8,000 an acre.[10]

As the land buying continued from spring into summer, more and more farms were being acquired. Without intending to, the company found itself in the farming business. The farms had to be tended and a farm manager was needed. Rouse hired John Shallcross, whom he referred to as "an Ivy League gentleman farmer." All Shallcross was told was that a large amount of land was being acquired and it needed to be cared for. He wasn't told about the new city, but he was asked to keep quiet about what was going on. Shallcross agreed to do what was asked of him. He helped with the secrecy by misleading his wife into thinking that when he left home every morning he was going into D.C., where he had taken a top-secret job.

Within months, the company had become the largest farmer in Maryland. It owned crops, barns, machinery, houses, corncribs, and pastures. To keep the land in good shape, active farming had to be carried on. John Shallcross and the crew he hired had a lot to do. Shallcross was perfect. He did all the things a large farm operator would do. He met with other farmers, became a member of the farm bureau, and hobnobbed with county officials. Among the properties the company bought were two tree nurseries. One of the former owners was hired to manage and expand them, because in the coming development there would be a need for thousands of trees.[11]

By the end of the summer of 1963 close to 14,000 acres had been acquired. When Rouse returned from Europe at the end of August, he realized the time had arrived for real planning. The planning for the new city was going to be different from the kind of planning that usually took place for a new development. He wanted to hear from a wider assortment of people than the usual crowd of engineers, architects, and contractors. As in other developments there would be plenty of concern with roads, sewers, utilities, houses, and public buildings. "But what about the people? What about community? What about consideration of those elements in the physical plan that could nourish and support, or diminish and deplete, the growth of family, neighborhood, and community?"[12] He had been disappointed by what he had seen both in America and Europe. Only passing interest had been paid to the amenities that really counted in people's lives. Invariably, the concerns that dominated development people were moving earth, laying pipe, raising girders.

Rouse went out to Berkeley, and gave the "It Can Happen Here" speech. When he got back, the public announcement was made and it was time to put specific plans on paper. The year before, Rouse had succeeded in luring to work for him the director of the National Capital Planning Commission, William E. Finley. Finley brought with him one of his top assistants, Morton Hoppenfeld. At first, Finley was charged with responsibility for the Village of Cross Keys. But soon Rouse had both men working on the new-city project. Finley's job was to produce an overall plan; Hoppenfeld was to focus on matters of design. They found themselves stumped by Rouse's many abstract statements of goals and intentions. They suggested to Rouse that they get help in the planning process by bringing in experts in the problems and issues that would be of importance to the new city's residents. A list was compiled of top people in such fields as health, family life, education, recreation, government, transportation, employment. The list was cut to thirteen, and invitations were sent out for a first meeting of what was called at first "the social planning workgroup."[13]

The first meeting would take place in November. Before the experts gathered each received a copy of the Berkeley speech and a cover letter by Hoppenfeld about the basic objectives of the new city. Hoppenfeld said, "The community should be designed to promote health, security, dignity, independence, opportunity, choice, growth, mobility, comfort, stimulation, and pleasure." To run the group's meetings, Hoppenfeld hired a social psychologist very experienced in working with brainstorming groups, Donald N. Michael.[14]

At the public announcement, which was made at a meeting of the Howard County Board of Commissioners in the county seat of Ellicott City, Rouse said that 147 parcels had been bought and that altogether 13,680 acres had been accumulated. He said the purpose was to build a planned city that would preempt the piecemeal development that was certain to take place soon. He promised that the concerns of the people of the county would be listened to and that plans would not go forward without the people's approval. It would take a year to develop plans in detail, but when they were ready they would be openly presented. If there was significant opposition, the company would not go ahead.[15] The dominant feeling in the room after the presentation was relief. The locals were relieved that the land had not been bought by some Texas oil millionaires or by a bunch of foreigners or by the United Nations. Rouse was elated. He felt that having arrived at the point of announcement was "proof again that big plans and ideas gain power and momentum of themselves, and that the possibilities are always far greater than conventional thinking would have them."[16]

When the Work Group met, Michael laid down some ground rules. Meetings would be held every other week for two days and one night. The thirteen invited participants had to attend every meeting, and that also went for Rouse, Finley, and Hoppenfeld. Everyone had to read all the distributed preparatory materials. Everyone had to be willing to accept the facilitated meeting format that Michael would use. And the group must not be pressed to arrive at conclusions or take votes; their purpose was only to explore issues.[17]

Before the first meeting, Finley and Hoppenfeld appealed to Rouse to please avoid using the word "love" in speaking to the Work Group. They did not think that a group of professionals and academics would let such a fuzzy word pass without scoffing. After opening statements about the project by Rouse, Hoppenfeld, and others, members of the Work Group tossed out one skeptical question after another. There was no cheerleading for the grand purpose. The gathered experts were very doubtful such a project could get very far. When the first meeting ended, Rouse was in the dumps. He said to the group,

> I'm going to be a very rude host, but I have got to tell you that this is the most disastrous evening I've ever spent. . . . You've all been invited to participate in this. . . . You're all being paid. You all professed that you believed in this idea, and right around the table, you all said it was impossible.[18]

From that beginning low point things had to get better. Rouse stressed that what he wanted were not ideas that were feasible but ideas that were the best solutions to unavoidable problems. The matters of feasibility and profit were matters *he* would worry about. Their job was to offer visions of the best. In the course of its explorations, consensus emerged on a number of points. The new city should be a real multi-faceted city, not a bedroom suburb. It should be possible for its residents to find everything they needed right there, including jobs, education, recreation, health care, and any other necessity.

What would be the component parts of this city? How should it be divided? What was the ideal size for the core component that would provide most of the essentials for the optimal growth of human beings? Rouse was not reluctant to bring up his home town of Easton as the kind of place that provided the best nourishment of the human spirit. Consensus formed around the idea that the basic subdivision within the new city should be the *village*, a unit of from 10,000-15,000 people. As participant Dr. Paul Lemkau, a Johns Hopkins Hospital physician, put it, "This number represented the best bet for a local feeling of identification to develop, where merchants could know their customers, ministers their memberships, and teachers their pupils and parents."[19]

Within the boundaries of the new city, Hoppenfeld projected the possibility of twelve villages[20]. Each village was to be like Rouse's Easton; it would be a central place where people of different income levels and types of housing would necessarily cross paths and mix. It would have most of the services and resources usually found in an American small town. It would have a middle school and a high school, a teen center, a supermarket, a library, a hospital, an auditorium, offices, restaurants, some specialty shops, and a few larger recreational facilities. It also would have a multi-denominational house of worship. The hope was that *one* building would be used by several religions. That would have the effect of preventing a competition among the different religions and sects, "reducing if not eliminating totally, the pursuit of prestigious land, buildings, and the monetary wherewithal."[21]

The elementary schools would be in the separate neighborhoods that made up each village. The elementary school, which would be pre-school through fourth grade, would be at the center of each neighborhood, within walking distance of every home. The neighborhood school would be another opportunity for racial and social-class mingling. In language that could earn its creator the honorific of Social Engineer, the facilitator summed up the group's vision this way: "We believed this approach offered opportunities to provide the early educational and social experiences needed by low income children and their families to prepare them for effective participation in the competitive middle class education of the middle and upper schools." Attached to the elementary school would be a day-care center that would be open from early in the morning until late in the evening.[22]

Each neighborhood should have a store of the kind that has come to be called a convenience store. Attached to the store should be an "eating terrace," where teens could congregate after using the neighborhood's recreational facilities, among them a swimming facility. There would be three pools: a wading pool for tots, a little deeper pool for older children, and a full-sized pool for teens and adults. There would be playing fields for team sports and also land set aside to accommodate individual sports. Finally, more recreation area should be set aside for "low income neighborhoods where there would be much less private land per capita."[23] In the end, Columbia was to consist of nine villages and within them a total of twenty-seven neighborhoods.

In addition to the villages there would be The Town Center. This would be the new city's "downtown." In it would be the central office of the city's governing body, the Columbia Association. In it would be the kind of resources "which require a 150,000 population and a sufficiently large geographic focus to make them practical." Here would be the main cluster of retail stores (as part of the inevitable mall), a hotel and conference center, movie theaters and a concert hall. Here would be the city's large religious centers. Also in the town center there would be a community college. In addition to offering academic courses, the college would provide programs and facilities to enhance the life of the city. It would have a major library, a center for continuing education, a center for family life education, a vocational training and guidance center, a community computer center, a fully equipped community communications center. All of these facilities would be "at the same time places to learn, to practice, and to serve." The facilities would be in a cluster, thereby facilitating "the exchange of ideas and the joint development of community programs and the best use of community resources."[24]

The city's major teen center also would be downtown. Ideally it would be located between the continuing education center and the main entertainment area, "to symbolize two major facets of adolescent life and to facilitate their expression."[25] The main entertainment area was to be known as Tivoli, after the entertainment area in Copenhagen.

> We hoped Tivoli might be a place where, under the benign influence of having fun and relaxing in familiar ways, people would have opportunities, especially attractively and conveniently presented, for discovering new ways to enjoy their free time—new foods, new visual and tactile aesthetic experiences, even new social relations.[26]

By February 1964, Rouse, Finley, and Hoppenfeld had heard enough, and the Work Group was disbanded. Most of what the three heard they put to use. The most important idea to be implemented was the three-part division into villages, neighborhoods, and town center

The Tivoli idea was taken very seriously by Rouse. The first step taken toward implementing this idea of an entertainment area was discussion about placing a carousel. From there the discussion within the company leaped to the idea of an amusement park. By 1966 cultural and arts facilities were added to the amusement park idea. Hochschild, Kohn, the Baltimore department store that planned to have a branch in the Columbia Mall, had asked Victor Gruen to come to Baltimore to discuss the project. Gruen looked at the plan for the Town Center and did not like what he saw. He wrote to Rouse and told him how he felt: "I must tell you with the honesty I feel one owes to a friend that the plan for the center is a great disappointment to me." The plan lacks "fusing"—"compaction."[27]

That is not the kind of honest opinion Rouse wanted to hear. He was badly hurt. It took him a month to put together an answer. What follows is part of Rouse's defense of what was conceived for the town center.

> The Town Center in Columbia will perhaps provide for the most comprehensive range of activities and services that has ever been contemplated in a new town center. In addition to 6 department stores and 1,800,000 square feet of retail space, we have provided for 1,500,000 square feet of office space, 800 hotel rooms, a concert hall, a university, a branch of the Peabody Conservatory of Music and the Maryland Institute of Art, the headquarters of Columbia Medicine, including a 300-bed hospital, a 25-acre culture-entertainment-recreation area (our Tivoli Gardens) that will include restaurants, bandstands, theaters, nightclubs and discotheques, amusement park, ice rink, roller rink, small boat marina—plus the Columbia Pavilion of Music as the summer headquarters of the Washington's National Symphony.

Take that, Victor!

Rouse continues,

> You may disagree with the manner in which we have related these components to one another, but you would not say, I think, that we have been inattentive. We have considered and rejected the compaction of these functions into a multi-level center because we consider it less human, less efficient, less economic.... There will be enormous variety and change in the Town Center of Columbia. It will be convenient for the automobile driver but not overwhelmed by the automobile. There will be a positive difference between the environments in which people shop and those in which they work, play, study, dream. We hope and believe it will be a place in which a person feels comfortable, stimulated, delighted, friendly—as well as a place in which business works well. We have the lake and the forest as integral parts of downtown. We will also have the enclosed mall, the roads, the walks, the plaza. Each will play an important part and they will be rationally and comfortably related to one another.[28]

Within the company, debate continued about Tivoli. Rouse wanted a Tivoli so renowned that it would be a *must* for tourists visiting Washington. At one point Greenwich Village in New York was thought of as something of a model for what a section of Columbia's downtown could be like. Wallace Hamilton, brought into the company to handle "institutional" matters, was given the unenviable chore of planning a Columbia bohemian quarter. In one 1966 memo, he wrote,

> For artists to want to move to and live in Columbia, there will have to be that quality which makes a city exciting. Time and again during the period of this survey, artists asked such questions as: "Will there be foreign films?" "Will there be different areas with different moods?" "Will the after-dark entertainment be in one, concentrated area, or spread around?"... Such queries indicate that the artist wants more than ideal working conditions and a community awareness; he wants a vibrant, vital, stimulating environment.[29]

As far along as 2007, such an environment is not to be found in Columbia. Not much was done to bring in a real arts community, even though at one point talk was going around about getting for Columbia a studio connected to D.C.'s Corcoran Art Gallery. Ontario Place along Toronto's waterfront opened in May 1971. Rouse was there in September. He returned full of enthusiasm. Ontario Place

> evokes ideas regarding what might be possible along Kittamaqundi [the manmade lake along which the plaza side of Town Center borders]. It reminded me once again of the significant point we simply must not forget and that is that we are at the center of a population of 4.5 million people growing to 6 million; that we are near by one of the greatest tourist attractions in the United States—the nation's capital; that we will have extraordinarily favorable access to Columbia; that we have much going here already including enormous national publicity to bring people to our "downtown."[30]

Alas, no Tivoli in downtown has arisen.

Downtown Columbia is not a regular stop for tourists, as Rouse had hoped it would be. A curious few come but not hordes. Gruen's critique has turned out to be correct. The Town Center suffers from a lack of "compaction." The downtown loop, made by Little Patuxent Parkway, separates the two parts of the Town Center. The enclosed mall, most of the restaurants, and the movies are on one side of the parkway and the main office buildings, the plaza, and the lakefront are on the other. At one point a pedestrian bridge goes over the parkway, but it provides only a minimal joining of the two parts. There is little strolling from one part to the other. To get from one part to the other, most people drive. Each part is indeed comfortable and stimulating, but the whole lacks compaction. By 2007, Downtown Columbia still was not a real downtown. In the view of many residents that makes Columbia all the better.

Chapter 12 Columbia: The Dream, the Plans

1. Autob, 68-69.
2. Autob, 68.
3. Autob, 72.
4. Autob, 74.
5. Autob, 74.
6. Robert Tennenbaum, ed., *Creating a New City* (Columbia, MD: Perry Publishing, 1996), 24-25.
7. Tennenbaum, 26.
8. Tennenbaum, 28.
9. Autob, 77.
10. Autob, 80.
11. Autob, 79.
12. Autob, 84.
13. Olsen, 149.
14. Olsen, 152.
15. Autob, 91.
16. Autob, 92.
17. Tennenbaum, 10.
18. Olsen, 152.
19. Quoted by Olsen, 157.
20. Olsen, 157.
21. Tennenbaum, 18.
22. Tennenbaum, 14.
23. Tennenbaum, 15-16.
24. Tennenbaum, 17.
25. Tennenbaum, 20.
26. Tennenbaum, 21.
27. Victor Gruen letter to JWR, March 1966.
28. JWR letter to Victor Gruen, 4 April 1966.
29. Wallace Hamilton memo to William Finley, 24 November 1966.
30. JWR memo to Richard Anderson, 8 September 1971.

Chapter 13
Columbia: The Next America

During the winter of 1964-65, Rouse and his staff worked on Howard County public opinion. They wanted broad public support for the new city before they took on the Board of County Commissioners. That support was uncertain. Howard County was rural, and there was no telling how widespread resentment ran toward the idea of placing a city in its midst. Rouse understood the anxieties of the county people, and he took very deliberate steps to try to lessen them.

But before that could be done the city had to be named. Rouse and his planning group had been on the lookout for the right name for months. At each of their weekly meetings possibilities were considered. No one name hit the spot. Many a literary or historic name was put forth. Indian names and names of local heroes were considered. None evoked unanimous enthusiasm. Time was getting short. Presentations about the city had to be made. Unanimous or not, a name had to be chosen. "Columbia" was a name that appeared on almost everyone's short list. Although it wasn't original and was already the name of some small cities in other states, it did have dignity and carried suggestions of the new. Rouse insisted that he be presented with a name. Columbia was brought forward. Rouse, glad at last to have a nomination, said, "Then Columbia it is!"[1]

Route 29 is a north-south state highway that cuts through the center of the land that had been bought. In a stone house on Route 29, an eight-foot by eight-foot scale model was set up showing the neighborhoods of a typical village, the downtown area, and the mall. After the public announcement, news about the project spread rapidly, especially since Rouse also had a flyer about it delivered with newspapers. Rouse and his staff put in long hours in the stone house. They wanted to present the project in the best possible light and respond to the concerns of the locals as sympathetically as possible. This was the technique that had worked so well for the Cross Keys project. Rouse and his staff met with small groups. They made dual presentations. First, they told about the hellish fate that lay ahead for the county if suburban sprawl from Baltimore and Washington just came about with no planning. Then they spoke about the rational growth that would take place within the boundaries of the new city and the benefits the rest of the county would see. The plan worked beautifully. The country people who instinctively opposed the idea of a city in their midst were brought around.[2]

The plan worked so well that in December 1964, the anti-Rouse Howard County Citizens Association did an about-face. In its newsletter, the Association said:

> We have seen enough, heard enough, pondered enough to be prepared to speak without equivocation. . . . Initially we had reservations. We now believe that Columbia will offer the people within its environs a superior place to live. Furthermore, we are convinced that James W. Rouse . . . intends to do what he says.[3]

In January 1965, the company proposed an amendment to the zoning regulations of Howard County. The kind of land uses the company had in mind for the new city had no precedent, and so to get County approval for what the company wanted to do changes had to be made. The proposed amendment called for the creation of a Planned Community district. Adoption would mean that upon given Planned Community district status for a project, a developer would not have to abide by the zoning regulations then in force. The proposed amendment was sent for an opinion to the Howard County General Counsel. After extensive study, Lewis S. Nippard, the County Counsel, decided that such an amendment would be illegal. What? "Illegal," you say? "Illegal" means not legal. If the proposed zoning plan was illegal, the project would be stopped dead in its tracks. All the plans for the new city would be left in suspension. Columbia would never have a single building.[4]

The County Counsel changed his mind. As Nippard later put it,

> The publication of my Opinion provoked strong reaction. Most of it was critical of me. I was accused of "killing Santa Claus" by appearing to prevent the development of Columbia. I was characterized as being inimical to Rouse and spoiling the opportunity for Howard County to lead the way in land use. Although not primarily intended to do so, my Opinion had the effect of smoking out the opposition. There didn't appear to be any. . . .[5]

So the amendment for Planned Community zoning went through, and Rouse could give his attention to getting on with the job of building a city.

Plans for Columbia's infrastructure were in place. Now the trenches had to be dug for all the piping—for water, sewage, electricity, telephone lines. Plots had to be laid out for the construction of homes. And builders had to be found who would buy the lots and build the homes. Rouse had to be very careful about the builders he brought in. Most would be skeptical about the mixing of white and black homeowners in the same neighborhood let alone the same street. When they completed a home, they would want to sell it quickly. Potential buyers would want to know who their neighbors would be. Builders, or real estate agents, would be inclined to tell buyers what they wanted to hear: that their neighbors would be of the kind the buyers wanted. But Rouse was adamant. He had announced that "Columbia would be a truly interracial market—an open city where every person or family coming to Columbia would be free to select any lot, house, or apartment without restriction, persuasion or influence because of race."[6] Not all builders would be willing to go along with the race-blind idea although they might say they would.

It was Rouse's policy that if a builder or real estate person discriminated or steered, no more lots would be sold to that builder. But things were going on that made him think he'd better re-state the policy. Because the policy might seem awfully strange to some builders and real estate people, Rouse thought he'd better head off misunderstandings and excuses. In a memo to all builders and sales people, he laid out the rules very plainly:

> Simply stated, we are "color blind." . . . All people will be shown the courtesy and attention by sales personnel that is appropriate to their interest regardless of color. . . . No agreement will be extended to any person or family that he will be "protected"against having a neighbor of a race different from his own. We really mean that Columbia is an open city. We are convinced that if this is clear to everyone—if all doors are really open—if there is no place for anyone to hide, then no one need be afraid; need seek protection; need knock down any closed doors. It is our hope that Columbia's policy as to race may be so clear and vivid from the beginning that it will be unmistakable to everyone."[7]

But some builders and sales people resorted to slick tricks. One was to refuse potential purchases in which the buyer wanted to get an FHA or a VA guaranteed mortgage. Such mortgages allowed for lower down payments, and were sought by people for whom the size of the down payment determined whether they could make the purchase; a higher percentage of blacks than whites would go after such mortgages. Thus, turning away buyers who proposed to get such mortgages, with the excuse that approvals for such mortgages would take too long, meant turning away less affluent blacks, which meant fewer blacks would make it into Columbia. Another tactic was the steering of black buyers to streets where other blacks had bought. The tactics of some builders and sales people led Mal Sherman, Director of Land Sales, to send out black and white testers, who would determine whether blacks and whites were being told the same things.[8]

On a trip to Pittsburgh Rouse found a builder who was in agreement with his ideals. Jim Ryan was the younger of two brothers who were partners in a Pittsburgh homebuilding operation. Ryan and Rouse really hit it off. Agreeing to Rouse's conditions, Ryan said he would buy 1,500 lots in Columbia. Years later

Ryan remembered his first encounter with Rouse: "I was young, high-energy, and I think he related. At some point when I said something about being the younger brother, he responded, 'You know, I'm a younger brother as well.'"[9] Ryan called his company Ryland Homes, and became the largest builder in Columbia

Just as he had got into squabbles over small points with the Gruen architectural firm in the building of Cherry Hill Mall, Rouse took exception to certain architectural touches regarding buildings in Columbia. He got into one squabble about a design that he considered too ordinary.

> We intend no crusade for contemporary architecture. . . . We expect Columbia to represent a wide range of architectural styles in its houses and buildings. However, in this prominent lakefront site and in Columbia's first presentation to the public, we feel it is important for the architecture to be in keeping with the overall Columbia spirit—that it be fresh, clean, warm, and human.[10]

The architect had to go back to his drawing board.

"The Next America"—that was the name Jim Rouse gave to the public presentation of what the new city would be like. The presentation was made in the Exhibit Building, in the area along the lakefront designated downtown. The Exhibit Building, designed by Frank Gehry, would be the showcase for Columbia. In Columbia, Gehry also would design the nearby music pavilion, ultimately to be named for Mrs. Merriweather Post; a Columbia firehouse; and, later, along Lake Kittamaquandi, the Rouse Company headquarters building.

The Exhibit Building opened on June 21, 1967. Within a year over 200,000 people saw The Next America exhibit. Eleven building companies were at work, and more than 1,200 families had decided to move to the three villages that were under construction. By the summer of 1968 the music pavilion was completed and so were numerous other recreational facilities: two lakes, two golf courses, three swimming pools, tennis courts, a horse center, and miles of pedestrian, bicycle, and equestrian paths. Also opened was the first office building, on the downtown lakefront adjacent to the Exhibit building. Called the Teachers Building, it honored Teachers Insurance and Annuity Association (TIAA) for its financial partnership in Columbia. A second downtown office building, to be called the American City Building, was under construction, and out in the industrial park a research firm and two light manufacturing companies were in operation. It was Rouse's hope that by 1980 business, industry, and education in Columbia would provide 30,000 jobs.[11]

Rouse was determined to attract colleges to Columbia. But he wanted at least one of them to be different, to have a special focus. In May 1966, he wrote to Bill Greenough, the president and chairman of TIAA, to tell him what he had in mind and to get some advice. "Here we are developing a new city at a time when urbanization and the problems that evolve from it have become major world issues," he wrote. "How obvious it is that we should establish in

Columbia a college or university focused on the urban environment—human development—the growth of the individual and the family."[12] Greenough told Rouse that Antioch College, of Yellow Springs, Ohio, was thinking of locating a branch on the East Coast. Rouse passed that bit of information on to William Hamilton, Columbia's director of Institutional Development, who contacted Antioch. In January 1968, Hamilton confirmed for Rouse that Antioch was looking for a site, and went on to say, "Antioch is one of the best small colleges in the United States, and one that has pioneered in the whole idea of the work experience in relation to education. It would be notably compatible to the Columbia environment."[13]

In March 1968 Antioch's president, James T. Dixon; vice president for academic affairs, Morris T. Keeton; and dean of the faculty, Albert Stewart visited Columbia. At this point in time, many college campuses across the country were in a state of agitation. The war was raging in Vietnam. Day after day, television showed American soldiers being killed. The year had begun with the Vietcong rebels' Tet Offensive, during which the Vietcong simultaneously attacked dozens of cities in South Vietnam, including the capital Saigon, where even the well-protected American embassy had come under fire. Although the Vietcong suffered far worse casualties than the Americans and their South Vietnamese ally, for the American people the losses were shocking. Within the year there were to be over half a million American troops in South Vietnam.

Although militarily, the Tet Offensive was a defeat for the Vietcong, a significant segment of American public opinion turned against the war. This was the year in which occurred three other events that contributed heavily to the buildup of the rebellious counterculture among American youth. In April the greatest African-American leader, Martin Luther King, Jr, was assassinated. King, who had become a strong opponent of the war, was in Memphis to support a strike of the city's garbage collectors. In June U.S. Senator Robert F. Kennedy, younger brother of the assassinated president John F. Kennedy, was assassinated in Los Angeles. He was in California as a candidate for the presidential nomination in California's primary election. He, along with Senator Eugene F. McCarthy, was strongly anti-war. In August hordes of counterculture youth were in Chicago to stage protests during the Democratic National Convention. The Chicago police force, under the direction of Mayor William Daley, did not treat counterculture types gently; many were badly beaten up. This caused further resentment among America's young people.

Students at Antioch College were in the vanguard of rebellious students, students who had contempt for the comfortable, self-centered way of life of America's middle class. In July, Jim Rouse went out to Antioch with his wife and 17-year-old son Winstead (Ted). The purpose was two-fold: to get a sense of whether Antioch College would be appropriate for Columbia and to let Ted have a look at a college that was a possibility for him. Rouse was happy with what he saw of Antioch, and he in turn was "exceedingly well received" by Antioch. Rouse was particularly impressed by Morris Keeton, the vice president for academic affairs. Keeton was a former Presbyterian minister, and his philosophies of life and of education apparently matched Rouse's. Rouse also was impressed by Ruth Keeton, the vice president's wife, who was deeply involved in social causes. On his return to Maryland he sent the Keetons a copy of Elizabeth O'Connor's *Call to Commitment*, which told about the Church of the Saviour in Washington, to which he and Mrs. Rouse had been going regularly on a weekday night as participants in its "School of Christian Living." He also told Keeton he would like him to meet Bob McCann, who was to be the president of the proposed Dag Hammarskjold College (named after the former secretary general of the UN), which also might locate in Columbia.[14] Indeed, Keeton met McCann when Keeton was an overnight guest at the Rouses. Jim Rouse bonded quickly with Antioch.

Negotiations moved along. As a first cooperative endeavor, five Antioch students began nine-month apprenticeships with the Rouse Company in September 1968. In November an Antioch delegation met with Rouse and his executives in Columbia—"the Antioch Weekend." Rouse heard things from the radical students in the delegation that dampened his enthusiasm.

In a letter to Keeton, dated December 9, 1968, Rouse reflected on the "Antioch Weekend." As he usually did before breaking the bad news, Rouse gave the good news first. He says, "The prospect of having you and Ruth in Columbia working alongside us building a college is a source of enormous exhilaration." He also says, "A very warm feeling for the Antioch interns who work among us nourishes the prospect of a special institution." However, he went on to say that he does not like having been made to feel defensive by the negative comments made by the visiting Antioch students.

Columbia executives are always under attack, he says.

> The practical people attack Columbia as absurdly idealistic and removed from the kind of marketplace considerations and hard market facts that must control development. The sentimental sophisticates attack it as "being built for profit" and therefore unimportant. The cautious white community whispers behind the back of its hand that "there are so many Negroes there." The black militants attack it as not being a true interracial experience because it represents only the black middle class. So it goes.

But he and the people he works with can handle it. "There is a fundamental integrity about what we are trying to do without which we would never be at the point we are now."

He goes on, pointing out that critics fail to take into account the context in which Columbia exists. They are after all in the midst of a conservative rural county. The locals are "fine, honest, good people"; still, it is something of a miracle that they calmly accept Columbia and work with us. Columbia needs their acceptance, and can't just fly in their face in order to avoid the charge that Columbia is just white middle class.

> I really am not interested in engaging in a continuing defense of Columbia's purposes against challenge by people who don't believe we mean what we say. We simply don't have time for that engagement. We have more problems and more opportunities than we have people to marshal for the struggle. And as much as I am sympathetic with the motivation of contemporary youth, I am not ready to encourage an institutionalization of their introspective cynicism in Columbia nor to dignify a "sub-culture" which represents to me another failure of contemporary urban life to meet the real needs of our people—in this case college students."

His hope is that Columbia will find a way to make its homegrown young people "hopeful, creative, contributing people instead of despairing, hand wringing, destructive people."

He also tells Keeton that he is sure "the Morris Keeton spirit, working with the spirit and struggle of Columbia, can produce an institution that will be creative in the growth of young people as well as in the growth of Columbia." But, Rouse reiterates, he does not have any use for Antioch's sub-culture of cynicism.

> I would like to think that the Columbia college task as it relates to Antioch places a high priority on replacing the sacred cow of the Antioch sub-culture with a new sub-culture of creative involvement, service to fellowman, fulfillment, growth, joy, love. I suspect that drugs, free love and existentialism have become the rebellious and cynical claims of gifted young people who have been denied the opportunity for larger, more demanding, more fulfilling claims on our society.

At about this tine, Rouse received an anonymous letter from Cincinnati. The writer warned Rouse about Antioch's radical students. He said that in a nearby school where Antioch students were doing an internship, they had "so antagonized students and the community that the interns had to be relieved." The letter went on to say, "the 'liberal' philosophy possessed by Antioch students and faculty members often resulted in intern teachers being critical and undermining our free enterprise system as we know it."

On Antioch Weekend Rouse had had first-hand experience with those attitudes, which he labeled "cynical." Nevertheless, plans for the joint venture went forward, and Antioch proposed opening the following fall a "field studies center" that would lead to "a semi-autonomous institution of higher education." Despite his reservations Rouse remained committed to Antioch. He sent to Morris Keeton and to Bob McCann a copy of a speech called "Toward a World University." The speech was by Harris Wofford, civil rights advocate and former associate director of the Peace Corps.

In the meantime, on the Antioch campus in Ohio there was strong opposition to the college's getting involved with Rouse and Columbia. Most of the opposition was by students associated with the Radical Students Institute. They saw Antioch's presence in Columbia as aiding and abetting the corporate way of life and the pursuit of profit above all else. They thought that placing

Antioch students in Columbia would put them on the sidelines in the struggle to aid the oppressed of America. They thought that living, studying, and working amidst the dominant middle class of Columbia would be of little benefit to the development of social consciousness among the students. All of their arguments were developed at length in the student newspaper *The Record*.[15]

In addition, the radical students put out a special issue of their newsletter *avanti popolo*, which on its cover featured a caricature of Jim Rouse as a killer capitalist smoking a foot–long cigar and wearing a tie with a big dollar sign on it.

> This issue of *avanti popolo* is dedicated to the dream city of the Rouse Corporation. Most of the articles suggest that Rouse's dream has many of the qualities of a nightmare. . . . Casually connected to the problems of our inner cities, but disconnected from their uncomfortable realities, Rouse City takes on surreal proportions.[16]

Almost all the radical students who took part in the caricature of Rouse were sons and daughters of the middle class who grew up lacking nothing. One wonders whether any of their parents asked them to do what Rouse asked his children of approximately their age to do. Robin, Jimmy, and Teddy Rouse were each given $1,000 for Christmas in 1969. But the gifts had a few strings attached. The money had to be given to poor families in need of food, housing, health care, or some other necessity. The money had to be given away directly, not through an intermediating agency, and it had to be done by Easter. Their father also said he wanted them to have a first-hand look at poverty and wanted them to experience the satisfaction of doing something to help people without the means to help themselves.[17]

Rouse read all the criticism by the Antioch students. He also read a rejoinder written by Judson Jerome, poet, literature professor, and member of Antioch's Columbia task force. Jerome answers every one of the radicals' arguments. With his usual black marker, Rouse made marginal comments on most of Jerome's points. To the right of one of Jerome's paragraphs, he wrote: "Hurrah! Guts, finally." That paragraph began with Jerome quoting the radicals: "Do we . . . wish to set up a college which can only affirm the present system?" Jerome then dealt with the question:

> If the educational design for the Field Study Center seems to affirm the present system, I would like to know what constitutes an alternative. So far we have heard only nay-saying, only typically middle-class resistance to change and experiment, only the appeal that we all stay in Yellow Springs and smother one another with competitive claims to social conscience, from those who talk about changing the system.[18]

As befits a college so largely devoted to the collision of ideas, the discussion drew much statement and counter-statement. In its statement in favor of Columbia, the task force argued:

If, after visiting Antioch, working with ten Antioch students on jobs in Columbia, seeing and hearing a selection of some 20 Antioch students at the November workshop, and reading the *Record* every week, the management of the Rouse Corporation continues to prefer that Antioch, rather than some other college, develop an educational program in Columbia, they would have to be extremely naïve to suppose that they could exercise control over an Antioch program. We will operate under the usual conditions of academic freedom, and we have reason to believe that we are expected—both by the corporation and the citizenry—to exert in Columbia the same kind of liberal or radical influence we exert elsewhere.[19]

For all intents and purposes "the management of the Rouse Corporation" was Jim Rouse, and, to his credit, he was not deterred: he wanted Antioch to come. There was cynicism at Antioch about him, but he refused to become cynical about Antioch. Representatives of Antioch came in the fall of 1969, and set up three programs: the Institute of Documentary Arts, the Institute of Contemporary Human Problems, and the Human Ecology Center. Students worked for pay within Columbia. They attended lectures and discussions, and they took some traditional college courses. But serious problems developed, and it wasn't long before the enterprise began to fall apart.

A problem that never was adequately addressed was housing. Students either rented rooms in Columbia homes or they shared houses that were built to be eventually sold to families. The typical Antioch student could not be comfortable in the midst of middle-class Columbia. As Rouse's liaison to the Antioch contingent, Peter King, Jr, saw early on, that Antioch students found Columbia irrelevant "to the learning experience of students and faculty who aspire to be agents of social change." Some students felt

> they indulge themselves too easily and too deeply in personal development to the exclusion of addressing themselves to organizational development "out there." . . . Given the insulating environment of Columbia, they could go on forever straightening out their own heads and never get around to doing anything for others.[20]

Antioch students in Columbia began to bail out, some as soon as the second year of the operation. They did their required work periods in the inner cities of Baltimore or Washington. Still, Jim Rouse and some of the Antioch faculty never lost faith that Columbia could offer beneficial experiences to Antioch students. When fewer undergraduates showed up in Columbia, Antioch began to focus its attention on educating Columbia homemakers who wanted a college education. When, in 1975, Antioch College found itself in dire financial straits and changed presidents, Rouse still kept faith. The new president, William Birenbaum, whom Rouse knew, wrote Rouse that he wanted to give the branch in Columbia his full support; he wanted to take it "far beyond what we have done heretofore."[21] Rouse wrote to friends in high places suggesting they meet with Morris Keeton and make pledges of financial support.[22] He himself, through Morris Keeton, gave Antioch a gift of $30,000 worth of Rouse Company stock.[23] Rouse had wanted Antioch to come—and he did not want to see it go. But Antioch's radical students were right. Columbia was not a good place for Antioch students with a strong social conscience; conditions were not bad enough for them to be useful. The 1970s were a time when things were stirring in America's inner cities, and Antioch students wanted to be of more direct help. The Antioch curriculum in Columbia devolved into a Visual Art Center that offered bachelor's and master's degrees for work in ceramics or fibers. By 1981 the programs were still operating at a loss, and the Antioch trustees closed them down.

On June 9, 2007, the Board of Trustees of Antioch University agreed that due to financial exigency Antioch College would suspend operations as of July 1, 2008.

While tranquility was not what Antioch students wanted, Columbia's tranquility is what Rouse and his team attempted to show the people from TIAA who were thinking of moving the giant pension operation out of Manhattan. Rouse very much wanted Teachers Insurance and Annuity Association to come to Columbia. For Rouse TIAA and Columbia were a perfect fit. Usually referred to jointly as TIAA, the company is actually two separate corporations. The other corporation is the College Retirement Equities Fund (CREF), which, as its name suggests, invests retirement contributions in equities; it has become the largest of its kind. TIAA, founded in 1918, provides a fixed-income annuity from its fixed-rate investments, whereas CREF provides variable annuities from its investments in stocks. CREF came into being in 1952 as a spin-off to make retirees' incomes more inflation-proof. It was the brainchild of one of TIAA's then vice presidents, William Greenough. Participation in TIAA-CREF had been limited to people in higher education or research organizations, but it has become a financial services company open to anyone. One reason Rouse hoped to land TIAA was that he and TIAA already had had a long, mutually beneficial relationship. TIAA had invested in a number of Rouse shopping centers as well as in Columbia.

In the late 1960s TIAA was considering moving from its long-time headquarters at 730 Third Avenue in Manhattan. It hired Fantus, a site-selection consulting firm, to make recommendations for a site within seventy-five miles of its present location. When Rouse learned that TIAA was thinking about relocating, he jumped in and made contact with Bill Greenough, who by then had become the company's president and chairman. Greenough was persuaded to visit Columbia. Rouse and his team then put on a full-court press. The decision took three months, but Rouse succeeded in persuading TIAA to exempt Columbia from the 75-mile move limit. TIAA made that decision knowing full well that the Rouse team would be relentless in pressing further. Despite the fact that Fantus had conducted its studies and recommended two sites in New Jersey and one in Westchester County, between March and August 1971 TIAA seriously considered moving to Columbia.

Rouse and his team went up to New York for meetings with the site-selection people. Rouse made a stirring presentation about his aspirations for Columbia. Visits were arranged for a team of TIAA top executives in Columbia. Every effort was made to impress the visitors with the advantages of doing business in Columbia and with the benefits to their families of living in Columbia. Interviews were done with four Columbia residents who formerly had lived in metropolitan New York. The interviewees were far from totally positive about Columbia; nevertheless, the Rouse people included in the packet they circulated among the TIAA people all that was said.

Some of the interesting things said are the following:

> Interviewee 1: We liked Columbia from the moment we saw it. It was a clean and safe place, full of talented people, a good place to raise our children. . . . We feel needed here and accepted here. We are involved in a lot of "turn on" activities, neighborhood committees. My wife feels fulfilled, useful. One of the things about living here is that Columbia isn't perfect. There is something here to overcome; something to be constructive about; to improve; and to be part of that improvement.

> Interviewee 2: The great thing about Columbia is not its visual satisfaction but its sense of community. . . . We really do live someplace where there's lots to do, where things are happening in a real way for the betterment of America.

> Interviewee 3: "Columbia is a children's paradise." There's almost too much to do. The freedom they have here is a problem as well as an advantage. We like to know where our children are at all times; and with as many activities and friends as they have, this is difficult for us . . . great for them. In New York a day camp was $500; here, it's like $15 and it's better. . . . We like the idea that Columbia is mixed racially and religiously, but we don't like the mix economically. We both grew up in racially-mixed neighborhoods in Manhattan, but I really don't like the idea of paying $450 a month for my apartment and having some guy paying $99 a month living up the street. I'm an economic snob, and I admit it. . . . The things a New Yorker will like most here are the open land, the richer, fuller life for those who need it, the low cost of recreation and entertainment. . . .

> Interviewee 4: There is a sense of belonging, of being wanted, of wanting to be involved . . . a constructive feeling where the barriers of "establishment" or "politics" are non-existent. Everybody is the "establishment" here. We are Jewish and we are socially acceptable everywhere for the first time in our lives. We are trying on new ideas. . . . Blacks have a real social problem in Columbia. They are suspicious to a point of paranoia. . . . There is segregation here economically rather than Black/White, and it's not good. . . . We have the opportunity to do many things with little wasted time. A New Yorker really doesn't have that many alternatives. His social and community life are very structured. We have an alternative . . . an unstructured life-style in Columbia.

When all the visits had been made, including one by a TIAA executive who, with his wife, spent time in Columbia on their own without Rouse Company supervision, and all the questions had been answered, the TIAA people were very favorably impressed. Rouse and his staff had executed their game plan very well. They were confident TIAA would come.

But TIAA decided to stay put. One of its main concerns was continuing access to a clerical labor force. In Manhattan, TIAA could count on a steady supply of women who would take the subway into midtown from Brooklyn, Queens, and the Bronx and perform their clerical duties for relatively low wages. TIAA executives were afraid that the mostly middle-class women of Columbia would turn up their noses at clerical jobs. They also were afraid that the closeness of higher-paid federal clerical jobs in the Washington-Baltimore area would push its wage scale up. Rouse insisted that the diversity of income levels in Columbia guaranteed that there would be a stream of lower-middle-class women ready to work as clerks; after all, Columbia provided homes for a company's janitor as well as its president. TIAA wasn't convinced. TIAA saw lower-income people gradually being squeezed out of Columbia. It saw Columbia becoming another Scarsdale.[24]

After all the time, effort, and money Rouse and his people had put into the campaign to get TIAA, the loss was very hard to swallow. They couldn't believe their new city had been rejected. They tended to accept the argument that in the end TIAA didn't want to rock its boat. TIAA had a special relationship with New York State regulatory bodies and with the Internal Revenue Service. To move to another state would endanger that relationship and might have severe economic consequences.

In 1967, Hunter Moss, Rouse's partner in Moss-Rouse, was back in Rouse's life. Moss had moved to Miami, Florida, and set himself up in the real estate development business. But back in Baltimore, executives of the Hochschild, Kohn department store (HK) decided they wanted a branch store in the mall that would go up in Columbia. They decided to hire Hunter Moss to conduct the negotiations with the Rouse Company, obviously counting on his former friendship with Jim Rouse to aid their interests. While he was kept well informed about what was going on, Jim Rouse kept his involvement with his old partner to a minimum. He had one of his vice presidents, Peyton S. Cochran, Jr, handle the deal. Nevertheless, Rouse was determined that the store his company was building for rental by HK open its doors in October 1968.

The negotiations with HK turned out to be very tedious and protracted. HK would be the first department store in the Columbia Mall, and there were all kinds of considerations about location, size, possible expansion, competing stores. HK wanted all the contingencies, power outages for example, settled before the deal was closed. Rouse, on the other hand, wanted to get the deal done as quickly as possible. Until everything was fixed with HK, it would be difficult to go ahead and negotiate with other stores.

In frustration, at one point, Cochran wrote a memo to Rouse telling him he was needed:

> I am sorry to get you involved, but Hunter and I have gone 95 yards and we need you for the last five. The Kohns feel that they have always dealt with JWR, and that on a project as important as Columbia that they should have an opportunity to discuss with you several points that bother them.[25]

Finally, both parties seemed ready to sign an agreement. On October 1, 1967, Rouse wrote to Moss, back in Miami, and told him that he had played an "indispensable" role in bringing about the agreement. "As department store negotiations go, this was a happy one," Rouse said. "The result is extremely fair to both sides under unusual circumstances. I thank you for your imagination and goodwill throughout the proceedings." Those are gracious and generous words although not particularly true. Moss wrote back to say that the distance between Columbia and Miami made it impossible for him to keep working for HK. Perhaps with tongue in cheek, he said, "I am delighted that you were pleased with Hochschild Kohn as your tenant in Columbia and I thoroughly enjoyed the negotiations." Moss also put in a word for the man he dealt with instead of the boss himself. "Skip Cochran is a real star and has that wonderful facility of demolishing stumbling blocks that could have held us up for many more months."[26]

In fact, the consummation of the deal was held up for many more months. In June 1968, Rouse still wasn't sure the deal would go through. He wrote to one of his aides that the Rouse Company simply had to have a schedule from HK giving dates for the decisions they had to make.

> To the best of my knowledge, we still have no schedule for this indispensable element [HK] of Columbia's downtown. We have reached a point where I think this must be lifted to absolute top priority. If Hochschild, Kohn is not coming to Columbia or if they are seriously delaying it, we should face that problem and start in a different course.[27]

As late as August 1969, HK had the Larry Smith consulting company do a market analysis.

And in March 1969 Rouse saw "real danger signals." HK had found out about the pedestrian bridge over the parkway. The bridge always had been in the plans but had gone unnoticed. Now HK thought the placement of the bridge would give an unfair advantage to Woodward & Lothrop, which was to be the second department store. It requested that the bridge be moved. Rouse was ready to blow his stack.

> I believe we must take a hard line with Hochschild, Kohn. "The bridge" is important to the whole linkage between the Mall, the Plaza, Tivoli, the Inn, and the residential community to the north. It is, and always has been, integral to the Town Center plan. It is simply too late for Hochschild, Kohn to be surprised.

This was November 1969.[28] Rouse was throwing up his arms. "What must we do to push this to signing?" he wanted to know.

The store finally opened in the summer of 1971, almost three years later than Rouse had wanted.

In the meantime, homeowners and tenants had been moving in. As is frequently the case, tenants mean problems. As one-year apartment leases approached expiration in the spring of 1968, some tenants were not offered renewals. One such tenant took her case to the landlord—Jim Rouse. In a letter, probably written for her by someone with an education much better than her own, a single mother explained why she thought she was being turned out. The woman who was the apartment manager had turned up to investigate a complaint about noise coming from her apartment. When the manager appeared, the nine guests in the apartment had unflattering things to say about her. "We were all indignant that she should consider our group too loud, and we thought she was being unfair and even a little ridiculous, and said as much." The tenant goes on to argue about the injustice of being evicted because of one incident. Then she attempts to play upon the heartstrings of the landlord.

> Sure, I kick up my heels once in awhile—I'd go out of mind if I didn't! If only people would try to have more compassion. Women who have husbands have more security, love (usually) and a helping hand making important decisions; they sometimes take these assets for granted and don't try to understand women who are alone, trying to be both mother and father to their children. . . . Columbia needs people like me too, Mr. Rouse. The only way I can stay here is to get married . . . but making such a serious decision in a state of desperation is not the way I want to enter matrimony."[29]

Rouse actually met with the woman and apparently persuaded her that she would be better off living somewhere else. After their meeting he wrote to her and sweet-talked some more: "It was fun talking to you and a great thrill to learn of your plans. I will assume that everything is working out successfully and that no action is needed on your letter. . . . Okay?"[30]

At the end of the first year, the company decided to raise rentals on its apartments. Some of its low-income tenants said they couldn't handle the 8% raise. Each of the hardship cases was given close scrutiny by the managers. Five cases were brought to Rouse's attention and his advice was sought. Which of these two approaches did JWR think was better?

> The first is to tell them that we're not going to raise their rents at this time, but that if they tell others in the project, we'll raise their rent instantly. The second, and perhaps more manageable approach would be to simply overlook these five people when it comes time to raise their rent. We say nothing to them and if one of them should bring it to our attention, we'll simply pass it off as a clerical error.

In the margin of the memo in which these two approaches were suggested, Rouse wrote a firm No! next to each.[31]

In his answering memo, he said, "What about an honest, open approach." He rejected the prevarications that had been suggested to him. His suggestion was that the executive with the best touch set up a meeting. Then several points should be discussed with the tenant.

> 1. Why the increase? 2. But aware you may be trapped 3. We don't want that to be so 4. Can you accept the increase? Would it be helpful if we staged it in steps? What else can you suggest? We want to be sensitive to your situation."

Then this compromise "in the most extreme case." If a similar apartment became available elsewhere in Columbia at the present rent, a switch could be made.[32] In other words, Rouse was saying, no lying or game-playing but no charity either.

As a landlord Rouse always tried to be compassionate and flexible. There also were a couple of problems with small businessmen in the villages. Harper's Cleaners was always in arrears with rent and always promised to make good. So too was Wiggins Home Improvement. Willie Wiggins played the race card, alleging that his company was suffering because the Rouse Company did not steer work to him to the same extent it did to white businesses. He threatened to file a civil rights suit against the company. Rouse took an interest in all these cases. But he did not let his compassion get the better of his basic business principles. Rent had to be paid, and when it was, a tenant always would be given fair value in exchange.

Chapter 13 Columbia: The Next America

1. Tennenbaum, 78.
2. Tennenbaum, 81.
3. Quoted in Olsen, 179.
4. Tennenbaum, 94.
5. Tennenbaum, 94.
6. Tennenbaum, 119.
7. JWR memo to "Developers and Their Sales Associates," August 22, 1967.
8. Tennenbaum, 121.
9. Quoted by Olsen, 187.
10. Quoted by Olsen, 188.
11. *Columbia Today,* July/August 1968.
12. JWR letter to William Greenough, May 26, 1966.
13. William Hamilton memo to JWR, January 22, 1968.
14. Olsen, 172.
15. *The Record,* Januy 31 1969.
16. *avanti popolo,* February 3, 1969.
17. JWR letter to his children, February 19, 1970.
18. Judson Jerome, "Columbia, Maryland: A Critical Appraisal," February 9, 1969.
19. "Supporting Pares re Columbia," January 27, 1968.
20. Peter King, Jr., memo to John Levering, February 8, 1970.
21. William Birenbaum letter to JWR, April 15, 1977.
22. See, for example, JWR's letter to Sidney Lansburg, Jr, December 30, 1975.
23. Author's phone conversation with Morris Keeton, November 19, 2003.
24. Memo by the committee that assessed why TIAA decided against Columbia, November 10, 1971.
25. Peyton S. Cochran, Jr., memo to JWR, July 11, 1967.
26. Hunter Moss letter to JWR, October 6, 1967.
27. JWR memo to Geotge W. Vrady, Jr., June 7, 1968.
28. JWR memo to Peyton S. Cochran, March 3, 1969.
29. Norma Dougherty letter to JWR, May 16, 1968.
30. JWR letter to Norma Dougherty, May 31, 1968.
31. W. H. Winstead memo to JWR, May 23, 1968.
32. JWR memo to W. H. Winstead, May 27, 1968.

Chapter 14
Columbia and the Vietnam War

The period of Columbia's development—let's say from the public announcement in 1963 to the tenth anniversary of the opening in 1977—is just a couple of years longer than the period during which the whole country was going through the trauma of the Vietnam War, the triumphs of the civil rights movement, the women's liberation movement, the growth of the counterculture, and the struggle between generations. As Jim Rouse focused on malls, Cross Keys, and Columbia, he was very conscious of the stirrings and changes that were taking place in American political and social life. Rouse cared about society's larger issues. It was his nature to be intensely interested in what was going on in America and the world. This was especially true during this period because his two sons, Jimmy and Teddy, were coming of age, Jimmy having been born in 1945 and Teddy in 1951. Also, he was married to a woman who also cared about the issues of the day and their broader context. And with the Antioch connection, he had some of the most culturally and politically sensitive students in America right there in Columbia.

Beginning with the riots in the Watts section of Los Angeles in 1965, for four "long, hot summers" almost every good-sized American city feared the spread of the Watts battle cry, "Burn, baby, burn!" All in all, 300 riots occurred through the summer of 1969.[1] The looting and burning by blacks seemed totally self-destructive to most Americans. But to many thinking students, the explanation for such behavior was rather different: it was self-preservation. Such behavior was the result of overwhelming feelings of frustration and futility. The people of the black ghettoes of America were at long last reacting against their oppression. Black militants such as Stokely Carmichael and H. Rap Brown claimed that since emancipation, blacks had been continually taken advantage of; the rioting was their way of saying they had had enough. Young people of compassion felt a compulsion to help inner-city blacks. Antioch students wanted to act.

The same young people saw the war in Vietnam as completely unjust. This war halfway around the world could not possibly be in defense of America. From a few hundred soldiers in South Vietnam in 1961 to 185,000 in 1965 to a high of 536,000 in 1968, America got itself more and more deeply immersed in the war against the Communist Vietcong and the army of North Vietnam. Only six months separate the opening of the city of Columbia, the huge anti-war demonstration in Washington in October 1967, and the Tet Offensive at the start of 1968. With Tet the futility of the war seemed completely apparent. Then, in March 1969, the massacre by American soldiers of 300 defenseless Vietnamese at My Lai became known, and there were more anti-war marches and rallies.

In early May 1970 the news spread that American forces had entered Cambodia, to the west and south of South Vietnam. To the anti-war people, this looked like another flagrant act of American aggrandizement. B-52s had been bombing the hidden supply caches of the North Vietnamese in Cambodia for some time, but now American ground forces had actually gone into the country. A new round of protests and demonstrations sprang up on college campuses. Then on May 4th at Kent State University in Ohio, where protests had become commonplace, the National Guard fired on a crowd of students, and four were killed.

The Antioch students in Columbia staged a protest rally in the village of Oakland Mills, where the Antioch offices were. The students had delivered leaflets announcing the rally to every Columbia home. About 500 people attended, including Jim Rouse. One of the leaders of the rally was the dean of Antioch in Columbia, Steven B. Plumer. He told the crowd that the deaths in Cambodia and in Kent should be observed "as if a member of our family" had died. An Antioch professor urged everyone to contact the President and other public officials with letters, telegrams, phone calls. An Antioch student got to his feet and held up a pistol, saying "I don't now how to use it, and I don't want to learn. . . . But times are changing. They're [defenders of American capitalism are] killing white kids now." Another student announced that over 3,000 colleges and universities were on strike and that Antioch was establishing a 24-hour strike information center. Another student held aloft a placard that said, "War Is A Rich Man's Game." A speaker announced that a demonstration was being planned for the following Saturday in Washington. Medical supplies and gas masks would be needed.

When Jim Rouse got up to speak, he read a letter he had just written to President Nixon.[2] His letter took a slant that must have been a surprise to his audience. He did not denounce. He did not foresee imminent drastic consequences as a result of Cambodia or Kent. For Rouse, the villain was war itself. The effort in Vietnam, he said, was being waged on the fringe of what is conscionable, "destroying over time the nation we seek to save and eating away the fabric of our society here at home. . . . Can we defend the freedom of the world by war—without destroying the very freedom and dignity and morality we wish to uphold?"

Rouse does not attack the president. He sincerely wants Nixon to grasp the larger, long-range consequences of the war: "Mr. President, isn't war itself our proven enemy—isn't war itself obsolete—isn't war an unreliable system for the protection of freedom and democracy? Isn't it, in fact, the greatest danger that confronts our people and our way of life?" Rouse appeals to Nixon to rise to the occasion. He urges Nixon to start immediately to build "a system of order throughout the world to replace war as an instrument for settling differences among nations."[3] That is something Rouse has believed since his service in World War II: that people can listen to one another and instead of hating work to bring about accommodation.

> Go before the nation, before Congress, before the U.N.; instruct your embassies throughout the world that the U.S. means business in ending war. . . . Enlist the resources of business, of youth, of the universities, of our vast technology in a massive effort to build a system to maintain peace without the threat of war. Commission a group of our most resourceful leaders to design the techniques of waging peace. . . . Let's start taking risks, Mr. President, on the side of peace—of morality—of justice. Let's align our nation with love and hope instead of hate and fear.

And what about those cynics and skeptics, the naysayers, who can't get beyond the idea that war is a part of human nature? They need to accept the idea that institutions change, that mankind "surges forward." So many bad institutions of the past were thought to be inevitable and could not be changed. But they are gone. "The time has come to destroy the most oppressive, extravagant, archaic, and irrelevant institution of all—WAR!" If only you will recognize this, he tells the President. "You will light up the young with hope. You will restore the revolutionary flame that has made America great."

It is safe to say that the gathered students did not know what to make of this message. They were frenzied, not in the mood to reason and reflect. Their enemies had acted, and the weak and innocent had been hurt. Such actions required actions on their part. They would go to Washington, where they would march and shout. Jim Rouse, the capitalist pacifist was too much—too heavy, too confusing. Cambodia had been invaded! Students were being killed! More than letters were needed. It was nice that Rouse had written to the president and paid for its publication, in *The Washington Post* of May 7th. But *action* was needed! Rouse, though, believed in the power of words, and, with contributions from people who thought the way he did, he had the letter to the president published again. This time in *The New York Times* of May 31st. He also distributed the letter to all the employees of the Rouse Company.[4]

Rouse's older son, Jimmy, entered Yale in 1963. He was two months shy of eighteen. He was only a few months older than both Bill Clinton and George W.

Bush. By the time Jimmy graduated in 1967, America had gotten much more deeply involved in Vietnam. The anti-war movement had taken a firm hold on many campuses, and young recruits to the counterculture were to be found in cities and hamlets all across the country. One was to be found within the Rouse household. When Jimmy Rouse left Yale, he was very uncertain about what to do with his life. When Bill Clinton graduated from Georgetown in 1968, he already was classified 1-A in the draft. In July of 1969, Clinton was ordered to report for induction. He never did. Through some shenanigans with the Army Reserve, Bill Clinton managed to avoid military service. When George W. Bush graduated from Yale in 1968, he leap-frogged over a long waiting list of applicants for the Texas Air National Guard and thereby managed to avoid some other type of military service that might have landed him in Vietnam.

As a political science major at Yale, Jimmy had to be deeply troubled by the war. Just six weeks before he graduated, large anti-war demonstrations were held in New York and San Francisco. Jimmy's behavior after he graduated indicates that, as with Clinton and Bush, he was determined to avoid any possibility of finding himself in the pipeline to Vietnam. When he graduated at the end of May, Jimmy planned to enter the Peace Corps. He went to Lubbock, Texas, and participated in the Peace Corps training program for Costa Rica. But on August 24, 1967, he wrote to Dr. Maurice Temerlin, Field Assessment Officer, informing him that he was resigning from the Peace Corps. The reason Jimmy gave was that he now had a greater enthusiasm for using his "newly acquired skills to attack the problem of poverty in the United States, especially among Mexican-Americans." He said his "past experiences and involvement in the problems of poverty in the United States" could be most effectively used by working with VISTA (Volunteers in Service to America). After a VISTA experience he would have more to offer the Peace Corps.[5]

While Jimmy was waiting for word from VISTA regarding his application, Jim Rouse wrote to a friend at the department of Housing and Urban Development, Dr. Leonard J. Duhl, thanking him for his kindness to Jimmy. He reminded Dr. Duhl that "these are tough days for the bright, sensitive, deeply concerned young men who are searching for identity and truth with great integrity and find themselves in conflict with some of the mainstreams of public policy."[6] With this description, Rouse also was describing most of the students in the Antioch contingent that would show up in Columbia. While waiting to hear from VISTA Jimmy lived at the family home on the northern edge of Baltimore, along with his older sister, whose husband was a Marine Corps captain in Vietnam.

When Jimmy finally did get a letter of acceptance into VISTA, he decided not to join. Instead he was going to enroll at the Maryland Institute College of Art in Baltimore. In his letter rebuffing VISTA, Jimmy says, "I have become anxious to test my enthusiasm for art by subjecting it to academic discipline. I have decided that at this point in my life it would be valuable to make use of this opportunity to try art school." Jimmy goes on to say that after a year at art school he may very well re-apply to VISTA.[7] On October 7, 1967, Jimmy wrote to the local draft board. He told the board that he is enrolled as a full-time graduate student and requested a student deferment.[8]

In the years that followed Jimmy had a rough time. He did not have a regular income, and a number of times had to borrow money from his father, who made him sign formal promissory notes. At one point he moved to Cambridge, Massachusetts, and lived with his married sister and her ex-Marine husband, Edward B. Norton, who was then attending Harvard Law School (One of their children is the actor Edward Norton). For a while he lived in a small rented house in Ellicott City, Maryland, only minutes from Columbia. He also lived in New Orleans and Wilmington, North Carolina. Jimmy was living a life that in the 1960s and early 70s was not that unusual for well-educated young men from privileged families. They did not want to join the establishment, they did not want to trade on the family name, and they did not want favors that the under-privileged could not get. Most of all they did not want to get caught up in an unjust war.

Jim Rouse was ambivalent about Jimmy. Jimmy fit the description of the typical hippie. He was laid back, seemingly without direction, and did some irresponsible things. It made him Jim angry that his son would borrow a Rouse Company car, get a parking ticket in Baltimore, and the father would have to pay the fine. In his circle of business associates and friends, Jim seemed to be the only father with a hippie son; other sons had managed to keep themselves on a straight and narrow career track. But while Jim was quite uncomfortable about Jimmy, he well understood the times and the circumstances that had knocked Jimmy off the track to a career, and he was not reluctant to defend Jimmy if he came under attack.

In the last week of March 1971, Jim and Libby Rouse attended a dinner party at which conversation about sons flared into confrontation. Paul Swett, a Baltimore attorney, was a long-time business associate and friend. At the dinner table, Swett let it be known that his son Tommy had kept on the straight and narrow. Swett was a little too proud of his son for Jim Rouse's taste. Rouse said some harsh things about young people who led their lives solely in pursuit of self-interest. He also praised young people who had chosen to live their lives in accord with far different values. Rouse regretted how the evening turned out.

In a peace-making letter to Swett, dated March 31, 1971, Rouse says,

> We had each drawn pictures of ways of life that were miles apart in life-styles and values. . . . I remember saying that if I had to choose between Jimmy's and that which you had described as Tommy's, I would choose Jimmy's. . . . Later, outside, you called me an "ass" for being "happy that my son was living in a slum."

The heart of Rouse's letter is a wonderfully eloquent defense of his son.

> A few years ago I might have felt much the same way, [he says to Swett.] It isn't a place I would choose for him now. But I respect him for what he is

doing. When, as a parent, you have lived with the intense and earnest struggles of these long-haired, grubby youth, you begin to understand the deep values and high integrity that motivates them. Libby and I have much trouble with the aesthetics. It brings us many unhappy hours, but we have come to understand and have a profound respect for their high sense of purpose and personal commitment to it.

Thus, when I supported Jimmy's life-style in preference to that which you described as Tommy's, it was not Tommy that I was belittling, but Jimmy whom I was supporting out of deep admiration for what I was seeing going on inside of him. . . .

Perhaps Libby and I are over-exposed to the strange and wonderful people who have reached adulthood recently. We have two of them in our family. We have been honed on hundreds of hours of tough, intense, exhausting dialogue about materialism, relevance, race, poverty, God, self, sex—and on into the morning. We have struggled—and still do—with ragged clothes, uncombed, uncut hair, dirt and disorder. But we have come to know that this is not some predigested academic pap they are selling from a living room soap box but a transforming way of life they are living out because they believe in it. Where it all leads I'm not sure yet, but I truly believe that Jesus, Gandhi, Lincoln, and King would feel close to their spirit and purpose.

What a thoughtful, patient, rational defense by a father of his nonconformist son!

This is approximately eleven months after the week of Cambodia and Kent State. This is about two-and-a-half years after Antioch students started coming to Columbia. If they had not been there, would Jimmy and his situation have received such a staunch defense?

Fast forward to 1992. Jimmy Rouse has been out of Yale for twenty-five years, and his classmates are putting out a little book called *Sixty-Seven at Twenty-Five*. Each member of the Class of '67 has been asked to tell what's happened to him over the last twenty-five years. Jimmy describes himself as an artist and the owner of Louie's Bookstore Café in Baltimore, Louie being the name of Jimmy's older son. He says his activities are "art, herbal medicine, psychic and spiritual phenomena." Then Jimmy lists "Things I have learned since leaving Yale":

—That we who have attended Yale comprise an extremely privileged and small segment of humanity.
—That with privilege comes responsibility.
—That I never knew what love was until I had children.
—That love is power.
—That oddly the most difficult thing is to love yourself.
—That art deals with that which unites us; and politics deals with the divisions between us.
—That through art you can travel through time and space and commune with souls who lived centuries ago on the opposite side of the world.
—That there is life after death and that we live again.

—That in a sense life is death and death, life. By necessity life deals with separation and barriers that death tears down.
—That we cannot solve our social problems by blaming the victims any more than we can solve our personal ones by blaming ourselves.
—That fear is the absence of love.
—That the responsibility that comes with privilege is the responsibility to learn to love.
—That there is much that I have yet to learn; more than a lifetime.

Chapter 14 Columbia and the Vietnam War

1. Abigail Thernstrom and Stephan Thernstrom, *America in Black and White: One Nation Indivisible* (New York: Simon & Schuster, 1997), 158-61.
2. An extensive account of the meeting is given by Glen M. Fallin in "Rouse, Others Blast Viet War," *The Baltimore News-American,* May 7, 1970, 1.
3. JWR's letter to President Nixon is on Company stationary and dated May 7, 1970.
4. Olsen, 222.
5. Jimmy Rouse letter to Maurice Temerlin, August 24, 1967.
6. JWR letter to Leonard J. Duhl, October 2, 1967.
7. Jimmy Rouse's undated letter is in the box with JWR's personal correspondence.
8. Jimmy Rouse letter to Local Board No. 11, October 7, 1967.

Chapter 15
A Downward Turn

Five years after its official birth, Columbia had two department stores, a branch of Baltimore's Hochschild, Kohn and a branch of Washington's Woodward & Lathrop. Construction of office buildings was moving along. Light industries and other businesses were moving in. But land sales were not good. The falling off in sales was largely a result of Hurricane Agnes. It came up the East Coast and hit Maryland in June 1972 and put out of commission a major sewer facility in Columbia. With sewer problems, the land sales contracts guaranteeing sewers could not be concluded. All in all, five years after its birth the new city was growing, but it was a drag on the balance sheet of the Rouse Company. The Rouse Company was making lots of money from its malls, but Jim Rouse was not content to be only a developer of malls. He wanted to develop more new communities, and he was determined to pursue opportunities to do so.

That is what was behind this statement to Rouse Company shareholders in 1972:

> Our growing knowledge of and experience with the American city continues to open new horizons for the longer range. Our people are competent, experienced, and highly motivated. They pursue big visions of what life can be like in America with conviction that our company can help to make it so.[1]

The opportunities that Rouse pursued in the early '70s were not fruitful, and they were costly to the company. Soon the company was in crisis, and the pursuit of big visions had to be suspended. In addition, Jim's marriage of three decades was unraveling. His habitual optimism was being sorely tested.

Let us deal with the personal first. Libby Winstead and Jim Rouse had been married since May 1941. In the early years of the partnership between Hunter Moss and Jim Rouse, before the outbreak of the war, Libby was part of a circle of friends centered around Hunter and Jim. In the changing dating pairings within the circle, Libby and Jim eventually were a couple. She was a young woman with a social conscience and a strong commitment to Christianity. During a year in New York, she had become a follower of Harry Emerson Fosdick, the well-known minister at Manhattan's Riverside Church, who believed a true follower of Christ must strive to make the world a better place for all. As Jim's wife, Libby clearly was a major influence in the formulation of his priorities. She reinforced his belief that people must come before profits.

In 1964, Libby and Jim together became followers of a charismatic minister in Washington. As Jim was building a new city, Newton Gordon Cosby was founding a new church, the Church of the Saviour. As Jim Rouse was an unorthodox developer, Gordon Cosby was an unorthodox minister. Like Rouse, Cosby, three years younger, was a veteran of World War II. Unlike Rouse, who had been safely ensconced in Hawaii, Cosby had seen combat. He had been a chaplain with the 101st Airborne Division in Normandy and had come under enemy fire. He had been awarded the Bronze Star for participating in an assault and rescuing wounded.[2]

Jim had to like Cosby's attitude toward money, which perhaps was best expressed in a 1987 letter to Jim. Cosby says we should let our faith talk to money, reversing the way it is for most people. "When faith talks to money, it uses money to express the person's deepest loyalty and love. When faith talks to money, our assets serve us . . . . We are not money's minions. Money must do our bidding, not us its bidding."[3] Even though Jim was not willing to make the kind of commitment Cosby wanted for full membership in the Church of the Saviour, the two men hit it off. Gordon Cosby did not measure Jim by his own very demanding religious criteria.[4] Jim was a good fellow, and the two became lifelong friends. Jim's will provided bequests for Gordon and his wife.

When Jim and Libby got involved with it, the small congregation did not meet in a church building but in an old mansion on Washington's Massachusetts Avenue that the church's members had been renovating. This was an off-beat congregation whose members were from all walks of life and who usually were drop-outs from other Protestant sects. Their minister did not care about class, rank, appearance, or wealth, and neither did the members. Libby and Jim knew about the church from *Call to Commitment,* a detailed history by church member Elizabeth O'Connor. Becoming a full member was not easy. It required a far deeper commitment than what was required in most Protestant churches, far deeper than what was required by the Rouses' home church, Brown Memorial Presbyterian Church in Baltimore. Regular attendance on Sundays was not nearly enough.

Gordon Cosby put his guiding belief this way:

> The encounter with the person of Jesus is basic and central—the narrow gate through which we go to become a corporate people with him. In that encounter with Jesus, if it's genuine, my inner being begins to die into the very being of God, and God's very being begins to flow into me. Something begins to happen

which is absolute central in that encounter, if I surrender to the Lordship of Jesus.[5]

Even though in the end he himself was unwilling to make the commitment, the idea of it had great appeal to Jim. He was quick to distribute to friends and associates copies of *Call to Commitment*.

Six courses had to be taken in the church's adjunct School of Christian Living, so that "rather than blindly accepting the claim that Jesus is the Son of the Living God . . . the student is to try living with him for six months." The emphasis is always on the experience of Christ himself. "The community keeps prayerful watch over the newcomer, to listen to him and to understand and encourage him. It is concerned with all the needs of a person." The hope is that the person "will experience confrontation with the living God." That is, the mind of the newcomer will become so focused that he or she, literally, will hear the voice of God and talk to God. The six courses taught in the School of Christian Living are designed to make such conversations occur daily. The six courses are Old Testament, New Testament, Doctrine, Stewardship, Christian Growth, and Christian Ethics. Undoubtedly, Christian Ethics was the course that had the greatest appeal to Jim Rouse. The course begins "with a look at the nature of God as revealed in Jesus Christ, and of the nature of man in relation to the demands of God." Can man do what is asked of him in the Sermon on the Mount? Not by himself. Eventually the course considers such matters as "the Christian attitude toward social problems, toward the state and politics, toward labor and economic issues . . . and the question of Christian responsibility and action in war and peace."[6] For five years, Rouse said in a 1974 oral history interview with Patricia J. La Noue, he and Libby had made a weekly trip to Washington to participate in the School of Christian Living. But he also said about his relationship with the Church of the Saviour, "I've never been able to be a member. I'm active. I participate but I'm not a member."[7]

Years later, in the course of delivering a sermon at the Unitarian Church of All Souls in New York, Rouse recalled the course on Doctrine and the book that was used, *Review of Life's Meaning* by Paul Jones. He said the course clarified his thinking "into a very simple understanding of life's purpose." He implied that he came away from the course believing what Jones believed:

> Creation not an event in time
> But a continuing process
> Man is God's instrument for carrying creation forward
> In the natural environment
> In the growth and change of institutions
> In relations with one's fellow man."[8]

And that "seen in that way, we are each co-creators with infinite potential" for creating new institutions and processes.

After the six courses a member had the duty to evangelize, "the task of helping others to be open to receive the gift of the Holy Spirit." "The need is for the person who can ask of God what he must do to be the one through whom new life breaks. What in me blocks the coming of the Holy Spirit?" There must be "a willingness to be out alone in a strange land, confident that God keeps us company there and with the faith that one day another will join us and then another...."[9]

The church had what it called "mission groups," small groups of members who reach out and evangelize but who also examine issues about themselves central to Christian living. One such mission was focused on housing and called Jubilee. That mission group was to lead to Jubilee Housing, which in turn led, in 1982, to Jim's forming the Enterprise Foundation. Another mission had to do with marriage. Elizabeth O'Connor says, "The group began by evaluating marriage materials and ended by evaluating their marriages." One member told her,

> We looked deep into our own marriages and related to the group things that no partner had told the other. We stirred up old wounds and our marriages were at one time or another in crisis. But today I have a better marriage because we worked out what we felt to be the essence of a marriage. You can't have a marriage if you can't talk about what is deep on your heart....[10]

It is a fair assumption that during the years Libby and Jim were involved with the Church of the Saviour their turn came to evaluate their marriage. If their issues were placed on the table and old wounds were opened, the result was not a better marriage; they would have been pushed down the road to the total split that soon was to occur. At this point in Jim's life, nearing sixty, he was too set in his ways to be able to make any major accommodations, let alone allow Jesus Christ into his marriage and into his life more generally. He was a workaholic. Columbia was Jim's mistress, Libby once said to her daughter. "No," Robin responded, "Columbia is daddy's wife—you are his mistress."[11] Most of the pleasure in his life came from thinking about and acting to make American cities livable, and in that way he probably came closer to fulfilling the exhortations of the Sermon on the Mount than any other American businessman. But to be a full member in the Church of the Saviour one had to employ self-hypnosis; one had to cultivate a state of mind in which the voice, image, and touch of God would seem real. A businessman overseeing numerous scattered enterprises couldn't do that. The will might be there but the time and the mood in which to make the effort would not. The wife who did not have daily professional commitments might be able to do it, and it was likely Libby did, but that would make the disharmony between husband and wife only greater.

Beginning in 1970 Jim often spent the night in a townhouse in Columbia. The Church of the Saviour couldn't save the marriage nor could marriage counseling. Jim gave up on the marriage. He moved his possessions out of the marital home in northern Baltimore in April 1973. Was it hope, embarrassment, or the need to pummel himself with words that led Jim to the dissembling letter he wrote just weeks before moving out? He wrote the following to the woman in Elkhorn, Montana, who owned land on which the family had vacationed:

> Our address remains 1 Overlook Lane, Baltimore—much to my regret. We are trying to build a house in Columbia, but it is not yet underway and, in the meantime, we continue to deny ourselves the fruits of the new city because we seem chained to the roots established at Overlook. But one day we will break loose.[12]

Four months after he moved out, he and Libby were divorced. Jim regarded the differences with Libby as "irreconcilable" and the divorce as inevitable.[13] For both husband and wife the divorce was a cause of great humiliation. Although Jim did his best to prevent the sorrow of the divorce from spilling over into his business life, how could it not have had some effect? Perhaps symbolizing the changes occurring in both his personal and business life was the noticeable change in Jim's signature. The change is clearly seen in his signature in the annual reports. The signature goes from big, ebullient clear letters, especially the initial J, to letters that are smaller, more angular, and less clearly defined.

In the early 1970s there was no assurance that the Rouse Company could avoid financial disaster. Survival, it was clear, depended on the cash flow generated by the shopping centers. It would not be until the end of the decade that Columbia would stop being a drain on the company's resources. In the 70s Columbia was owned by Connecticut General Life and Howard Research and Development, which was a subsidiary of the Rouse Company, so that a firewall was in place separating the growing Columbia debt from the Rouse Company. Additional borrowing was necessary to support Columbia, and Rouse managed to sell $30 million in ten-year notes to Connecticut General, Manufacturers Hanover, and Morgan Guaranty. The annual report for 1970 proclaims, "The Rouse Company has no liability on the above debt of Howard Research and Development." On the other hand, in 1970, Rouse took pride in the fact that within three years of officially opening, there were well over 100 businesses in Columbia, including such big names as General Electric, Bendix, Head Ski & Sports, and Merck, Sharp & Dohme. Still, as he said in the annual report of the following year, "We will not be 'over the hump' financially until the debt peak is passed," an acknowledgement that debt was still going up.

In his "President's Report to Shareholders" in 1972, Rouse noted that Columbia "has celebrated its fifth birthday and has become, in almost every respect, an important city." From a broader perspective, he saw "the restoration of the American city to a healthy, livable, successful human environment as the most vital domestic issue in the nation—a challenge to all business and financial institutions." He saw the Rouse Company playing a major role.

> Our civilization must discover how to fulfill the essential requirements for successful urban living. . . . It is the purpose of the Urban Division [of the

Rouse Company]to harness and focus the full range of the company's experience in city building, planning and financing toward the revitalization of existing cities, the orderly expansion of their metropolitan areas, and the building of new cities.

Back in 1968 the Rouse Company had formed a subsidiary called The American City Corporation. Through its Urban Life Center, "a conference and membership organization for thought and action on the American city," American City's purpose was to give advice to older cities and to help formulate plans for new cities or towns based on the Columbia experience. One of its first tasks was the presentation of six workshops in which were discussed the crucial steps in the process that led to the building of Columbia—the "Columbia Process." Rouse hoped other developers would take the cue and follow the trail he had blazed with Columbia. By 1972, approximately fifty public and private organizations had contracted to make use of what the American City Corporation had to offer.[14]

In 1970 Hartford, Connecticut, asked for help. The insurance companies, the city's main industry, and its middle class had been leaving turbulent Hartford for the tranquility of nearby suburban towns. Hartford had all the pathology that afflicted older mid-size and smaller American cities in the last decades of the twentieth century—bad housing and schools, unemployment, drugs, crime, disillusionment, bitterness, and an overriding feeling of futility. Jim Rouse eagerly accepted the challenge of helping the decaying city. He and Leo Molinaro, American City's CEO, went up to Hartford and told the men in the city's power structure that what was needed was a comprehensive approach to the city's and region's problems.

The Hartford business community signed a $3 million contract with American City, and American City went to work. It formed Greater Hartford Process, Inc., which would "examine the region, set forth the goals . . . and design specific proposals to bring about a region that 'works.'" Its board of directors was wide-ranging, with representatives not only of business but labor, local governments, planning agencies, and residents of the region. Rouse Company representatives were called "Senior Consultants." Besides Jim Rouse and Leo Molinaro, they were Bill Finley, who was Rouse vice president for urban development, and Michael D. Spear, Rouse vice president for community development and research. Also formed was The Greater Hartford Development Corporation, which "will obtain financing, acquire land, and engage in site planning, development and management of the community development proposals suggested by Process. . . ." This set the stage for DevCo to take actions very much like those that were taken by Howard Research and Development for the development of Columbia.[15]

After a staff of forty carried out and processed hundreds of interviews and engaged in other forms of research and discussion over two years, American City and Greater Hartford Process made three main recommendations. One was for the rehabilitation of the city's slums, principally those of the black North

End; another was a plan for controlled growth in the suburbs; and the third was for the building of a new town on open land. Other recommendations included participation by all affected parties; developing a consensus on realizable goals; gaining firm commitments for carrying out plans; recognizing the inseparability of social, economic, and physical planning and development; working on a large scale; acting on the basis of shared economic, social, and political values; and establishing a continuing process.[16] These are ideas that Jim Rouse had been advocating for twenty years.

Not much happened as a result of the Hartford Process. More than thirty years later the city of Hartford still struggles with many of the same problems that were enumerated in the report. Connecticut, unlike Maryland and most other states, does not use the county as a political subdivision; instead, it has home rule. Connecticut has 169 towns, separate governmental jurisdictions with their own board of education, police department, and municipal administration. This means that every town is capable of blocking any regional cooperation that it thinks is not in its own interest. The interests of wealthy bedroom suburbs are rarely in accord with the interests of the much poorer cities in which most suburban breadwinners work. Thus, the education provided in a Hartford suburb such as West Hartford is far superior to the education provided in city schools. The cost of social services needed by Hartford's Puerto Rican and West Indian communities is only minimally shared by the much wealthier surrounding communities. Home rule fortifies towns but is disastrous for cities. Jim Rouse and American City put forth a plan for reducing pernicious divisions, but in the end the suburban towns were unwilling to make the sacrifices required of them. Rouse and his colleagues had, in effect, wasted their time.

Rouse also was approached for advice by the New York City Planning Department. It wanted to know what to do about the sparsely populated southern end of Staten Island, the New York borough across the harbor and closest to New Jersey. Rouse jumped at the opportunity to have input into the process of developing 9,000 acres of land. New York City offered $330,000 for a plan.

Rouse provided three different plans for balanced communities of three different densities—low, medium, and high. The plans for South Richmond provided for housing, commercial establishments, and open space. Falling back on the Columbia model, the plan laid out a number of neighborhoods and a downtown that would serve the whole area. The recommended plan projected a population of 400,000 and medium-density housing. The housing would be a mixture of single-family homes, townhouses, and apartment buildings. Because the land was owned by the city and there was no direct opportunity for profit, Rouse also recommended that a special public development authority be created. The Rouse Company might get involved in management but there was only a very limited opportunity for ownership. The creation of a public authority required state legislative approval. John Marchi, Staten Island's the long-time popular Republican state senator, took on the job of introducing and guiding the proposal through the legislature in Albany. And there the plan met its death.[17]

More time and effort had been wasted. Just as Rouse might have predicted, development spread piecemeal across southern Staten Island. In the absence of a comprehensive plan, much of the housing that was built was not a good match to the housing already there and special zoning and re-zoning was necessary.[18] For one thing, development proceeded without a plan for a sewage system. In 1995 the city's Department of Environmental Protection had to ask for bids on sanitary and storm-water control systems. One bidding company described the situation it encountered this way: "A variety of pollutants, mostly originating from household wastes, mix with uncontrolled stormwater runoff, impacting the area's abundant surface waters and flooding the suburban streets, recreational areas and residences."[19] This was the very kind of problem Rouse-style comprehensive planning would have prevented.

Another opportunity for a planned community was within the city of Memphis, Tennessee. Ten miles from the city's center were 4,450 vacant acres known as Shelby Farms. Fearing piecemeal development, local officials asked the Rouse Company for a plan for comprehensive development. Jim Rouse was enthusiastic. He said Shelby Farms was "the best opportunity we've found in America to take what we learned at Columbia and do it again." Rouse's planners laid out two villages and a town center for Shelby Farms. In June 1973 the county commissioners gave the project its approval. The plan provided for 40,000 residents in 12,000 units of housing.[20]

But local developers and environmentalists blocked implementation. The former did not want the project to go to an outside company, and the latter wanted no development at all. Shelby Farms was a jewel of open space within an urban environment, much like New York's Central Park. Shelby Farms, though, was five times larger. It offered at least as many recreational opportunities. People walked dogs and strolled around its lake. They picked strawberries. They watched the geese and ducks and bison. They flew kites, rode bikes, and hiked the trails. They sailed on the lake. There were locations for shooting and for archery. It was the venue for an annual Great Outdoors Festival, for concerts and Civil War reenactments. It even hosted a farmers market.

In the years since Rouse was turned away there have been two big issues regarding Shelby Farms. One involved the plan to take management of Shelby Farms away from Shelby County and give it to an independent conservancy. The conservancy would take over with a privately funded $20 million endowment. It would make numerous improvements and keep Shelby Farms a mostly quiet, free park that would be off-limits to developers forever. Naturally, local developers and officials who saw huge money-making potential in the land opposed the conservancy. Another interest group wanted to see a parkway cut through Shelby Farms. Such a road would make it easier to get into the heart of the city from points to the east. The parkway too had its opponents. Jim Rouse usually took the position that development was inevitable. To prevent piecemeal sprawl, he urged that large vacant tracts be protected with a plan for comprehensive rational development. Sometimes, though, simply stating that idea injected the local population with a fierce determination to prevent all development.

Something similar happened with Rouse's plan for a planned community on the Eastern Shore of Maryland. Wye Island sits about five miles below the bridge connecting the western and eastern shores of Chesapeake Bay. If you can imagine a plucked chicken held flat in the palm of a hand with its head dangling at a forty-five degree angle to the left, you've got the approximate shape of Wye Island. Located in Queen Anne's County, it is about ten miles north of Rouse's native town of Easton. What with his continuing investment in the Rouse-developed Talbottown shopping center, Rouse, through the years, kept alive his interest in the Eastern Shore. In 1968 he had been approached by one of the owners of almost the entire island of 2,800 acres. Frank Hardy tried to persuade Rouse to buy his property and develop it. At the time, Rouse had his hands full with Columbia. When, in 1972, he took a drive to the island, he didn't find much on it. A wealthy couple lived in a mansion and two other families were there to take care of the house and grounds. All the island except for the mansion and its grounds was owned by Frank Hardy and his brother Bill.[21]

On May 1, 1973, Rouse signed an option with the Hardys to buy 2,500 acres. By this date, Jim had left his wife and the divorce was in process. It is doubtful that he experienced much of the sense of liberation that some other men might feel in such a circumstance. The Wye Island option had to be exciting, had to help lessen the weight of the marital trauma. It focused him on ideas for making this planned community the best of its kind.

Wye Island was not going to be a multi-racial, multi-class real community. It was off the beaten track, away from jobs. Its main asset was the water that surrounded it. The thinking and planning that went into Hartford, Staten Island, and Shelby Farms would not be applicable. Wye Island would not be a development for people who were concerned about earning a living; it would be a recreational community for the well-off. Rouse had his doubts about building an enclave that would benefit people already privileged. Company executives also wondered about the redeeming social value of such a project. But Rouse liked the challenges the project presented. He also thought that all in all the county would be better off as a result of the kind of development he would bring it.[22] If he did not do it, sooner or later another developer would, and the development would be of lower quality.

Shoreline development was tricky. All kinds of unintentional damage could result. He needed to find out just how much development the island and the waterways could sustain. For that he needed studies by planners and environmental scientists. Costs would run into hundreds of thousands of dollars, but he was willing to spend the money. Once his mind was made up, as with Columbia, he felt it essential to communicate with all whom development might affect. Thus, following announcement of the signed option to buy, he wrote a letter to the people of Queen Anne's County.

He addressed the issues he knew were of greatest concern. He gave assurance that growth could be managed in a way "sensitive to the land, the water, and the people of the community." He said the island would offer "educational, cultural, aesthetic, and economic benefits." He promised to discuss plans for the island as they evolved and to back off from the whole project if it "does not have the enthusiastic support of the preponderance of the community." He invited the community to let him know their ideas. In July he let the county commissioners know that the company would pay for any consultants the county might want to bring in.

The preparation of plans was done mostly by the firm of Wallace, McHarg, Roberts and Todd. The firm came up with twenty-three alternative plans and produced many more topographic layouts of the island. For each plan, the implementation costs were staggering. Problems with regard to sewage were not easily resolved.[23] Rouse had a hard time deciding which plan to go with. The deadline to exercise the option to purchase the 2,500 acres for $8,850,000 was only four months away. With much uncertainty, Rouse decided upon one of the plans.

On March 14, 1974, Rouse was ready with a mock-up. The eight-feet-by-twelve-feet model was set up at an open meeting held by the County Planning Commission. It had miniature houses and stores and white sailboats on the blue waterways. It showed Wye Village, where 706 housing units would be clustered around two coves. It showed one large town dock where all the community's boats would be berthed; no individually owned docks would be allowed. It showed the offices for doctors, lawyers, and tradesmen, and also the 200-room inn. It showed the golf course and the outlying areas where estates of five acres would be permitted. Rouse explained that while the estates would use individual septic tanks, the village would be served by the very latest wastewater treatment system and that none of the effluent would end up in public waterways. He pointed out that even with the village development and the five-acre estates half of the island still would remain undeveloped.[24]

The response from the small audience was unanimous opposition. Rouse finally said, "If the people of Queen Anne's County say they don't want our development, we'll never file for rezoning. And someone else will develop the island in the conventional manner." That was Rouse's main point: development was inevitable, and development done by others will be piecemeal and bring problems Rouse development would avoid.

With the June 30th deadline for the purchase rapidly approaching, residents and officials of the county were indifferent at best. Initial opposition did not turn to enthusiastic support as with Columbia, although Rouse's own initial doubts had turned to enthusiasm. Within the Rouse Company there was no support. The preliminary work on Shelby Farms and Wye Island had eaten up millions. The country was in poor economic condition, and so was the company. With the company's common stock worth little more than 10% of what it had been only two years before, taking on the burden of Wye Island development looked very foolish. With naysayers all around him, Jim Rouse decided to give up. The effect on Rouse, as Boyd Gibbons puts it, was that he "was disheartened, almost depressed. Though he had initially been skeptical about the project, he had become its most energetic advocate. 'This is a real sad day for me,' he told his board members."[25] He had signed the option to buy at a low point in his personal life. The project's potential had boosted his spirits. Now, after a year's enthusiasm and a lot of expense he had nothing to show.

Two years later, the state of Maryland bought the Wye Island property owned by Bill and Frank Hardy for $5.3 million. The property was turned over to the Department of Natural Resources State Forest and Park Service, and became known as the Wye Island Natural Resources Management Area. It is a waterfowl and wildlife habitat and also a low-impact recreational area. There is bird and wildlife watching but also controlled hunting for deer. Trails are maintained for hikers and cyclists. Boaters drop anchor in coves and inlets. Camping and lodge accommodations are available at reasonable prices. Despite Jim Rouse's predictions, Wye Island has remained undeveloped, and the general public has a place to enjoy open space and nature.[26] The people of Maryland and others have a resource they probably never would have had if there had not been a determination by Eastern Shore people to prove Rouse wrong in his firm belief that development is inevitable.

The fruitless work on Shelby Farms and Wye Island was explained in the 1974 annual report this way:

> During the year, considerable effort and dollars were expended in an attempt to gain support for the development of two new community projects. . . . Delays and difficulties in gaining the necessary public support and approvals led to our withdrawal from both projects. Efforts to seek other opportunities to develop new communities have been suspended for the foreseeable future.

Suspended for the foreseeable future. Those are not Jim Rouse's kind of words. Would *he* ever say that about the possibilities for new communities?

In 1973, Mathias J. DeVito, 16 years younger than Rouse, was promoted to President and Chief Operations Officer, and the focus of the company changed. The "Letter to Shareholders" in the 1973 annual report blatantly states the new emphasis in its very first sentence: "The heart of our business is the development and operation of regional shopping centers." The second sentence underscores the message: "This has prospered." From 1973 on, the lead item in the annual reports is jointly signed by James W. Rouse and Mathias J. DeVito.

In 1974, the Rouse Company owned twenty-four shopping centers and nine office buildings. Thirteen additional shopping centers were under development.[27] Still, in October Jim Rouse had to take on a painful task. He wrote to Bill Greenough, the president of TIAA to inform him of what was going on with regard to Columbia. TIAA had $15 million invested in Columbia, and now loans had to be re-financed. "I want you to know of my deep personal regret," Rouse says, "that circumstances make it necessary for us to seek this unusual cooperation on the part of the major lenders." He reminds Greenough that Columbia is no ordinary real estate project the success of which is measured in dollars and cents. No, he says,

> It has been a venture of faith on your part and your associates in the philosophy behind it and in the economic prospects which that philosophy supports. It is as important now as in the past to prove that urban growth can be rationally accommodated in new communities that are sensitive to the physical environment, to the people and to the institutions that provide support in our society—and to show that such communities can be developed with economic returns sufficient to justify the investment that is required to bring them to completion. . . . We will move out of the present storm and Columbia will regain its momentum, pay its debt, and produce an acceptable return to its investors and stockholders.[28]

The "present storm" was the stagnation and inflation that battered the American economy beginning in late 1973. The rate of inflation hit 13% and the prime lending rate was more than 11%. The Arab oil-producing nations refused to sell oil to the United States because of its support of Israel in the war that began in October 1973. The building and real estate industries in America were hard hit. In Columbia, the sale of land for homes and businesses was far below projections. Income with which to pay off debt was not coming in. As part of the refinancing of Columbia, Connecticut General became a larger and larger owner of Howard Research and Development. At one point in 1975, Connecticut General owned 85% of HRD.[29]

But it wasn't only Columbia that was in trouble. New towns elsewhere in the country were also in bad shape. In 1970, Jim Rouse was overjoyed with the passage by Congress of the Urban Growth and New Community Development Act. With Title VII, the act created a corporation to dispense incentive funds to developers moving to create new towns. Title VII pushed developers toward replicating Columbia. Specifically, Title VII sought to encourage rational, orderly, efficient growth, whether in cities, suburban, or rural areas. Three main objectives were focused on: creation of a national growth policy, providing subsidies for planning initiatives by states, and the underwriting of large-scale planned new towns. Among the requirements for the new towns were that they fit in with regional and local plans and that they seek a balance in residential, commercial, and public developments. Residential planning had to include housing for people of low and moderate incomes. Planners were to rely to the maximum on private enterprise.[30]

The New Communities Corporation, between 1970 and 1973, gave the go-ahead to fifteen new towns and was considering about fifty more. Each of the fifteen was more or less following the Columbia template. The recession of 1974 seemed to stop the program cold; only a few of the single-family homes, town houses, and apartments under construction could be sold. Bloom explains the failure this way:

> The mixture of market-rate single-family homes with unconventional architecture, high-density housing, industrial parks, racial integration, and subsidized housing that had proved successful at Columbia and given it much fame alienated many potential builders and residents in a less sensational context.[31]

The biggest part of that sensational context at Columbia was the person of Jim Rouse. Even at Columbia, no ordinary developer would have been able to get blacks and whites and people of widely different income levels to live in close proximity. Jim Rouse liked it that people on different income levels lived in the same neighborhood. Unfortunately, most Americans would not. Those who liked it found their way to Columbia. There weren't many more left. When it was written, Rouse believed Title VII provided just what was needed in the way of government support for more quality new towns to spring up. When it didn't happen, he took the position that in hard times such as the 70s Congress needed to be more generous.[32] But Rouse had been chastened. New towns seemed like extravagance. Rouse's focus turned elsewhere.

How strange life can be. Just as he was enduring a losing streak in business generally and in his favorite kind of venture, Jim Rouse won big in his personal life. In June 1973, while his divorce from Libby was in the works, Jim met Myrtle Patricia Traugott. Jim was visiting friends in Norfolk. They needed a fourth for doubles tennis. The Norfolk friends called a friend to be the fourth, and Patty walked into Jim's life, an event he called "a divine accident." She played tennis, Jim's favorite form of recreation. She was a commissioner on the Norfolk Redevelopment and Housing Authority. She also was pursuing a master's degree in Urban Affairs and once had heard Jim Rouse give a speech. She was divorced, and she was available. They saw each other during the summer and fall of 1973, and it wasn't long before Jim knew he had found a new life partner. His enjoyment of Patty seemed only to grow. They were married in the Church of the Saviour on November 2, 1974. A couple of months later, in a letter to a friend, Jim said this about his new bride: "Patty is richly compatible in faith, energy, temperament, goals for life and living. She is bright . . . likes people, is resilient to life's trials and challenges, full of zest and, miracle of miracles, loves me. It is a wondrous new life."[33]

The tenth anniversary of the opening of Columbia occurred in 1977. In ten years, the new city had drawn 46,000 residents. Where there had been none, there were 20,000 jobs in 770 businesses. The new city had a comprehensive health care program. It had interfaith religious centers and schools at all levels. Its own local government provided a wide range of recreational activities and facilities for entertainment while preserving over 1,000 acres of open space. These, and other, facts are merely *listed*—not *celebrated*—in the Rouse Company annual report for 1977. You would expect Columbia's achievements to be the featured story. But the cover of the report is given over to a full-page photograph of the opening of another shopping center, The Gallery at Market East in Philadelphia. Columbia is not even mentioned in the jointly signed "Letter to the Shareholders." Columbia does get a full-page picture, but it's on page 14, and the progress report on Columbia is given only two-thirds of the opposite page.

There is nothing of Jim Rouse's gushiness about the new city. Nothing about Columbia being "the next America." Nothing about its being a "venture of faith" well on the way to being redeemed. Nothing about the next Columbia. Nothing about Columbia's importance to our civilization.

Chapter 15 A Downward Turn

1. The Rouse Company's 1972 Annual Report.
2. Elizabeth O'Connor, *Call to Commitment* (New York: Harper & Row), 1963, 10.
3. N. Gordon Cosby letter to JWR, November 19, 1987.
4. On this period in JWR's life, www.enterprisefoundation.org/about/whoweare/history.asp. Accessed April 2004.
5. vineyardusa.org/publications/newsletters/cutting_edge/2001_fall/cosby. Accessed April 2004.
6. O'Connor 25, 27.
7. Available at the Maryland Historical Society in Baltimore, Maryland.
8. In the La Noue interview, JWR attributes the lines to Paul Jones in *Review of Life's Meaning*.
9. O'Connor 86-87.
10. O'Connor 51.
11. JWR letter to Philip Klutznick, October 11, 1971.
12. JWR letter to Grace, March 1, 1973. 1. The Rouse Company's 1972 Annual Report.
13. La Noue interview.
14. 1972 Annual Report.
15. Report of American City Corporation, April 1972.
16. *Hartford Courant* editorial, May 30, 1972.
17. Olsen 204.
18. *Staten Island Advance,* November 20, 2002.
19. www.figure8communications.com/images/Richmond_Creek.pdf. Accessed April 2004.
20. Olsen 208.
21. Olsen 208.
22. Boyd Gibbons, *Wye Island* (Washington: Resources for the Future), 21.
23. Gibbons 45-46.
24. Gibbons 11-12.
25. Gibbons 186.
26. www.dnr.state.md.us/publiclands/eastern/wyeisland.html. Accessed April 2004
27. Gibbons 20.
28. WJR letter to William Greenough, October 18, 1974.
29. Paul Lockwood, "Connecticut General," *Columbia Magazine,* June 1987, 36-39.
30. Bloom 140-42.
31. Bloom 144
32. Bloom 146.
33. Quoted in Olsen, 255-56.

Chapter 16
Festival Marketplace: Boston

For an exuberant personality a downward turn is rarely purely downward. Even as things are going wrong, the optimistic mind continues to see prospects for new achievements. In the early 70s, Columbia was struggling, and neither Hartford, Staten Island, Memphis, or Wye Island brought a profitable return to the company. Still, in June of 1973 Jim met Patty, and a year and a half later he was in a wonderful new marriage. And in the meantime, the Rouse Company was getting closer and closer to landing the big Boston contract.

In March 1972, Jim Rouse and Ned Daniels went up to Boston to see an architect named Ben Thompson. Thompson had a proposition for Rouse. He wanted the Rouse Company to be the developer—or redeveloper—of Quincy Market. It was an idea that already had been acted upon by Boston officials, gone into the development pipeline—and gotten stuck.

In the spring of 1972, Rouse was 58 and Thompson 54. Both had been in the Navy during World War II. Thompson had gone to Yale; Rouse hadn't but his son Jimmy had. Thompson, like Rouse, was a visionary and a lover of cities. Thompson was fascinated by the vitality of markets in public squares. So was Rouse; his favorite was Farmers Market in Los Angeles. The year before, Thompson had written in *The Boston Globe*,

> The natural pageantry of crowds and goods, of meat, fish, and crops from the fields, of things made and things grown, all to be tasted, seen, and touched, are the prime sources of sensations, experience, and amusement in the daily lives of whole populations—were and still are, in most nations except our own.[1]

As he had with Gordon Cosby, Rouse quickly hit it off with Thompson. According to Ned Daniels, "The two of them took off into fantasy land. . . .

They'd each met their match, and Jim Rouse got so stirred up and so excited, so intrigued . . . and that was the beginning of their romance."[2]

Until the migration to the suburbs began in the 1950s, Quincy Market had been Boston's main food market. Before Quincy Market, Faneuil Hall, the building in front of it on the downtown side, had played that role. Faneuil Hall was built by Boston's wealthiest merchant, Peter Faneuil, as a marketplace for farmers and fishermen and various kinds of other merchants. Only a short distance away is Boston Harbor, where in 1773, irate colonists dumped those sacks of tea into the water. Faneuil Hall's second floor is different; it is given over mostly to the Great Hall, where early Boston's town meetings were held and where to this day lecturers and politicians may hold forth. In 1826 the structure on the waterfront side of Faneuil was built. The new market was named after the then mayor of Boston, Josiah Quincy. When, after the middle of the twentieth century, more and more city people moved to the suburbs, business at the market declined, and little was done to keep it up. Nothing was done to bring in new business. The nearby population continued to fall off, and, as people's tastes changed, Quincy Market, as well as the adjacent North and South Markets, became dingy, derelict, decrepit. Quincy Market was at the center of Boston's Waterfront Urban Renewal District. But as the 200th birthday of the United States approached, not much renewal had taken place.

In 1964, the Boston Redevelopment Authority (BRA) purchased the property. In 1970, the BRA solicited proposals for the restoration and revitalization of what it referred to as the Faneuil Hall Markets. On July 1, 1971, a Philadelphia developer, Van Arkel and Moss, was given the contract, and it chose Ben Thompson as its architect. But seven months later the BRA revoked the contract with Van Arkel and Moss; it had become apparent that Van Arkel and Moss "lacked the organization and the financial ability to proceed."[3] About a year later, the BRA awarded another contract it later revoked. This one went to the Falzarano Construction Company for external work. In the meantime Architectural Heritage, a local firm, came forward as a development company and wanted the contract. This was the unsettled state of affairs that led Ben Thompson to Jim Rouse.

For Rouse this was a project that would enable him to continue his mission to do something about cities. Here was an opportunity to bring back to life a dying section of downtown Boston. It had been the conventional wisdom among developers that combining historic restoration and profit-making wasn't possible. But that wasn't going to turn Rouse off. Yes, he would submit a proposal. He and Ben Thompson would team up—the innovative architect and the risk-taking developer. If the Rouse Company got the job, it also would work with the other members of Van Arkel and Moss's Boston team, the real estate brokerage firm of R. M. Bradley Co. and the contractors B. H. Macomber Co. Trouble is Architectural Heritage (AH) also wanted the contract.

AH already had done work in Boston. It had converted the old city hall into an office building and preserved the old Sanborn fish market in that building. Its officers were historians and preservationists, not businessmen, which looked like a good thing for people running a restoration project. Bursting with energy and enthusiasm, Roger Webb, the AH president, described his firm as the city's "agent" and claimed his proposal would bring more money to the city than would Rouse's. The competition between AH and the Rouse Company was largely between a local organization that promised to put the public interest first and a private company that ultimately would be driven by the profit motive[4].

The pros and cons of the competing companies were analyzed in a *Boston Globe* article of January 7, 1973. While AH had no equity and its financial planning was weak, the Rouse Company would have little difficulty raising the money needed to see the project to completion. In the restored Quincy Market building, Rouse would devote 60% of the space to retail and 40% to offices; AH's plan was for a 50-50 division. Jim Rouse had done the arithmetic and could say with confidence exactly how much would be needed for the various facets of the total job. It would total $16.3 million, which included expenditures for construction, land, utilities, interiors, exteriors, landscaping, etc. Rouse was able to say that there would be an annual operating budget of $700,000 for a total of 354,000 gross square feet. Despite the obvious disparity in experience and ability to do long-range planning, that Rouse would get the contract was no sure thing, especially since the director of the BRA, a college classmate of Webb, Robert T. Kenney, was expected to recommend AH.

The *Globe* article prompted Ben Thompson to spring into action. He wrote an impassioned memo to the president of the Boston Society of Architects. He wanted the society to get involved. Thompson didn't say it should support Rouse over AH, but he did mention "our plan," which would put the emphasis on small merchants and "a colorful diversity of life and events competing on a day to day basis—around the clock and in all seasons." Thompson asserts that the decision about the developer was of the utmost importance. He had not been associated with any project more significant, because this one "encompasses the urgent question of what the American city is about." He asks about the market, "How can it be restored not only to its valid condition but to the popular function and urban spirit that have been lost through Twentieth Century decay?"

"Most American cities today," he continues, " are looking for a direction, a prototype from which to draw confidence in the rebuilding of downtown." He hopes that others in the society care as much as he does about what will happen. "A positive solution," he says, "could set precedents for many years to come."[5]

Thompson's memo had the desired effect. The board of directors of the Boston Society of Architects unanimously approved a resolution calling for an open discussion of plans by the competing developers. They sent the resolution to Mayor Kevin H. White. They urged that the contract not be awarded until after "a thorough and public analysis of the professional, financial, and business qualifications of the respective parties has been presented and publicly commented upon." They also urged that the BRA get the opinions of its committees on real estate and architectural design and bring the Boston Landmarks Commission into the discussion.

On February 26, 1973, both Webb and Rouse appeared before the Boston City Council. Webb played on the idea that his firm presented a deal that was for the long-term good of the city, whereas the Rouse plan was governed by considerations of the long-term profits for the company. After costs, Webb said, he would give all profits to the city. He told the Council that Quincy Market "does not have to be given away for $1 per year." The market, he said, is a $2-million asset that really does not need much work. Under his plan, the city would get about $2 million a year in the last 88 years of a 99-year lease. When Jim Rouse took the floor, he said Webb's figures were "wholly irresponsible, completely naïve and reveal a lack of knowledge." He denied asking for the Quincy Market building at $1 per year. What he wanted was a 99-year package for all three buildings, the Quincy building and the North and South Market buildings. The heart of Rouse's pitch was this:

> It's absolutely impossible to reproduce unless the three buildings are locked on as one. If the city allows this to go forward with North and South Market streets as individual programs, it would have simply squandered one of the greatest opportunities available for all times.[6]

The city already was paying for external renovation. Whereas Webb said he planned to spend $500,000 on the interior, Rouse said he would spend $2.5 million "to make Quincy Market what it should become." Rouse said he would give the city a guarantee of $600,000 after the third year or 20% of gross, whichever is larger. Webb said nothing about a guarantee. With America's bicentennial approaching, Rouse also said that as part of the deal he would give $500,000 for promotion of Boston's celebration of the birthday.[7]

Architectural Heritage still was not out of the running. Rouse went back to Boston to see Mayor White. In the mayor's office, he got up and went to the window. In front of him were the waterfront and the blighted market. He invited the mayor to go for a walk with him through the ramshackle streets adjacent to the market. As they were strolling along, Mayor White turned to Rouse and said, "I hear you are like a bulldozer. If you want to get something, you push over everything to get it." Rouse responded by saying, "If I am trying to do something and I believe it is right, then I do my best to persuade other people that it is right. . . ." Rouse was bringing the mayor under the influence of his exuberance. He said to the mayor, "The only thing that being discouraged should do is make you think of new answers. You can't give up."[8]

In late March, after both the mayor and the City Council recommended it, the Boston Redevelopment Authority designated the Rouse Company as the developer of the Faneuil Market Area. The designation, however, was tentative, and would not become final until a formal lease was signed. Several months went by and the parties still had not signed a lease. One issue was that the BRA did not have control of the North and South Markets. Control had to be given by the City Council, and there were signs of Council reluctance and the possibility of demands regarding other parts of the lease. Another possible snag hinged around the question of what would happen to the vendors currently renting space. In addition, the Rouse Company's project director in Boston, Roy E. Williams, discovered that the structural condition of the buildings was not as good as had been assumed. He was afraid that fixing up the buildings before the project even began might cost as much as $750,000. In late November, Jim Rouse had to write to Mayor White. He urged the mayor to get involved and inform city officials that they had to deal with the fact that the buildings needed to be made basically sound before the Rouse Company could begin its work. Procrastination made it more and more unlikely that the desired completion date of April 1975 could be met.[9]

When the lease was finally done, it provided for the renovation of all three buildings and a 99-year term. The company would pay to the city, in lieu of taxes $200,000 in the first year of operation, $400,000 in the second year, and $600,000 per year thereafter. Merchants who were already in the Quincy Market would be allowed to stay for three years without an increase in rent. Prospective new tenants who had been displaced from the Quincy area or some other renewal area would be given preference in the leasing of space in the project of other comparable merchants. All planning and design would be done by Benjamin Thompson & Associates of Cambridge.

On June 27, 1974, Ben Thompson wrote to Jim Rouse in Columbia. Thompson now wanted to formalize his role in the project that hereafter was to be called Faneuil Hall Marketplace. Thompson had been in Columbia the week before to discuss his role. It could be said that without Ben Thompson the Rouse Company would never have been involved in the Boston project. Thompson wanted formal acknowledgement of "our untypical role as initiators and entrepreneurs responsible for the Rouse Company involvement in the Faneuil Hall Marketplace project." Thompson asserts that he has been involved in ways not usual for an architect-designer. He states,

> We recognize that there is an important element of pioneering in our creative collaboration on this job, both in the broader scope of the Owner-Architect teamwork, and in the handling of sensitive aspects of developing historic public buildings in an inner city context.

And Thompson wants Rouse to agree that in the years ahead Thompson & Associates will handle all matters of Marketplace design. Should the Rouse Company's involvement in Boston be enlarged to include other downtown properties, Thompson will get favorable consideration.

Another letter from Ben Thompson, also dated June 27th, was addressed to the Rouse Company. In it, Thompson states that for his contribution to the Marketplace's development he should get a payment of 1% of each year's gross receipts to the developer. He then raises the possibility of a buyout arrangement.

He proposes that "the agreed royalty be payable annually for an established start-up period of seven years free of the buyout option, whereafter the buyout might be exercised in any third year after notice is given of intention to exercise the option." Thompson is acting as his own lawyer. Obviously he's doing all right.

The renovated Quincy Market wasn't ready by the desired April 1975. Nor was it ready by July 4, 1976. But it was ready late in August. Not long after the opening Rouse sent an exhilarating memo to company employees:

> It is already apparent that Faneuil Hall uplifts those who come to use it. It is of the good city. The flower shops, the trees and benches, and public spaces, the openness through the canopies and the colonnade, the richness drawn from the heritage of old buildings, the little shops run by their owners and the personal exchanges across the counters between the owner-merchants and their customers, the smallness, intimacy, smells, sounds and sights that are uniquely those of a market have all served to tap some deep yearning. . . .[10]

People did not arrive at Quincy Market by car; they walked. The business people were not franchisees of national chains; they were individual proprietors. Ben Thompson had sought "individual proprietorship with immense chaotic variety," and he got it. But much was going to change.

Jim Rouse had made a wise decision in giving Thompson a free hand. His creativity was a major part of the project's success. Throughout the marketplace, "Ben Thompson's unmistakable decorative touch declares itself," Jane Davison wrote in the *Globe*. He created a rotunda under the central dome and in it a revolving group of short-term renters lure passersby. The line of vendors extends outward and continues under Thompson's ingenious canopies, meant to be imitations of the awnings used in the early days of the market. There is no air conditioning. Thompson took out all the windows and hoped the market would be cooled by breezes off the water. In winter, there is minimal heating. The canopies are heated, but the vendors lining the external walls have to bundle up, just as they did in the past. Thompson "has plumped for high standards in multifarious details, less architectural than decorative," Davison wrote. You can see his devotion, she says, to the idea of keeping the past alive in the present in the letter he sent to tenants. Do things, he told them, that will reflect the city's past, its present, and its future. Establish a tradition that can be carried on by future merchants and designers. In 1977-78, the Faneuil Marketplace was completed with the re-opening of the North and South Markets. While they, like Quincy, had restaurants, most of the businesses were non-food specialty shops. The main attraction remained the Quincy Market, standing between the other two, a massive Greek Revival temple dedicated to good eating and the pleasures of the senses.[11]

But the reflection of the city's past was short-lived. The one-of-a-kind small shops had difficulty surviving. When their three-year lease was up, most were not renewed. As Bloom puts it, "The festival marketplace became the

Trojan horse of the suburban reentry into the center city."[12] More and more of the small shops went under or were forced to become fast-food operations. For those who cared about the past, chain-store creep was in full play. Much of the retail space was taken over by the upscale chain stores the Rouse Company liked to have in its malls. Despite the entirely good intentions of Thompson and Rouse, the original vision for Faneuil Hall Marketplace was vanishing. The people who came just weren't interested in the products of the old-fashioned fresh food marketplace.

In 1978, Thompson wrote to the Rouse Company complaining about, among other things, the "homogenization" he saw taking place as small owner-operated businesses were replaced. He wanted Rouse to take steps "to reassert the market's identity as a viable, convenient place to shop for groceries of an unusual and quality kind."[13]

But Faneuil Hall Marketplace was making money for the company and the city. The millions who came voted with their dollars, and "groceries of an unusual and quality kind" were not getting many votes. Even with the loss of the sense of the past, shoppers, diners, tourists, browsers gather at the Marketplace day and night, over ten million in most years. In good weather, the throngs are entertained by street performers. What had been a run-down, blighted section of town was transformed into an area bursting with life. When Jim Rouse attended the 1976 opening, he turned to Patty, his new wife, and said, "Why this is like a festival!" And the term stuck. Rouse was now in the business of creating festival marketplaces, even if it meant giving the masses who came what they wanted.

Chapter 16 Festival Marketplace: Boston

1. Quoted on the website for *Shopping Centers Today Newswire.* Accessed May 2004.
2. Quoted by Olsen, 242.
3. Robert T. Kenney memo to The Boston Redevelopment Authority, March 1973. All the documents related to Faneuil Hall Marketplace can be found in CA.
4. Bloom,156.
5. Ben Thompson memo to John Harkness, January 9, 1973.
6. *Boston Globe*, February 27, 1973, 14.
7. *Boston Globe,* February 27, 1973, 14.
8. Autob, 102.
9. JWR letter to Kevin White, November 26, 1973.
10. Quoted by Bloom, 160.
11. *Boston Globe,* October 26, 1976, 74-78.
12. Bloom, 158.
13. Bloom, 168.

Chapter 17
Festival Marketplace: Baltimore

In 1960 Jim Rouse did not get the contract to build the Charles Center in downtown Baltimore. It was an enormous disappointment. Rouse was one of the country's leading spokesmen for urban redevelopment, and his own city chose not to give him the contract for its biggest redevelopment project. By 1976, he felt he could try again. The Quincy Market phase of the Faneuil Hall Marketplace had received nothing but raves. The new city of Columbia was up and running. What more could be asked for in qualifications? If he had the right project, why shouldn't he get to do it? Since 1960 there had been a vast improvement downtown. Blighted warehouses and wharves no longer lined the Inner Harbor, the downtown waterfront. During the bicentennial year of 1976, the parade of tall sailing ships had brought festive thousands to the Inner Harbor. The oldest U.S. Navy ship, the *Constellation*, was now permanently berthed there. Diagonally across from the *Constellation*, the Maryland Science Center had recently opened. Rouse saw an opportunity for a Faneuil Hall-type marketplace on the vacant land between the *Constellation* and the Science Center.

Even before the opening of the renovated Quincy Market, Rouse was taking soundings in Baltimore. He was in contact with Martin Millspaugh, the CEO of Charles Center-Inner Harbor Management. He drew out of Millspaugh this statement in a letter of August 2, 1976: "We believe that there exists an excellent opportunity within the Inner Harbor to create a major commercial attraction which will service not only local traffic but draw the business visitor and the tourist." While that wasn't exactly what Rouse wanted, that statement was good enough. But the road between vision and actuality would be the usual long one. The enthusiasm that Rouse felt had to be transferred to others. Rouse had had the support of Theodore McKeldin when he was mayor in the 60s and he had the support of the present mayor, William Donald Schaefer, but now he also needed to persuade the Housing and Community Development Commission and the City Council. And some persuasion was needed even within the Rouse Company.

The degree of enthusiasm within the company for going ahead varied. L. B. (Monk) Askew, Jr., the Vice President for Design and Development was not exactly thrilled. He had taken a look at the site and summarized his reaction: "I didn't get flag waving enthusiasm. However, I did not get completely turned off either; but we would need all the help we could get—access, location, visibility, and contributions. Let's try it!"[1] The reaction of Scott Ditch, vice president for marketing, was more positive:

> I believe Baltimore is ready for the Quincy Market kind of project we could put together on this superb site. Nowhere in the entire metropolitan area is there a place where the community can really come together for many reasons—for shopping, dining, entertainment, browsing, or just to "be," in a warm, exciting place. I strongly recommend that we proceed with the program. . . .[2]

This was the reaction that had to be evoked in the outside constituencies who would have a say in whether the proposal went forward. An important endorsement came from the Baltimore chapter of the American Institute of Architects. Its president, James R. Grieves, wrote to the commissioner of Housing and Community Development, M. Jay Brodie, and he said just the right things. The west side of the Inner Harbor "desperately needs" a two-story structure that would help link the Science Center to the *Constellation* and make the waterside promenade more exciting. He said the Rouse Company, over twenty years, had proven its leadership in reviving downtown environments with exciting and profitable shopping places.[3]

When word got out about the Rouse proposal, opposition quickly developed. One objection was that the Rouse development would hurt other new commercial developments. South Baltimore was already in the revitalization process, and plans were afoot for redevelopment north of the harbor.

> The last thing downtown Baltimore needs, [Irwin J. DuBois, president of the South Baltimore Business Association, wrote in *The Sun*] is the construction of a new shopping center placed between the Howard and Lexington retail district and South Baltimore. . . . The Rouse proposal threatens the emerging potential of the downtown neighborhoods. These neighborhoods must be allowed the promise envisioned by our city administration.

DuBois also made the point that was to be picked up by many others: the Inner Harbor was popular because of its openness. The Rouse structures would take over much-needed open space. Open space and grass should not be transformed into glass and steel.[4] Rouse, to show what could stand in place of some of the harbor's open space, brought the entire City Council up to Boston.

Another point made by opponents was that the Quincy Market project was the restoration of an old building. Nothing was built in previously open space. While a campaign was carried on, under project manager Bruce D. Alexander, to gain the backing of various influential Baltimore community groups, the infringement on open-space became the opponents' main argument. A zoning change was needed by Rouse, and a hearing was held before a committee of the City Council. Opponents came out in force. Brodie, the housing commissioner, and Grieves, the architect, gave presentations in favor of the zoning change. But they were met with the scorn of Louise Alder, chairwoman of Citizens for the Preservation of the Inner Harbor. Her response to the experts was, "We've been treated to a slick sales pitch. . . . The city has made the Inner Harbor area an open-space area for all, then they want to take it away." She had much support. A majority of the speakers were opposed to the zoning amendment Rouse needed to go ahead.[5]

Minority participation in the project became an issue. Alexander told Brodie minorities would get jobs, first, in construction and, later, in retailing. He committed the Rouse Company to hiring a general contractor who was as interested as the company was in having a significant number of minority workers. He pointed out what the company had done in Boston, where the company and the general contractor working together hired more minority journeymen and apprentices than required by federal guidelines. He said the Rouse Company had insisted that the general contractor also hire for its staff a person "who is schooled in available equal opportunity programs, is in touch with minority communities and contractors and with federal, state and city officials, and who will spend time dealing with minority groups to achieve these goals." Alexander acknowledged the difficulty the company would have in finding minority businesses that met the qualifications for renting space, but, he said, space would be provided for smaller businesses—space for kiosks and pushcarts—that would enable small minority businesspeople to build their credit and a track record as retailers. At a future date, those would be important recommendations and help minority retailers gain access to larger rental space.[6]

In January 1978, the City Council gave Rouse the change he wanted, and Brodie gave the company exclusive negotiating rights for the property. Opponents of the project struck back. They got over 12,000 signatures to a statement saying they wanted to keep the Inner Harbor free of commercial development. The statement also supported an amendment to the city charter, which would be voted on in the November election. If the referendum passed, all of the waterfront area would be designated parkland and further development would be stopped. Mayor William Donald Schaefer then outflanked the Rouse opponents. He proposed his own amendment to the city charter, in words very similar to the opposition's. It said that the city would retain all the Inner Harbor waterfront area as public parkland—except for 3.2 acres, the land required by Rouse for his two pavilions. Louise Alder, leader of the opposition, accused the mayor of deliberately trying to confuse the voters.[7]

Mayor Schaefer's plan was to get his amendment on the ballot not through the drawn-out, tedious process of accumulating the requisite number of signatures but by getting City Council approval for placing it on the ballot. At a City Council hearing, Jim Rouse made a compelling case for his project and Mayor Schaefer's amendment. Harborplace, Rouse said, would be an expression of the unique personality of Baltimore. It would not block views of the harbor but would "frame and give scale and shape to harbor views." It would enable more people activities to take place in the "spirit of festival—a continuing 12 months fair." It would support the other attractions at the Inner Harbor and provide new opportunities to local small businesses. The architecture would be "light, airy, sparkling." He insisted that the idea that there would be a loss of open space was completely mistaken.[8]

By August things did not look good for the Rouse proposal. Rouse was told that the opposition's argument that parkland was being given away for commercial development was getting a very sympathetic hearing by voters. If the vote were held in August, Rouse would lose. In a memo to his top people, Rouse underscored the urgency of the situation. Speakers who favored his proposal had to get on the calendar of neighborhood organizations. More had to be done to make the campaign for the proposal look like the work of Baltimore citizens rather than city officials. A slide presentation had to be prepared for showing very quickly. The legal limitations on what the Rouse Company could do to influence the election had to be checked out.

Within the next month the campaign for the Rouse proposal got rolling. The company could provide information but could not lobby—and inform the Rouse people did. The main vehicle was "Citizens for Harborplace," led by twenty-six community leaders and assorted bigwigs of union and civic organizations. The president of the Interdenominational Ministerial Alliance, Rev. Wendell Phillips, wrote to the city's clergy to announce that his organization had "voted overwhelmingly to endorse and support the construction of Harborplace." Members of the alliance placed great importance on the promise of 400 construction jobs and 1,000 permanent jobs the Rouse project would bring to the city. It was pointed out that "James Rouse is a man of great integrity and ability who has always been sensitive to the problems of the black community."[9] Over the years Rouse had been a strong ally of the black community; it was only right that he be helped now. It was expected that recipients of the letter would urge their congregations to get out on Election Day and vote for Question K and against Question N.

As Election Day approached, the alliance between Jim Rouse and Mayor Schaefer became even closer. Rouse sent Schaefer a copy of his 1964 letter to the then Mayor Theodore McKeldin. The letter spelled out what Rouse thought should be done at the Inner Harbor. Now Mayor Schaefer wrote back and said that Rouse's ideas were "prophetic" and that "your vision was, and still is, impressive." In addition, he said, "The harbor is the source of our material and spiritual strength. We owe it to ourselves and future generations of Baltimoreans to build on that strength with all the sensitivity we can muster."[10] The latter statement certainly is a classic statement of political pap. It would have been just as useful to the opposition.

On Election Day, Question K, Mayor Schaefer's amendment, won and Question N lost. While the citywide vote for K was 58%, in black neighborhoods the favorable vote was 72%. The project went ahead.

It was not to be a renovation project as in Boston. But the objectives of the project were the same as those for the Faneuil Hall Marketplace. Rouse and his designer, Ben Thompson, would again try to capture the flavor of a bygone era in the life of a waterfront city. Rouse insisted that Harborplace would be a Baltimore place and not another place for a conglomeration of chain stores. Harborplace would be a place for local owners selling local products. The two two-story pavilions that make up Harborplace had their grand opening on July 2, 1980. At noon on this hot and humid summer day the schooner *Pride of Baltimore* sailed into the Inner Harbor with a contingent of Maryland grandees. Speeches were made at dockside in the sweltering mid-day heat. Then the dignitaries moved inside to cut ribbons at Harborplace shops. Bruce Alexander, the project manager, had been involved in a running debate with Rouse. Alexander wanted air conditioning; Rouse, remembering Faneuil Hall Marketplace's success without air conditioning, did not. Rouse produced data showing that summer temperatures in Baltimore were not much higher than Boston's. Alexander produced figures on humidity in the two cities—and won the debate. Now Rouse, his large brow covered with sweat, told Alexander that air conditioning was indeed a good idea.[11]

When it opened Harborplace did have a local and old-time flavor. On sale in the fresh food area were Chesapeake Bay seafood, poultry and melons from the Eastern Shore, dairy products and vegetables from western Maryland, and the crafts of local artisans.[12] But as in Boston the vision of the developer and designer did not last more than a few years past the opening. Two nearby fresh food markets—Lexington and Cross Street—continued to be the prime markets for local food shoppers, mainly the poor from nearby streets. Plenty of people came to Harborplace, and they forced it to become something else. In his initial vision, Rouse saw the corner of the Inner Harbor he wanted to develop as containing, in addition to the food stalls, "sidewalk cafes, dozens of eating places, large and small, many fronting on terraces overlooking the harbor." That part of the vision came to dominate. Rouse also foresaw a "democratic, embracing, comfortable place for all people—rich and poor, young and old, of all races—a place which the diverse people of Baltimore can be proud to share."[13] But the local poor people showed up in relatively small numbers. The people who did come were, by and large, middle class; people looking for a pleasant place to stroll, enjoy the passing parade, and then have a good meal, not particularly caring whether the restaurant was local or a franchise of a chain. They had no problem with the likes of Pizzeria Uno, Planet Hollywood, Hooters, and the Cheesecake Factory.

The Rouse Company saw what was happening. A 1981 study reported that Harborplace "is attracting a clientele which is affluent and proportionately more white than metropolitan Baltimore." It noted that Harborplace drew "more shoppers from the suburbs than from the city, and there is a distinct dependence" on areas to the north that are primarily suburban. Bloom observed that white suburbanites made it a more financially successful place than it would have been otherwise but at the cost of its originality. As in Boston, homogenization set in.[14] Bloom contended that the Rouse Company did not pay enough attention to the needs of the fresh food sellers. As a fresh food market, Bloom argued, Harborplace could have been as successful as Seattle's Pike Place, but the Rouse Company was "insensitive" to those needs. "In their rush for profits and cutting-edge management, Rouse and his managers lost sight of half of their vision."[15] That was true enough.

On the other hand, the part of the vision that was realized should not be minimized. The Inner Harbor is much more powerful as an attraction than it would have been without the Rouse development. Baltimore has gained economically, and so have the spirits of visitors. About 15 million visitors have been coming to the Inner Harbor every year, many of them drawn by the restaurants and shops at Harborplace. Between the two pavilions set back from the promenade, is a wide-open, easily accessible amphitheater, a place to meet friends or just to sit, relax, and people watch. On weekends when the weather is mild, there is likely to be a succession of street performers eager to please. Throughout the summer there are regularly scheduled concerts on Friday and Saturday nights and Sunday afternoons. There are ethnic festivals and competitions of one kind or another. On Halloween afternoon, kids look for candy handouts at Harborplace stores. At Christmastime tubas play. On New Years Eve, there is a fireworks spectacular.

On any day of the year when the weather is not wet or cold, there are people on the promenade. On a sunny Tuesday in April of 2005 when the author last visited, the Harborplace corner was thronged. On birthdays and anniversaries and graduation days, people from all over the area come to the Inner Harbor. It's what people in the Baltimore area do on their special occasions. And after they've strolled for a while, they look for a table in one of Harborplace's restaurants; local or chain doesn't matter. It would be hard to find anyone who would say that the people of Baltimore would be better off had Harborplace not been built. Harborplace is a happy place.

Chapter 17 Festival Marketplace: Baltimore

1. L. B. Askew. Jr. memo to K. A. Gorman, March 17, 1977.
2. Scott Ditch memo to K. A. Gorman, March 16, 1977.
3. James R. Grieves letter to M. J. Brodie, September 13, 1977.
4. *The Sun,* October 8, 1977, A15.
5. *The Sun,* May 25, 1978, A1.
6. Bruce Alexander letter to M. Jay Brodie, January 23, 1978.
7. *The Sun,* May 25, 1978, A1.
8. JWR memo to Mathias DeVito, June 19, 1978.
9. Wendell Phillips letter to Fellow Clergy, October 25, 1978.
10. William Donald Schaefer letter to JWR, November 2, 1978.
11. Author interview with Bruce Alexander, July 7, 2003.
12. Bloom, 172.
13. Bloom, 171.
14. Bloom, 175.
15. Bloom, 178.

Chapter 18
The Social Entrepreneur

When Harborplace opened, Jim Rouse, having turned sixty-five, was a year into his official retirement as Chief Executive Officer of the Rouse Company. While he remained as chairman of the board, his last day as CEO was May 23, 1979. That was the day of the company's annual meeting of stockholders. Rouse addressed the meeting and reflected on "a way of thinking" that, he said, had emerged within the company over the years. It was a way of thinking that had three main goals: "to improve the physical environment and the quality of urban life . . .;" "to provide continuing opportunities for personal growth and fulfillment for people working in the company"; and "to increase earnings annually at a rate sufficient to provide adequate rewards to our stockholders . . . and to attract the capital required to finance our operations." The company's guiding principle was to "put 'the bottom line' where it belongs—at the bottom. . . . It is when the bottom line is made the top line—the object of the enterprise—that business gets mixed up, off the track, loses its way."[1]

On that occasion he passed on to Matt DeVito, his successor as CEO, a framed poster that said, "When life gives you lemons, make lemonade." He also gave him a card that had sat on his desk and said, "Make no little plans, they have no magic to stir men's blood." The third item he gave DeVito was more personal. It was a Bible with a note inside the front cover. The note said, "Give your best; use your gifts; respect the dignity of all men and women; know from whence this earth, its people, this business comes—and know that as it reaches out and works for the good of mankind it is right."[2] One wonders about these gestures. Having worked closely with DeVito for the past half-dozen years, does Rouse not have full faith in DeVito's readiness to carry on the Rouse way of thinking? Does a mentor who has full confidence in his protégé, who has confided in him regularly and discussed goals and methods—does such a mentor need to put on display such reminders? Well, when one is a CEO, it is not difficult to lose sight of the idea that the business is on the right track only when "it reaches out and works for the good of mankind."

When the meeting adjourned Jim Rouse was no longer obliged to concern himself daily with the business of the Rouse Company. That burden was off his shoulders. He could do as he pleased. But, of course, he was not the kind of man to indulge himself in luxury, pampering, or the self-centered pursuits so traditional to American retirees of means. He wasn't going to spend his remaining days on the golf course, on the Bay sailing, or even writing a book about his accomplishments. He was on the lookout for a new way of putting into practice the spirit that he told that last stockholders' meeting pervades the company: the spirit of caring—helping people. While he remained as chairman of the board, essentially he was separated from the company and without a base of operations. He traveled, gave advice when asked, spoke at conferences, thought about teaching, thought about going into politics. And waited for a firm push toward a new endeavor.

A few days after Harborplace opened, an article in *The Washington Post* took his thinking down a new path. The article pointed out the disparity between shiny, new Harborplace and the blighted Sandtown-Winchester neighborhood only about two miles west of the harbor. Sandtown was a neighborhood without hope. But at this point in his life what could Rouse do about it? Still, his blood was stirred and his mind was making connections. He thought about Jubilee Housing and the Church of the Saviour. In 1972, members of the church's mission group that was focused on housing bought two decrepit apartment buildings and, with a lot of volunteer help, corrected 940 code violations and made the apartments livable.

In his oral history interview in 1974, Rouse related how that took place. The mission group, usually ten to twenty people, emerges "out of somebody's call to do something. The church never sits down and decides that we ought to engage in this mission. . . . The church then financially supports it, and spiritually supports it, and it becomes a little congregation."[3] Rouse associated himself with the Jubilee Housing mission.

> We rehabilitate housing for poor families, and they have these two apartment houses they wanted to buy—ninety apartments. I bought the apartments and leased them to the Jubilee Housing Corporation. . . . They have gotten families to come in—white, suburban families, church groups—to come in and rehabilitate an apartment—clean the floors and paint the walls.

They did it at a cost of about $800 an apartment; the FHA had said it would cost $10,000 an apartment.[4] And in this way the mission group made these apartments habitable for working-class black families. Jim called what had been done "a Christian performance."

It took two years to do all the fixing, scrubbing, and painting, but Jubilee ended up with ninety affordable apartments. Jim had helped with the financing, and he and Patty had been placed on Jubilee's board. Since 1972 Jubilee had rehabilitated four more buildings and gone on to provide some of the social services a neighborhood like Adams-Morgan needed. All of which led the retired Jim Rouse to wonder, Why couldn't more of that be done? Why couldn't more of that be done on a large scale? Well, for one thing, it would take a constant infusion of cash. Where would the money come from? In any case, it was watching the successful work of Jubilee that led Rouse to think about getting involved in such work on a larger scale. He reports saying to his wife, "If these people can do this, there must be thousands of people in the U. S. who would do it, too, if they only had the process in which to work."[5]

Rouse was aware of an operation in England that was doing good works supported by self-generated cash. Near the Dart River in the southwestern corner of England was a 1,000-acre estate that dated back to the Middle Ages. In 1925 Dartington Hall was bought by a wealthy arts patron and social activist, Leonard Elmhirst, and his wife, the American heiress Dorothy Payne Whitney Straight. Dorothy Straight's son Michael would eventually become the editor of the American journal of opinion *The New Republic*. After several years of reconstruction and renovation, Leonard and Dorothy founded several businesses on the estate, and used the profits to fund a cultural center that became internationally known. After their deaths, the Dartington Hall Trust continued the work. The business ventures—a sawmill, a textile company, a glass company, a construction firm, gardens, and various farms—provided the revenue to support the cultural center and associated educational activities.[6]

Jim Rouse had found his purpose in retirement. He would establish a for-profit development corporation to help non-profit Jubilee-like organizations provide housing for the poor. He would do what he did well—develop retail projects—to generate the funding needed to start the process that would end with more decent housing. With more decent housing, the quality of life in cities would become a lot better. As Rouse said a few years later, "I had two objectives, and they fit very well. One was to do something about housing for the poor, and the other was to use the real estate development process to create a flow of money for a social purpose." He wanted to use his skills and knowledge "for the poor instead of the rich." Thus, Rouse became a social entrepreneur.

So in 1980, in his enthusiasm for linking profit and good works, he decided to call the dispensing arm the Robin Hood Trust. The enthusiasm carried to the point that Patty Rouse got a supply of little green Robin Hood caps that would be worn by supporters at the time the two-sided project was announced.[7] Patty Rouse had not seen Dartington. On a business trip a few years later, Rouse made a point of getting his English host to set up a trip to Devonshire so Patty could see Dartington for herself. He gave a full explanation to his host:

> It was my trip to Dartington Hall . . . that inspired The Enterprise Foundation, a charitable corporation, and its wholly owned subsidiary, The Enterprise Development Company, a for profit tax-paying commercial real estate

developer, the earnings from which will flow to the foundation and out to housing for the poor.[8]

Rouse was under no illusions about what he was getting into in trying to improve the quality of life in the black ghettoes of America. He knew that though housing was a large piece of the overall problem, housing was only one of several pieces. He frequently spoke about "the urban jungles at the heart of our cities . . . the pestholes of our society." In May 1985, he cited the figures for joblessness, 30-50% of black men without jobs. "Graduating from high school in the U. S. today for young black men gives about equal opportunity—hustle or work. Hustling to survive—alcohol, drugs, crime. One out of every two black children is now born and raised in poverty." In December in a speech at the Harvard Center for Business and Government, he said, "We have slipped into a kind of anesthesia in the United States." About housing for the very poor, "we see so much of it. . . . We just become anesthetized by the figures. . . . They don't penetrate anymore. They don't make us feel it. . . . We know but we don't feel the life of the poor." We think the problem is unsolvable, that "there's nothing we can do about it." And so with all the crime that is partially caused by lack of decent housing, "we are a nation living out of fear, and we kind of accept it. . . . We're said now to be the most violent country in the world. We are said to be that country in civilization that has by far the highest per capita of people in jail. What a judgment on us that this is our civilization. . . ." Rouse challenges American corporations to see what needs doing and to start doing.

> What would happen if Xerox or IBM took over the prison system in a state, took in these people with the responsibility to turn them out fit for life in the city. . . . One of the great losses is that you know business does wonderful things, in hospitals and symphonies and universities and private schools . . . but we don't have the structures in America today by which business people can enter leadership in the areas of deep human needs and that's what we have to create. . . . Business for the most part is insensitive to the problem because it doesn't know it and doesn't see any answers because they are not there. . . . We must change that state of mind, and as we do, we will ignite the business system into a cooperation with government to achieve a whole new world.[9]

Rouse was certain Enterprise Development would be profitable, would become a "money factory" for the foundation. The means would be festival marketplaces set in smaller cities; he would not go into larger cities because he wanted to avoid any possible competition with the Rouse Company. He was absolutely convinced that the successes of Faneuil Hall Marketplace and Harborplace could be duplicated in smaller cities. He told a Tokyo audience in 1986 that the marketplace "is the democratic, unifying, universal place which gives spirit and personality to the city and provides, at its best, the most appealing entertainment available. A city is hollow without a lively, effective retail core." He explained the success of his two large festival marketplaces by saying they are a response to the suburban explosion and its subdivision-type segregation, to its fractured living, and to the high-tech, computerized, televised, cellophane-wrapped, chain store society. . . ." [That society has] generated a yearning for the warm, the intimate, the personal relationships with small merchants . . . a yearning for the color, fragrance, texture, and variety of the true marketplace.[10]

In the meantime, money would be raised for the foundation by asking for it, from the usual group of rich people, rich foundations, and rich companies that supported good causes. A substantial contribution would get the giver named to the new organization's board of directors. One of those looked to for a contribution was John W. Gardner, nominally a Republican, who had served as Secretary of Health, Education, and Welfare for President Lyndon Johnson and was the founder of his own good-works organization—Common Cause. Gardner was a doer and an optimist like Rouse. Among the pronouncements for which he is known is the Rouse-like, "What we have before us are some breathtaking opportunities disguised as insoluble problems." But Gardner knew that in order to raise money from the rich, Rouse would have to tone down his enthusiasm—and give up the Robin Hood image; the rich might give voluntarily but would not like the idea of somebody "taking" their money. Rouse accepted Gardner's advice, and the Robin Hood Trust, in March 1981, was re-named The Enterprise Foundation.[11] Among others who agreed to be on the board were Gordon Cosby, pastor of the Church of the Saviour, who also served as vice president; another friend, Senator Charles McC. Mathias of Maryland; former Secretary of Defense and president of the World Bank Robert S. McNamara; and Andrew Heiskell, the former chairman of Time, Inc.

Rouse's plan was one of the first in America in what has come to be known as "social entrepreneurship." With the enthusiasm appropriate for a new type of venture in America, Rouse spelled out the plan for potential donors: "The combination of the work of the Development Company and the Foundation becomes a demonstration of the capacity of the free enterprise system to work directly to support important social action."[12] While the plan called for Enterprise Development to be the money-maker, it too would have beneficial social effects. In June 1985 Rouse predicted that Enterprise Development's projects would create 5,000 new jobs. Of that number, one-half would be filled by people who had been unemployed, and of those 80% would be minorities. He expected the projects to launch careers for fifty minority businessmen.[13] A few years later, with great pride Rouse was to tell a hearing of the House Ways and Means Committee that Enterprise Foundation

> is exposing new ways to harness the creativity and disciplines of the free enterprise system to encourage the initiative and effort of neighborhood groups. It is adapting self-help programs that work in its network of neighborhood groups and finding ways for corporation and other private-sector groups to participate in a responsible, meaningful way. Finally, it is seeking to establish a larger model of a city-wide public/private partnership that can eliminate all unfit housing in that city over a predetermined number of years.

Norfolk, Virginia, was to be the scene of the first development. Rouse had had some previous experience with Norfolk, a city with open space along its waterfront. He managed to work out a deal with city officials. The city would put $9 million into the first stages of the project. In return, after taxes and operating costs, the city would split the profits with Enterprise Development. City officials were to understand it would probably be five years before a profit was turned. The Norfolk project, named Waterside, was really little more than a one-pavilion Harborplace set in a park area close to a marina. It opened in June 1983 and was an immediate hit.[14]

Another small festival marketplace, Portside, was developed in Toledo, Ohio, along a bank of the Maumee River. Rouse believed that waterside settings were special: "Water is magic to people." In a Toledo speech, Rouse said his riverfront project there would have a very dramatic effect on "the spirit and life of the city and for the merchants who will make it a lively beautiful intensely human marketplace." Rouse saw this type of project being emulated across the country. "American cities," he said, "really are ready for a new life at their heart." He saw Portside appealing to "all people, young and old, rich and poor, black and white, singles and families. . . ."[15] With exuberance that had a good streak of the Pollyanish, Rouse predicted that Portside "can and will trigger an explosion of activity that supports other activities, and as each activity supports the other there begins a new cycle."

In Richmond, the capital city of Virginia, the 6th Street Marketplace was somewhat different, not being close to water. The marketplace here was but one piece of a larger redevelopment effort. He built a multi-level arcade and a bridge across Broad Street that connected not only the two competing downtown department stores but also the city's main downtown attractions. At the groundbreaking Rouse said, "We believe this to be the new urban form for the American City—the street transformed into an atrium—a marketplace of shops, kiosks, pushcarts, eating places and above all lots of people." The resolution of all the competing interests affected by the project has "set an example for the nation of how a city can be brought together for a brighter future." Rouse went on to do similar projects in the non-water Michigan cities of Flint and Battle Creek.

On November 19, 1984, Rouse spoke in Chattanooga, Tennessee. He was the final speaker in a series on quality-of-life issues. For Rouse, of course, that meant two themes: revitalizing downtown and housing for the poor. Located on the Tennessee River in the southeastern corner of the state, Chattanooga already had taken tentative steps toward revitalization. The activism of the alliance between the city's business and civic leaders, called Chattanooga Venture, reminded him of the work that had been done by the Greater Baltimore Committee. And the city had a riverfront. Chattanooga hadn't heard Rouse before. He fired up its leaders when he told them "Water is magic" and "the greatest resource you have is that waterfront." He advised putting as many of their attractions as possible on the waterfront and connecting it to the city's center. Without implying that he wanted the job, he pushed the festival marketplace as the key element in making the waterfront come alive. And he challenged the city's leaders on housing. What were they doing to see to it that *all* the city's people had decent housing? If helping the poor was really a part of Chattanooga Venture's agenda, why did they not set the goal of making all the housing in the city fit and livable within ten years? In essence he asked Chattanooga to fulfill the plan he had scripted for Washington thirty years earlier: No slums in 10 years.[16] Bob Corker, a young real estate developer, stepped forward. Rouse persuaded Corker to persuade Chattanooga Venture to enlist the Enterprise Foundation in making a study of Chattanooga's housing needs. Enterprise's report, called The Chattanooga 10 Year Plan, pointed out that the poor people of the city required 14,000 housing units, most of which could be provided by rehabilitating the existing stock. It reported that only one in five low-income households were receiving help for housing costs, and it provided a scale of realistic rents and mortgage payments. It recommended subsidies for rehabilitation, training in home maintenance and repair, and strict housing code enforcement.[17] In an accompanying letter to Bob Corker, Rouse said, "We believe the program presents a rational schedule for how Chattanooga will become the first city in America to take on the challenge of making all its housing fit and livable."[18] Enterprise provided the plan and the exhortations; Chattanooga had to do the rest.

Chattanooga's leaders were enthusiastic. To implement Enterprise's recommendations, the business community raised over $2 million for Chattanooga Neighborhood Enterprise, Inc. (CNE), which began operating in late 1986.[19] Chattanooga became a model of what a city with enlightened leadership could accomplish. Rouse took to referring to the work in Chattanooga as "our pinnacle of hope" and "a lighthouse to the nation." Chattanooga had set "a challenging but achievable goal . . . to make all housing occupied by very poor families livable and affordable within 10 years."[20] Such a decision will cause "the people of a city to truly face up to their task."[21]

Having the *will* to get the job done was the crucial factor. With the will, Rouse had no doubt that challenging goals were achievable.

> This is the wealthiest country in the world, with the greatest problem-solving capacity in the history of mankind. We have the capacity to provide decent housing for all our people. We need the will to do so. No other country in Western civilization has the disgraceful conditions that mark the neighborhoods and scar the people of American cities.[22]

CNE did not eliminate Chattanooga's slums in ten years, but it did become what amounted to a non-profit mortgage company and within ten years helped with 1,486 home purchases. Its record in that role was so good that it was allowed to approve FHA mortgages without review by the agency.[23] Rouse was especially pleased by what had been done in a mixed-income neighborhood called Orchard Village. It is, he wrote,

> a wonderful testimony to Chattanooga—and the rest of the nation—that housing for the poor doesn't have to look like 'poor housing' but can blend compatibly into the rest of the community. Not only does the design have incredible visual impact, but also the mortgage financing makes this attractive housing accessible to first-time homebuyers with very-low to moderate incomes.

Ten years after CNE's founding the city received a "Best Practices" award from the United Nations Conference on Human Settlements, not only for its housing but also for its clean air, electric buses, and open spaces.[24] In the sixteenth year after its founding, in 2002, with Bob Corker as mayor, CNE assisted in 119 home purchases, rehabilitated more than 200 rental units, and owned or managed 741 rental units. It had rehabilitated a larger percentage of inner-city housing than any other city in the country.[25] By the year 2000, Chattanooga had built an aquarium that became a major tourist attraction and had begun significant development of Tennessee Riverpark and its numerous recreational facilities. It had launched "The 21st Century Waterfront Plan" for further waterfront development, which will include a national park. Much of the impetus for all this change came from Jim Rouse's speech in 1984. Even though Chattanooga was not going to get its renovation done in the "predetermined number of years" Rouse thought necessary, he rejoiced at what was happening. When he said, however, that if Chattanooga could get it done "then every city in the country will follow their example," he was allowing his exuberance to carry him altogether too far.

Bob Corker, who was instrumental in the early stages of the city's improvement, in 2006 was elected to the U. S. Senate.

For its first three years Norfolk's Waterside development seemed to be doing well. But despite the throngs it drew during the summertime, Waterside could not realize the profits for Enterprise and the city that had been envisioned.[26] In Richmond, malfunctioning heating and air-conditioning systems caused a huge public relations problem. After a year's operation, the 6th Street Marketplace had a revenue shortfall of $1,750,000 and had to be refinanced. Toledo also was a big disappointment. In his zeal to have on-going sources of funding for the good works of the Foundation, Rouse had plunged ahead in Flint and Battle Creek without the kind of market research he had relied upon early in his career as a retail developer. Those cities, it seems, had been chosen as marketplace locations mainly because they were the home bases of the Charles Stewart Mott Foundation and the Kellogg Foundation, foundations that might be generous to the Enterprise Foundation. The story of Flint, a city tied to the ups and downs of the auto industry and General Motors in particular, was especially interesting. The biggest investor was William S. White, who was the head of the

Mott Foundation, which had given a million dollars to the Enterprise Foundation. Rouse was determined that the Flint marketplace, called The Water Street Pavilion, succeed. With its performance below the level anticipated, Rouse, in October 1987, wrote a reassuring letter to White. He pointed out that Water Street means much more to Enterprise "than just a business deal." Water Street is "an important part of our business history, our spirit, and our purpose." Rouse tells White that when, in 1983, his colleagues doubted the wisdom of going into Flint, he wrote a memo arguing for the importance of doing it. Flint, he said then,

> is a troubled city with a badly deteriorated downtown, a tough economic situation and high unemployment. . . . Its need happens to be on our threshold and we have the capacity to do something about it. Every business has some responsibility toward needs that rationally come before them. Most businesses ignore those needs unless they fit most comfortably into their economic purpose.
>
> We are a little different, because we are individuals who care about cities and because we are organized in a venture which is specially infused with that concern as a fundamental purpose. . . . If it is possible for us to fit Flint's needs into our financial disciplines then shouldn't we be stimulated by the opportunity to bring new life to a troubled city?[27]

Rouse had come to truly believe that the mere presence of a downtown festival marketplace enhanced a city's quality of life. People enjoyed coming to festival marketplaces just to stroll and hang out. The marketplace was a place of recreation. That was the secret of the successes in Boston and Baltimore. But it took time for the people of a region to realize that they could have a good time by going downtown. Pedestrian traffic at the smaller marketplaces was bound to increase. The merchants who could hold on would eventually be rewarded. People would come—and they would buy. Rouse truly believed.

Despite the disappointing results at home, Enterprise Development was asked to help with festival marketplaces overseas. Rouse went to Australia in 1984 and came home with a deal with Thomas Hayson for Enterprise Development to be a consultant and partner in a Harborplace-like project, Harbourside, at Darling Harbour, along the waterfront in Sydney. Also in 1984, Rouse received an inquiry from William J. McNally, executive director of The Ireland Fund, about the possibility of doing a festival marketplace in Belfast, Northern Ireland. Despite the contribution to peace and reconciliation such a project might offer, Rouse did not want to be the developer. He thought that at this early point in EDC's life getting involved with Belfast would be a further diversion from EDC's main purpose. He was willing, though, to have EDC get involved in a consulting capacity. His response to McNally offers insight into what Rouse thought EDC could do without actually getting involved in building a marketplace. EDC would help "to designate the location, conceptualize and detail the overall plan, the elements of the marketplace, its design, the merchandizing of the space, the allocation of uses, the leasing program, the promotion and management processes."

Rouse also lets McNally know what Enterprise Development would want as payment for its consulting services.

> We would be reimbursed for all out-of-pocket expenses (travel, etc.) and for the time of our people on the project. Our standard allocation of the people cost to a project is at a rate of 3 times the daily rate of compensation in order to cover benefits and home office overhead. This would work out to an average people cost of roughly $1,500 per man-day. . . . We would require a fee to compensate for the time away from our projects, for lost opportunity, and for justifying this deviation from the work which really demands our attention. Following our examination of this role we have set this fee at $500,000 in addition to cost.[28]

Nothing came of the exchange with McNally.

Rouse and the Australian Thomas Hayson got along famously. Hayson loved the festival marketplace concept. He envisioned successful marketplaces in a series of cities in Australia and Great Britain. In 1987, he proposed a deal Rouse couldn't resist. With his English partners, Hayson would invest $11,650,000 in Enterprise Development stock, with EDC selling an additional $5 million in stock to American investors. The English and Australian investors, called Merlin International Properties, Ltd., would own 25% of EDC and other investors would own a total of 17.5% but the Enterprise Foundation would continue to own a majority interest. The great benefit would be that EDC would be the consulting developer in the new festival marketplace projects, for which it would receive an annual retainer of $500,000. This would enable Rouse to make earlier, larger, and more consistent cash payments to the Enterprise Foundation than could otherwise be made.[29]

In America, centers of cities were dead or dying. In the smaller cities into which Enterprise Development had ventured, the festival marketplace slowed down the process only a bit. At first, as poor performance drove home harsh facts, Rouse thought that more had to be added to the marketplaces. Entertainment was needed, "the next rational leap in central city marketplaces." He told his staff they had to think of " 'pay-at-the-gate' entertainment (Disney, 6 Flags, movies, theatre, concerts, etc.) as enhancement of the marketplace and feeder off its traffic." There were "unsatisfied needs and yearnings of the community" that they had to get a better grasp of. "What might we do NOW at Norfolk, Toledo, and soon at Flint, Battle Creek, Richmond, as well as what might we do in Dallas, Pittsburgh, etc."[30] But midway through 1988, of the original developments only Norfolk's Waterside and Battle Creek's McCamly Place still remained under EDC management. Despite Rouse's continuing optimistic forecasts, EDC had "disengaged" from the projects in Richmond, Toledo, and Flint. A dozen years later, EDC president Aubrey Gorman summed up the losing struggles he had been in the midst of: "They were tough. I mean, nothing would work. There were constant negotiations. We were constantly trying to settle people down, constantly trying to get money. We didn't have any money."[31] Rouse, commander of EDC as chairman of the board, explained the failures this way: "What went wrong is that the metropolitan areas weren't large enough; therefore the markets weren't big enough and the attractions of the center city were not sufficient."[32] Perhaps if he hadn't been so carried away by the sense of the small festival marketplace as a veritable magnet, drawing people from their other activities, perhaps if he had been capable of more realism at this point, he might not have been so badly hurt.

Rouse still maintained his belief in the festival marketplace, but he now realized it could not save most cities as a stand-alone attraction. In September 1988, he was asked to take a look at the dying heart of Newark, New Jersey. A new performing arts center was in the works for downtown. Would it bring vitality back to Newark? By itself, Rouse concluded, a performing arts center wouldn't work. He wrote to Charles L. Hirsch of New Jersey's Wesray Capital Corporation.

> Center cities that are serious about revitalization must use every possible resource in the most effective way. . . . Performing arts centers need hotels, restaurants, transportation as close as possible. Hotels and restaurants want entertainment and educational facilities close by, as well as offices and transportation. Retail shops depend upon the pedestrian traffic generated by the offices, hotels, restaurants, and entertainment/education centers. . . . Planned and developed to produce a convenient, lively, new downtown, they will do that.[33]

All the while he was fighting to make a success of Enterprise Development, Jim Rouse was also hard at work as Enterprise Foundation's number-one fundraiser. In addition to everything else he had to attend to, he was busy writing letters and making visits to all the rich people and foundation executives he thought might make an offering to the Foundation. He wrote and made visits to the likes of John F. Akers, Mrs. Brooke Astor, Robert M. Bass, Warren Buffett, Katharine Graham, Austin Guirlinger, John W. Hechinger, Carl Ichan, Ed Lowe, H. Ross Perot, Milton Petrie, Abe Pollin, Richard Ravitch, David Rockefeller, Andrew C. Sigler, and Louis Wolfson, among others. If he got a negative response, a year later he would lay out the Foundation's accomplishments and ask again. Buffett said about having Rouse visit: "It's always refreshing to talk to Rouse. It's like drinking a chocolate soda."

He devoted himself to the work very conscious his remaining work life was getting shorter and shorter. Every day he would turn down interview requests, invitations to speak, invitations to award dinners, requests to be presented with honorary degrees. He had no time to indulge his ego. He pushed on, determined to make Enterprise Development a more productive "money factory." He pushed on, determined that Enterprise Foundation be a more productive provider of homes for the poor.

Rouse's post-retirement work with Enterprise had a profound impact. Ten years after Rouse's death, American graduate students are studying Social Entrepreneurship, wanting to have an impact on society, wanting to make a difference. More than 30 graduate schools of business have developed courses in social entrepreneurship.[34] Duke University began the first such program in the mid-1990s with the creation of its Center for the Advancement of Social Entrepreneurship. The Harvard Business School was soon to follow. In 2005, Jane Wei-Skillern, a professor at HBS, said about the school's students:

> This generation of students expects more out of their careers, beyond the initial business success and financial gain that people generally assume business students are interested in. . . . They envision community engagement as a core part of what they do."[35]

Chapter 18 The Social Entrepreneur

1. JWR speech, May 23, 1979.
2. Olsen, 288.
3. La Noue interview.
4. La Noue interview.
5. JWR letter to Robert Longley, December 12, 1988.
6. www.dartington.u-net.com. Accessed May 2004.
7. Olsen, 298.
8. JWR letter to Maurice Ashe, April 23, 1985.
9. JWR speech to New York City's Planning and Housing Council, May 1, 1985.
10. JWR speech in Tokyo, "How to Revitalize a Society," September 10, 1986.
11. Olsen, 299.
12. Quoted by Olsen, 303.
13. JWR speech, May 1, 1985.
14. Olsen, 307.
15. Olsen, 317.
16. Quoted in *Chattanooga Venture News,* "Riverfront is city's best asset," January 1985, 2.
17. Olsen, 342.
18. JWR letter to Robert J. Corker, July 21, 1986.
19. JWR letter to Raul Yzaquirre, October, 15, 1986.
20. JWR letter to Mary Tyler Cheek, November 6, 1986.
21. JWR's sermon at New York's Unitarian Church, October 5, 1986.
22. JWR letter to Mary Tyler Cheek, November 6, 1986.
23. www.enterprisefoundation.org/model0/020documents/e532.htm. Accessed May 2004.
24. www.chattanoogafun.com. Accessed May 2004.
25. Ellen Lazar speech at Conference on Neighborhood Concerns, May 22, 2003.
26. Olsen, 318-19.
27. JWR letter to William S. White, October 14, 1987.
28. JWR letter to William J. McNally, December 14, 1984.
29. JWR memo to top Enterprise officers, June 23, 1987.
30. JWR memo to top Enterprise officers, June 17, 1985.
31. Quoted in Olsen, 328.
32. JWR to Enterprise Board of Trustees, September 15, 1988.
33. JWR letter to Charles L. Hirsch, August 9, 1988.
34. Alan Finder, "A Subject for Those Who Want to Make a Difference," *New York Times,* August 17, 2005, B9.
35. Finder, B9.

Chapter 19
Back to Baltimore

In Chattanooga the goal was decent housing for all. Then the goal was expanded. Rouse realized that decent, affordable housing wasn't enough. If the misery in the nation's black ghettoes was to be eliminated, a lot more had to be done. More was needed than food and shelter. More and better social services had to be available. A comprehensive plan was needed; housing was major but was only one part. Rouse remembered the contrast in Baltimore between spiffy Harborplace and down-and-out Sandtown two miles away. He remembered the comprehensive planning that had gone into Columbia, and, he asked himself, Why not do it for Sandtown? But to put a comprehensive plan to work in Sandtown, Baltimore's mayor would have to take the initiative. Rouse and Enterprise would have to work with city government, and that would not be easy.

Rouse had managed the placing of a total of 171 modular homes on lots donated by the city in four low-income neighborhoods, working with Jim Ryan's Ryland Modular Homes.[1] This was good, but it was piecemeal and limited. In the spring of 1986, with the help of Marion W. Pines, Baltimore's Commissioner of the Neighborhood Progress Administration, Rouse tried to drum up support for a larger project. The result was an "absolute impasse." William Donald Schaefer, the mayor, did not want to go forward unless the project was in a white neighborhood. Rouse did not want to go forward if the housing was to be restricted to one race. Rouse let the project drop, acknowledging "that bringing blacks into that neighborhood would cause real trouble."[2]

Prospects for a comprehensive project in Baltimore changed on December 8, 1987, when Kurt Schmoke became mayor. Schmoke was a graduate of Yale, for which he was a football star, a graduate of Harvard Law, and a Rhodes Scholar. He was Baltimore's first elected African-American mayor. During his campaign he had promised a community organization called BUILD to do something about the Sandtown-Winchester neighborhood. BUILD—Baltimoreans United in Leadership Development—was a faith-based organization of forty-five churches, and it wanted big changes in Sandtown.[3] That was exactly the kind of project Rouse wanted for Enterprise.

But a year after Schmoke's inauguration there had not been much of a response to prodding by Rouse. The new mayor was taking his time and being distant. Rouse was not happy. He was approaching seventy-five and could drop dead at any time. His brother Bill died suddenly at sixty-one. His father had died at sixty-three. Schmoke was sorely trying his patience. After a year of Schmoke, he told his people at Enterprise, "The next step is to find out whether or not the city of Baltimore will be a serious partner or whether we should go to another city."[4] And three months later, on March 10, 1989, he wrote,

> As we left it with the Mayor, the next step on Sandtown is his. It would seem that we should be spending no time or money on Sandtown until we know what he wants to do. We should not assume any part of a 'comprehensive neighborhood program' until we hear."[5]

Rouse's goal now was to transform a whole neighborhood. In a short while his exuberance would lead him to expand that goal to three neighborhoods in three cities.

> We will raise up models for people to look at, so they can see this is what the neighborhood was and this is what it is and this is what it cost. And it's a reasonable hunch that it would cost less to correct the conditions in such a neighborhood than to pay to sustain them. . . . It's not just to do a neighborhood. It's to be a model of what the city can be.[6]

But Mayor Schmoke was on another page.

In the meantime, Rouse began a campaign to raise money from wealthy people and institutions in the Greater Baltimore area. He wrote, for example to Harvey M. "Bud" Meyerhoff, son of Joseph and nephew of Jack Meyerhoff, now a realtor-capitalist himself. Bud had become a trustee of Johns Hopkins University and Johns Hopkins Hospital; he had lots of money. Rouse explained at length what the Enterprise Foundation did and then hit home: "Is it reasonable to ask that you commit $100,000 a year for five years. That would give a great lift to our work."[7] In this way, he appealed to all the really wealthy people he could think of. He also tried to pry large chunks of money out of the country's major foundations. Thornton Bradshaw had recently been elevated to the chairmanship of the MacArthur Foundation. Enterprise already had received grants from MacArthur of $500,000 and $1,500,000. Rouse was not shy about asking for more: "We come to you now . . . because we believe that our recent progress has brought us to a new threshold of possibilities for changing the systems by which the very poor are housed, for altering national policy on housing in America...."[8]

On April 24, 1989, Rouse celebrated his seventy-fifth birthday. He was honored at the Capitol in Washington, and his family staged a weekend bash on the Eastern Shore. This birthday reminded him again that his time was getting short. He launched into a frenzy of fundraising efforts, and made plans for an official campaign start with a gala at Washington's Union Station. The fundraising was to be a five-year program to raise $50 million. By January he was able to count on advance contributions of over $10 million. He and Patty kicked in $1 million, and he succeeded in getting the Rouse Company to contribute a million.[9] At first there was a plan to turn the fundraising over to the Ketchum Company, specialists in fundraising. But Rouse disagreed with their tactics, and wanted all the fundraising kept in-house: "It would be a burden for us to have a Ketchum agency guiding us with continuing conflict between our purpose and capacity, our strengths, and their image of an institution which we are not."[10] So even though a new person was hired at Enterprise with the title Director of Resource Development, Rouse himself kept going at the fundraising. He wrote to and visited the likes of William Coors, Pamela Harriman, Stanley Marcus, Albert Ratner, and Sanford I. Weill.

He was on a mission. He was responding to a "call." Rouse seldom referred to his religion or faith. But he did so in a letter to Sue Bender, who had given him a copy of her book about the Amish, *Plain and Simple*. In the book, Bender tells about the impact on herself of having spent time living among the Amish. Rouse tells Bender that she was "drawn by the call that the Amish lived out values missing in your own life." He believes that responding to

> that call so directly and faithfully says something very important about who and what you are. . . . That you felt it . . . is your inner secret, your special vested power. . . . Just live with your secret vested power—in peace. It is of faith itself. If there is more for you to do, it will speak to you.

If God has more to say to you, "know that you have the receptivity to hear it."[11] Rouse, of course, is speaking about himself. He has heard the call to use his special knowledge and abilities to try to alleviate the plight of blacks living in America's cities. That is what is driving him.

In thinking about the Amish, Rouse was reminded of the people who make up the Church of the Saviour. "They live, in values, not unlike the Amish," he went on to say to Bender. It was they who taught him the best way to respond to the needs of others. One should stand in "reticent willingness" to help. "Don't reach in offering, perhaps unwanted," help. Don't dish out unsolicited advice. Stand with all antennae tuned—ready to respond to the need as the other communicates it—and then to serve, to help." And that was the way to respond to the needs of poor city blacks.

In June 1987, his old friend Alan Cranston, who'd been head of the United World Federalists and was now the senior U. S. Senator from California, asked Jim Rouse to serve as chairman of a national task force on housing. Cranston was a member of the Senate's Banking Committee and chairman of its subcommittee on housing. The task force would be an unofficial private body financed by a grant from the Mott Foundation. The charge to the task force was "to identify what is working in our housing system, what is not, how to correct flaws, what resources are available, how to use them effectively, what new government and private programs are needed to make decent affordable housing available to all our people."[12]

Cranston wanted the task force to meet twice a week in Washington between September and December. For Rouse that meant three days a week, because as chairman he would have to devote one day to preparing for meetings. He had been turning down all kinds of invitations that would distract him if only for a few hours from his Enterprise work. But if legislation could come out of the task force's work, it could have a great impact for the cause. Also, his being away three days a week would allow for the beginning of the transition to the time when he would be away *all* the time.

He had been grooming F. Barton Harvey III to be his successor as head of Enterprise. When Bart Harvey accompanied him to speaking engagements, Rouse usually pointed him out. He liked to tell an audience that Harvey had been making big money working on Wall Street for Dean Witter when he realized there had to be better satisfactions in life than making money. Harvey took a leave from Dean Witter and first came to Enterprise as a full-time volunteer. Then, in 1985, taking an 80% cut in compensation, he was put on Enterprise's payroll. Soon he was named deputy chairman of the Foundation. But early in 1986, Harvey got Rouse ticked off to the point that the boss wrote him a zinger of a memo. Rouse was a workaholic who would never get caught up with all he wanted to do. Sometimes he would make an attempt at it by staying away from the office. He wanted no intrusions on that time.

He called the days he stayed away "briefcase days." He didn't like it when someone thought a briefcase day was a day of relaxation. And so he felt compelled to write a memo telling Bart Harvey about it in no uncertain terms.

> Briefcase day is not a soft spot in my schedule—it is essential. It is like an important appointment. As you know, I have no time to read letters and memos that come to me, no time to respond, no time to work out schedule complications. No time to think except at night. Thus, I use every night to keep up. But trips out of town, meetings or dinners at night, or other interventions often block out these nights. Even then I try to cover the briefcase material when I get back to Waterfowl [his house on Waterfowl Terrace] no matter how late. This means I do the simplest, quickest things, setting aside anything that is more than one page or requires any amount of thought, time or writing. This piles up when this is followed by a second night. After a third, it piles higher. My only way of dealing with this is "briefcase days." They are always under assault. . . . Sorry it must be this way, but that is how it is.[13]

The National Housing Task Force did not complete its work until March 1988. Senator Cranston was pleased with the report sent to him by Jim Rouse. He had material now that could be discussed in the 1988 presidential campaign. The principal recommendation was for the creation of the Housing Opportunity Program—HOP. Based on his experience with Enterprise Foundation and the success of Chattanooga's Neighborhood Enterprise, Rouse now believed that decisions about housing for the poor should be made at the neighborhood level. He hoped for legislation that would allow federal funds to be channeled directly into the neighborhoods. The funds then would be allocated to different entities within a comprehensive plan. If liberal Democrat Michael Dukakis beat George H. W. Bush in the 1988 election, getting the legislation passed would be a lot easier.

Bush won the election. He named the former NFL quarterback and Buffalo-area congressman Jack Kemp as Secretary of Housing and Urban Development. Even before the Inauguration Rouse began to cultivate Kemp. He invited Kemp to the January meeting of the Enterprise Foundation board. Afterward, he wrote Kemp: "It was an exciting meeting and filled us with new hope and confidence for what you will bring to HUD." And he concluded his letter by saying, "We have had three meetings. It is increasingly clear to me that you are the right man at the right time in the right place. You have one of the great opportunities in America today. The Lord has put you there. What a wonderful responsibility."[14]

In March Rouse had Kemp visit Jubilee Housing with him. He was proud to point out what "strong, creative, dedicated people" had done in providing places to live, jobs, and health care. In June a rumor was afoot that Kemp was considering a position with the National Football League. Rouse wrote to persuade him to stay on at HUD. "You have lifted the spirits of many people. . . . No one in my lifetime has lit such hope. To dash it now by pulling out would shroud the housing struggle with disillusionment and despair." Kemp stayed on. He gave the principal address at the fundraiser for Enterprise at Union Station on September 20th. Encouraged to do so by Rouse, Kemp also gave an address to the leaders of the project in Chattanooga. "The stage is set," Rouse had written to him, "for a ringing Jack Kemp exhortation mixed with applause for their triumphant beginning and challenge for them to move faster, better; to set the stage for programs throughout America."[15]

The recommendations of the Housing Task Force were before Congress, and the Bush administration was supportive. Rouse testified before the Senate committee and sought bipartisan support. "The issue of decent, affordable housing is neither Democrat nor Republican but rather a test of the Congress to respond to a critical national need." On November 28, 1990, President Bush signed the National Affordable Housing Act, sponsored by Cranston and Texas Congressman Henry Gonzalez.

Just as with the Housing Act of 1954, during the Eisenhower Administration, Rouse can be heard in the language and philosophy of this legislation. Among the stated purposes of the act are "to expand the supply of decent, safe, sanitary, and affordable housing . . . for very low-income and low-income Americans" and to provide federal assistance to make feasible "new construction, rehabilitation, substantial rehabilitation, and acquisition." The act will "promote the development of partnerships among the Federal Government, States and units of general local government, private industry, and nonprofit organizations." For each participating jurisdiction, the act will provide a HOME Investment Trust Fund with a line of credit for investment in affordable housing, with repayments to be made available for reinvestment. Finally, the act will "assist very low-income and low-income families to obtain the skills and knowledge necessary to become responsible homeowners and tenants." From leadership of the task force to the signing into law, Jim Rouse could take enormous satisfaction in what his investment of scarce time had produced.

Rouse met five more times with Mayor Schmoke. Finally, at the end of October 1989 he came out of a meeting that was different: "A really astonishing meeting with Kurt Schmoke." He explained to Paul Brophy: Schmoke "has been reserved, cautious, interested but very uncommitted." This time Rouse let him speak first, and now Schmoke was ready. "He came out firing." No more reserve and caution. He said about Sandtown: "I am absolutely committed to this. . . . This will be the most important project in Baltimore."[16] On the National Housing Task Force, Rouse had worked with Paul C. Brophy, who was executive director of the Pittsburgh Urban Redevelopment Agency. When the work of the Task Force was done, he hired Brophy to be the Foundation's president while he continued as chairman of the board. The Rouse memo to Brophy about Schmoke went on to say: "There is little doubt in my mind about his spirit, his enthusiasm for this project. He seemed to smile with excitement as he talked about it"

Sandtown-Winchester was a very big challenge. It would be hard to find a neighborhood in an American city in worse shape. Abandoned houses pockmarked every street. Of the houses that were lived in, 80% were in need of serious help. Average household income was $6,900. Forty-four percent of the men were unemployed. Sandtown was at bottom or near bottom on all the statistical indicators. The spirit of the people was way down. Working with the worst, Rouse could demonstrate how much could be done.

> We need to hold up a vision of the doable. We should push every city toward undertaking a Chattanooga-scale effort—to feel, at least, that that is where it is headed. . . . We must not settle for a little effort. . . . We are engaged in a national campaign to transform the lives of the poor in America.[17]

Enterprise, BUILD, and the city joined forces. The mayor went after federal funding for housing through what came to be called the Nehemiah program. The reference is to the Old Testament prophet, who spoke about his return to the destroyed city of Jerusalem: "Ye see the distress that we are in, how Jerusalem lieth waste. . . . Come and let us build the wall of Jerusalem that we be no more a reproach. . . . Let us rise up and build." A task force was formed consisting of two people from Enterprise, two from the mayor's office, three residents of Sandtown, and a few from relevant city departments. Nine work groups were formed, each chaired by a resident, to consider different aspects of community life, such as schools, job readiness, health care, security, community governance. This was part of the "visioning process." Rouse wanted people to think about "what the neighborhood would be like if it worked in the best possible way." Neighborhood meetings on two successive nights drew 600 residents.

Enterprise is a community development intermediary. Its work is to arrange financing, bring in experts, and facilitate action. It provides the wherewithal to community nonprofit organizations. It helps new nonprofits get started. Enterprise's workers do not pick up shovels; they don't work with bricks and mortar. Enterprise makes it possible for contractors to be hired and to set their people to work. Once there was consensus about what the community wanted to be like, Rouse brought in seven specialists: in housing, human services, health, health care planning, economic development, and budgets. Despite having a project manager based at Sandtown, Rouse himself was making the big decisions and keeping the process moving. Just about every decision was important, because Sandtown would be the model for the two other model neighborhoods and the three together would be models for neighborhood transformation across the country.[18] Within two years, Enterprise had poured $6 million into Sandtown.

But without the right leadership, Rouse feared, there might not be much permanent return. Mayor Schmoke's enthusiasm, he decided, could not be counted on. Rouse would have liked to see more boldness. From his perspective there was too much at stake to rely upon the mayor. In July 1990, Rouse wrote to a long-time confidant: "He must bring all his departments, all his leadership on board for a major effort. An incremental strategy is doomed . . . before it ever gets underway." And Rouse feared that progress would be incremental if the mayor were relied on. The stakes were too high for that. "I believe that there are many people at the bottom who are frightened, frustrated, fed up, ready to join a revolution for change—to follow a vision of a decent life—many more people than there were a few years ago."[19]

A year later Rouse still did not see the persistent, aggressive leadership he hoped for. While in theory the mayor and the city were in charge, in reality all the initiatives were coming from Rouse and Enterprise. Rouse, in a long memo to Paul Brophy, explained why he disagreed with Brophy's idea that there should be a sharper division of responsibilities between the city and Enterprise. The responsibilities on the city's side would not be carried out in a timely way. "It is we who must maintain the creative initiative in the planning and doing." It is Enterprise that "must remain in effective control of the doing for the program to succeed." If the city's role was more sharply defined, Enterprise could lose the capacity to lead, and "the transformation will sink into disappointment and failure."[20]

Sandtown was a community made up for the most part of people with very limited language skills and many personal grievances. Of most importance to many residents were such issues as garbage collection and litter, the open-air drug dealing, the dangers to children. The big picture was of limited interest. Communication was difficult, and there were sharp limits to people's determination and ability to stay focused.[21] "The transformation will not be easy," Rouse wrote to Paul Brophy. "It will require strong leadership, persuasion, marshalling of support, winning confidence of the neighborhood, political, business, labor, church, and civic leadership." And again the matter of leadership: "The leadership must be strong, caring, sensitive to the people and government and aggressive in pursuit of sound, legitimate, but, in many cases, unproven goals."[22]

The job was getting done. Enterprise, BUILD, and the city, working together, called the Sandtown project Community Building in Partnership. On the grounds of an abandoned bakery more than 200 new homes went up. They were prefabricated brick rowhouses; each cost $87,000 to build. They were sold for $37,000. The two-story, three-bedroom houses were bought for as little as a $256 monthly payment; people with incomes as low as $11,000 a year were eligible to buy. More new homes were built and old ones rehabbed. Social services were being provided. People were participating and trust was being built. Progress was taking place in the schools, in skill training, in finding work, in health care, drug and alcohol prevention, in deterring adolescent pregnancy, in preventing crime and providing security.[23]

On April 29, 1992, rioting broke out in Los Angeles. The verdict had been given in the trial of the four police officers who beat up Rodney King. While one of the officers was found guilty of using excessive force, the other three were acquitted. The black community was furious and many took to the streets. Burning, looting and random killing, mostly in Watts but also in other sections, went largely unchecked for three days. It was a replay of the Watts riot of 1965, the worst riot in American history. With more "Burn, baby, burn!" this was much worse. Schools and businesses closed; a curfew was imposed. National Guard troops patrolled the streets. When the rioting was over, there had been fifty-two deaths and 2,500 injuries. Property damage to 1,100 buildings and 2,300 stores came close to $1 billion. In the wake of the murder of Martin Luther King on April 4, 1968, rioting had broken out in Washington and Baltimore as well as many other cities. While only six deaths were reported in Baltimore, there were thousands of fires and over four days 5,000 people were arrested. Those riots close to home twenty-four years earlier had not receded in Rouse's consciousness.

On May 24, 1992, Rouse was to give the commencement address at the University of California at Berkeley. But on that day he was recovering from quintuple bypass surgery. Nevertheless, he had been able to put together the speech. He sent his son Jimmy Rouse out to Berkeley to deliver it in his stead. The speech was particularly important to Rouse, because twenty-nine years earlier he had given a Berkeley speech in which he spoke about his plans to build a new city. Now he would talk about the glorious outcome of those plans, and go on to show the logical progression of his work from brand-new Columbia to down-and-out Sandtown. In the wake of the L.A. riot, Rouse feared similar outbreaks in places like Sandtown.

Rouse did not accept the notion that the cause of the riot was the unjust verdict. The cause, he said, "was deeper than that—much deeper—more serious." He said he agreed with Martin Luther King that "riot at bottom is the language of the unheard." "Too many have been unheard—unheard because they eke out survival in the 'other' America—the forgotten America of the poor." He gave the familiar statistics: about the highest child poverty rate of any industrialized nation; about homeless families "living like stray animals"; drug-addicted babies; the high incarceration rates. He said millions of Americans were alienated, "living helpless, hopeless lives—feeling no stake in our country—tinder for a radical torch." He shocks himself with his account of the misery: "This is America! Can you believe it?" But most Americans "have not looked into the saddened sullen faces; felt the hopelessness, the distrust, suspicion, and separation" that pervades the lives of the poor."

He is convinced that the conditions he has described "are the breeding grounds for a new America that we don't want to face—an impoverished, suffering, hostile people living in violence and in fear. It threatens our stability—threatens our survival as a civilized nation. . . . This is what Los Angeles is screaming to our country." And this is what he feared could happen in Baltimore. In Rouse's mind, it would only take one incident of police brutality or one unfair verdict for Baltimore to go up in flames.

Americans must wake up. The "massive indifference" of people in the middle and at the top must end. "We must shake ourselves and our collective systems by the collar. We must make life work for people at the bottom as it works for people in the middle and at the top." And then Rouse gets to Sandtown, "a representative neighborhood of persistent decline, loss of hope, fear, and violence." That neighborhood will be transformed. All the needed social services will be provided. And block by block,

> all the housing is to be made decent, attractive, livable, and available at rents and prices the residents can afford. The physical amenities that speak to the neighborhood's quality of life—sidewalks in good repair, trees, gardens, playgrounds, community meeting places

—all will be there. What is being done will help "the community build its sense of belonging, caring, self-respect, pride, and hope." And that must be done in a hundred neighborhoods across the country.[24]

The surgery had slowed him down. But it wasn't long before he was back on the streets of Sandtown. On December 2, 1993, the ABC TV program "Prime Time" featured Rouse and Sandtown. The residents seemed to worship Rouse, the elderly white man who, with his attractive wife, wandered the streets in shirt and tie and beat-up bucket hat. "He's been Godsent," one resident said. "He's 77 and a millionaire. He could be taking it easy on a boat somewhere. Instead, he's here." In answer to a question by the interviewer, Rouse said, "I feel the hand of the Lord on my shoulder all the time. . . . It's just not rational that there should be such poverty in America." He was in a hurry, he said. He wanted to see what was going on in Sandtown repeated across America. And he was enjoying himself. "My wife, Patty, and I laugh about how we are as comfortable with the people of Sandtown . . . and have as much fun at any event in that community as we do at a cocktail party with friends in Columbia."[25]

In September 1994, Jim Rouse, eighty years old and in declining health, wrote a letter to his friend William Donald Schaefer, mayor of Baltimore 1971-86 and, at the time, governor of Maryland. He spoke about the work being done in Sandtown-Winchester. Rouse told Schaefer that Sandtown "is the most important work I have ever undertaken in my lifetime. Patty and I give it all of our available time and energy—days, nights, and weekends."[26]

Nicholas Dagen Bloom does not think much of what Rouse did in Sandtown will last.

> Against great odds, Enterprise and its partners are trying to create an island of private sector social democracy in an impoverished city, without similar governmental and private resources for surrounding areas. As laudable as their efforts are, it is difficult to imagine how a neighborhood demonstration project can become a successful piece of utopia with transient and impoverished populations, lack of access to good jobs, and surrounding neighborhoods lacking equivalent social investment.[27]

To which it can only be said that if Jim Rouse had not created this project, nothing would have been gained and those whose lives have improved would never have got out of the muck.

The numbers were proof that the project was worth doing. In the ten years since Mayor Schmoke made his commitment in October 1989, average household income was up by over 40%. Property values were up by 500%. The unemployment rate was down from 22% to 14%. Crime was down about 20%.[28] Anyone taking a tour of Sandtown can *see* the results. House after house and street after street look good. You would think one particular street with a cul-de-sac was out in suburbia. One big negative, though, is that many abandoned houses remain. With windows and doors sealed to prevent addicts and vandals from getting in, they do pockmark a street. They mark that street as being different from the kind of city street where white people live.

Chapter 19 Back to Baltimore

1. "Enterprise Housing Venture," an undated Enterprise fact sheet about Franklin Terrace community.
2. JWR Enterprise letter to Marion W. Pines, April 22, 1986.
3. Kurt Schmoke, "What's God got to do with it?" (Washington: Brookings Institution Press, 2000), 67-68.
4. JWR letter to Leo Molinaro, December 27, 1988.
5. JWR memo to Paul C. Brophy, March 10, 1989.
6. Quoted by Edward Gunts, "Home Sweet First Home," *The Sun,* July 21, 1991, 9.
7. JWR letter to Harvey M. Meyerhoff, March 8, 1988.
8. JWR letter to Thornton Bradshaw, November 2, 1987.
9. JWR letter to Arnold S. McKinnon, December 22, 1989.
10. JWR letter to Raymond S. Chambers, August 14, 1989.
11. JWR letter to Sue Bender, June 18, 1990.
12. Letter from Alan Cranston to JWR, June 1987.
13. JWR memo to F. Barton Harvey III, February 10, 1986.
14. JWR letter to Jack Kemp, June 5, 1989.
15. JWR letter to Jack Kemp, January 7, 1991.
16. JWR memo to Paul C. Brophy, November 1, 1989.
17. JWR memo to top Enterprise staff, November 27, 1989.
18. Gunts, 9.
19. JWR letter to Siobhan Oppenheimer-Nicolau, July 9, 1990.
20. JWR memo to Paul C. Brophy, December 9, 1991.
21. Pat Costigan memo to JWR, May 24, 1990.
22. JWR memo to Paul C. Brophy, December 9, 1991.
23. Barry Yeoman, "Left Behind in Sandtown," *City Limits Monthly,* January 1998.
24. JWR speech, May 24, 1992.
25. Autob, 4.
26. Quoted by Olsen, 358-59.
27. Bloom, 105.
28. Susan Fingerman, "Sandtown-Winchester: Then and Now," November 1991 report for Enterprise Foundation.

Chapter 20
Last Years

On April 26, 1991, Jim Rouse turned seventy-seven. The previous October he had devised a plan for the transition at the Enterprise Foundation. He thought very highly of Bart Harvey, who was serving as deputy chairman, but he also thought very highly of Paul C. Brophy, who in 1988 was named president. He wanted both of them to be his successor, but *he* still wanted to remain engaged, as chairman of the board. The board of Enterprise did what Jim Rouse wished and named both Harvey and Brophy as vice chairs who would become co-CEOs.

Rouse was an avid sports fan, so he knew that coaches who made two quarterbacks equals usually regret having done so. But he seems to have persuaded himself that given the different strengths of Harvey and Brophy a division of tasks and authority could work. Harvey would be in charge of fundraising, public policy, and public information; Brophy would be in charge of program development and operations, financial controls and management, and general Foundation operations. The two would share responsibility for budgets, loan and grant approvals, and oversight of Foundation subsidiaries.[1] Rouse knew this arrangement would present problems. Since he was continuing as chairman of the board, he was afraid that his two successors would show excessive sensitivity to him as the founder and the head since the beginning. He was afraid that he, "no matter how good my intentions," will be tempted "to assert myself where I don't need to be—and don't want to be—suction from the past and continuing concern which I must step on."[2]

The changeover was to take place on July 1, 1991. On June 26th, Rouse put out a memo to "Everyone in the Enterprise Foundation and our affiliates." He felt it necessary to remind people of Enterprise's basic mission. It is to help people at the very bottom of society. He was afraid the mission would creep upward. It is the job of "each of us who works here to transform the conditions at the bottom of our society." It is a job that requires "deep and passionate commitment." Working with people who had more stable lives would be easier; he didn't want that to happen. "The simple truth is that our purpose is the very poor. If we cannot fulfill it, we must acknowledge that we cannot—stop soliciting funds on that basis, and reduce our operations to the level of support available for a less compelling purpose." He dreaded the idea that in his absence Enterprise would become just another bureaucratic foundation.

On the same day he sent a memo to a top Enterprise executive, with copies to Harvey and Brophy. It dealt with the way a job applicant had been treated. Rouse was upset. "This is a human being who was not treated as a human being but as a number or an object. . . . All people who deal with us, from funders to poor people to job applicants, should be treated as important people." He hates the idea that some people are treated "as routine, unimportant, a bother." How the individual person is treated moves the world toward being worse or better. "We want to add to the warmth and joy of the world, not to the negative, machine-like pattern that molests us at all times."[3]

Even after the changeover Rouse got involved in small operational matters when he thought a large principle was involved. He complained to Bart Harvey about a report that will be widely distributed.

> You may not have had the opportunity to review this—and I do not want to place blame anywhere—but this does not meet the standards of excellence we must expect of ourselves. If we don't demand excellent performance, we will never get it. But if we clearly seek it, people will demand it of themselves; will be proud of their work and proud of their foundation.

One of the offenses is the choice of type. The fonts are too small. The small type is difficult to read and is insulting to the people listed. He doesn't like the copy either. It tells from whom money was raised and how much, but it doesn't tell what was *accomplished* with the money. Rouse says donors will want to know, "Why did you need my money and what are you doing with it?"[4]

Rouse had always been a stickler about writing and the appearance of a page. "Every proposal, every letter, every piece of writing is a sales piece." Sentences should be short and clear. There should be no wasted words. Writing "is persuasive because it is rational, clear, to the point, tells the story." Format is important too. "The appearance of the page is critical to drawing the reader into the content—short paragraphs, wide margins—underscoring key phrases, particularly at the beginning of paragraphs."[5] In any case, with Rouse getting involved in such operational matters, Enterprise in effect had *three* co-CEOs. The upshot was that the co-CEO who was less tied to Rouse left. Paul Brophy resigned after being co-CEO for a little more than two years.

In his last years Rouse became more and more interested in the plight of the homeless. He did not see them as faceless persons worthy only of pity. He saw the lack of affordable housing as a frequent cause of homelessness.

The new homeless are those who are on the street simply because there is no place for them to live where they can pay the rent. Family problems, poor health, loss of a job all contribute to this. But, for many, it is just no place to live they can afford.

He sees the work of Enterprise as part of the solution. He is appalled that for families with incomes under $10,000 a year one-half of their income goes for rent. "This means very little for the rest of life, nothing for reserves."[6]

> As a society [he goes on] we must learn to regard the whole range of horrible disorders as deserving of our attention—not believing that we can correct it all, that everyone can be happy and non-suffering—but that as we work on the most clearly correctable or relievable conditions, we are lifting people out of misery into decent living. We are reducing the misery at the bottom, making more and more of our people effective workers (which we badly need), and relieving or eliminating the cumulative social sense of being people left out, abandoned, with no hope of the good life."

Typically, Rouse believed the problem was solvable. He and the Foundation were working on two fronts. First, they were working to make the people in power—"corporate, wealthy, political"—aware of "the breadth and depth of the problem; to understand the suffering, fear, hopelessness of millions of people living in wretched housing, paying rents they cannot afford, and knowing that one setback can put them out on the street."[7] Second, they were demonstrating there really are solutions. They were working on new systems to house the poor, raising money, showing how costs could be cut.

Jim Rouse always took the trouble to explain himself and to try to make sure that his position on an issue would not be misunderstood, even on relatively small issues. This is seen in innumerable letters he wrote in answer to requests that came to him out of the blue. He answered all requests for handouts or personal loans. He answered requests from people asking him to join their pet causes. In the summer of 1991, he answered a letter asking him to give his support to "Baltimore City Homeowners' Coalition for Fair Property Taxes." Rouse's answer is a testament to his honesty, fortitude, and the strength of his commitment to justice for all. Rouse explains that taxes are higher in older, central cities than in their surrounding suburbs because the cities are forced to assume the burden of the poor.

> This is true for many reasons, high among which is the many years of racial segregation during which the poor black immigrants to the city were packed into the cities with too little housing at too high cost, resulting in overcrowding and derelict slums, too little in services which were available to the suburbs. Over the years we manage, unwittingly, in America to cultivate a society of persistent, spreading poverty with the outfall from which we all now suffer— nearly 50% school dropouts, meaning that about half of the young people in the city enter adulthood unqualified for work—thus, joblessness at rates of 30% to

50% in center cities, homelessness, drugs, crime, violence (more people in jail in the United States than any other country in the world)."[8]

The burden of high taxes is thrust upon the backs of more fortunate city dwellers as a result of "our national neglect," and Rouse cannot support lowering them.

A few years earlier, Rouse received a check from a farmer who worked several properties on the Eastern Shore, one of which was acreage Rouse maintained as a vacation spot. Rouse's land had paid off for the farmer and, contractually, Rouse was due a payment. But the farmer's other sharecropping arrangements had not turned out well. Rouse was unwilling to accept the reward that the free-market system said was rightfully his.

> I don't think it is right that I should profit from your work when, because of weather, your operation as a whole is not profitable.
> You are a good farmer and a fine man. As you stated in your letter, you give your life to farming. You are entitled to make a living from it. I am simply a landowner who gives no toil to the crop, and I do not deserve to share in its yield at a price that is the result only of fortunate weather on my farm when your other farms had poor weather.
> If you were lazy or a poor farmer, it would be different. But that is not the case, and I do not feel it is fair or right that I should prosper—doing nothing—and you should struggle while working hard and doing a good job.[9]

So Rouse returned the check he had been sent.

It is easy to be cynical about anyone in America who has made a lot of money. After all, it's part of the American creed that you're supposed to pursue your own self-interest. So for some people that's what everything is about. Anyone's behavior that on the surface is free of self-interest is just camouflaged self-interest. No matter what it might look like, it's all about self-interest—money. Or it's about fame, which is a stop on the way to money. Or about power, which will be used to enrich oneself. Yes, there he is —Donald Trump, who obviously puts self and wealth above all else. And, yes, there are innumerable others in the American business hierarchy with the very same goals, pursued both legally and illegally.

Some commentators don't believe there are any other kind. A half-dozen years after the founding of Enterprise, a long article about Rouse's past career and present work appeared in a Norfolk newspaper. Rouse was astounded by its tone of cynicism and its misunderstanding of his motives. He felt there was little appreciation for what he was doing—or for the principles that had guided his career. He was described as "Well-schooled in the uses of publicity" and as a master in the use of hype. He was said to be trying "to wash the blood from his hands" with his present work; the blood was on his hands for having made millions from suburban malls that "sapped the life from center cities, leaving the poor behind." "Less CEO than guru," the article said, "Rouse seems to have built Enterprise on his personal celebrity, his wealth of connections and his inexhaustible supply of dreams."[10] *Guru*—implying that his foremost motive was to mobilize a flock of devoted followers. He was also offended by the idea that he was an idle dreamer with nothing to show for his efforts to help the poor and something of a charlatan for pushing plans so ambitious as to defy reality. In responding to a note from the reporter, Rouse reaffirmed that his goal to house the poor was earnest and serious. He pointed out that neither he nor Patty receive compensation for their work but in fact contributed money to the cause.[11]

Rouse was hurt and disappointed by the article. Being accused of having self-interested ulterior motives really hurts when your motives are neither self-interested or anything but what they seem. Rouse had an aversion to cynicism and here he was being accused of being cynical. Ironically, the reporter's tone is undercut by the words of Rouse with which she closed the article:

> I don't understand how men spend their lives in a particular kind of work, and then when the time comes for them to retire, they go fishing or play golf. It's as if they are passing judgment on their lives—that really what they wanted to do all along was play."

What Rouse was really saying is that he can't understand how some men can play while there is so much work on behalf of others that needs to be done. He is indirectly attacking the indifference to the misery of others that he has seen so much of. Cynicism and indifference—they go together, don't they? Rouse would never want to be accused of either.

With financial help from his father, Jimmy, Rouse's older son, opened Louie's Bookstore Café in downtown Baltimore. After a few years he sold it and concentrated on his art work. Rouse's younger son, Ted, became a partner in the Baltimore development firm of Struever Bros., Eccles & Rouse, specialists in "adaptive reuse." Ted hadn't been sure that he wanted that kind of career; earlier he had been a music student. Jim Rouse and Ted did not see too much of each other. They kept in touch through the mail, and Jim occasionally sent Ted a document or clipping he thought would be of interest. In the summer of 1990, he sent Ted the report of the Social Venture Network conference. Ted was moved to respond. The report

> has given me a new boost of enthusiasm and motivation for the work I am involved in. . . . I have at times this summer wondered whether all the frustrations of business are really worth the effort. Reading your words about business goals and realizing that there is more than one business person who wants to make capitalism a positive force on earth for improving the quality of human life inspires me and makes my work seem worthwhile.[12]

That was the meaning of the latter half of Jim Rouse's life—his relentless endeavors to make capitalism a positive force, a force for a more equitable America.

When Rouse was able to resume activity after his 1992 heart surgery, he plunged wholeheartedly back into the Sandtown project. Here's what his on-site project manager, Pat Costigan saw:

> He provided the determined energy. He sought to communicate that vision to the key partners—the mayor, the key players in Baltimore and the community. He drove every little bit of thinking about it day in and day out.... He was literally involved in every element of it—the conceptualization, the visioning, the writing of the vision, articulating the process, going to the stakeholders, doing behind-the-scenes encouragement.[13]

But the physical breakdowns that inevitably accompany old age were beginning to assert themselves. First, in 1994, there was a minor stroke, which left him with slurred speech and only partial use of his left arm. Then he fell and broke his shoulder. Not long after, back pain forced a visit to his doctor, who had him see an oncologist at Johns Hopkins Hospital. His back was full of cancerous tissue, and he underwent an arduous round of chemotherapy. Finally, the doctors also found amyotrophic lateral sclerosis—the dreaded Lou Gehrig's disease.

In late 1995, he could no longer go to the office. He tried to carry on at home, rolling his wheelchair to his desk in the kitchen. For a while he was able to receive visitors, read reports, and with help answer correspondence. But the paralysis was spreading and soon he couldn't speak. He was in his wheelchair one morning and made it into the kitchen. When his nurse came in to check on him, he was dead. That was on April 9, 1996. He had lived to within seventeen days of his 82nd birthday.

Chapter 20 Last Years

1. JWR memo to Trustees, January 7, 1991.
2. JWR memo to Harvey and Brophy, April 15, 1991.
3. JWR memo to Mark Sissman, June 26, 1991.
4. JWR memo to Bart Harvey, November 11, 1991.
5. JWR to Everyone, July 6, 1989.
6. JWR letter to Billie K. Press, June 26, 1989.
7. JWR letter to Robert H. Smith, December 7, 1988.
8. JWR letter to David B. Rudow, July 15, 1991.
9. JWR letter to Robert Garrett November 22, 1987.
10. Ellie Novek, "Developer Rouse works to house poor," *The Virginian Pilot,* November 1, 1987.
11. JWR letter to Ellie Novek, December 8,1987.
12. Ted Rouse letter to JWR, August 3, 1990.
13. Quoted by Olsen, 358.

Chapter 21
Columbia Fully Grown

In the commencement address that Jimmy delivered for him at Berkeley in 1992, Rouse recounted the story of how discouraged he was after the initial discussions of the Columbia work group in 1963. But from feelings of futility and despair his mood became upbeat when one of the scholarly participants said, "You know we are all missing the point of these discussions. We are being asked how in a new community—to nourish love."[1] The foremost goal of the discussions then became specifying ways in which the city and its villages could encourage, could nourish love. After those moments of epiphany there was no further talk of love. The term that came to be used for what Rouse had in mind is "community." The work group planners focused on ways in which community could be nourished. So in assessing what has happened in Columbia between its birth and its coming into maturity, the important question is, How much has *community* grown in Columbia?

In places that are comprised of only one ethnic or racial group, community is much more likely than in places that are diverse. Rouse wanted Columbia to be diverse. He wanted a mix of income levels and a mix of races. The blending of races has worked out much better than the blending of people on different socio-economic levels. From the beginning, about 20% of Columbia's population has been African-American. In Columbia, just about every street is integrated. In that Berkeley speech, Rouse guessed that there are more bi-racial couples per capita in Columbia than in any other American city. Non-white people living in Columbia have said again and again that they feel more comfortable there than they would anywhere else in America. As a barrier to community, race is not an issue in Columbia.

Indeed, some middle-class African-Americans feel that race relations are too good. They see a problem in that. They fear that when Columbia-raised African-American children go out into mainstream America they will be unprepared for the racism they'll meet. In 1991, a black mother, Alice Cornelison, spoke about the Ph.D. dissertation she was doing. She was comparing the experiences at college of black students who had gone through Columbia's schools with students who had gone to school in largely black Prince Georges County. She argued that Columbia-raised students need to learn more about the hostility their skin color will bring upon them in the outside world. "I want to warn parents here that when you turn the entire education of your children over to the public school system, they don't learn about their culture. . . . That's easy to do when you get comfortable."[2] But almost every one of the Columbia students told Cornelison they would want to raise their own children in Columbia. One student put it this way: "Columbia instilled in me that there is a chance to live with people in harmony. Because if it can happen there it can happen on a larger scale."

Jim Rouse had heard Cornelison's position before. Columbia doesn't reflect the real world; therefore its children are not adequately prepared. In a 1987 interview he said:

> To the contrary, young people here are better prepared for the outside world because they have grown up experiencing what life ought to be. You don't have to only know the worst there is to be prepared for life. Knowing the best there is is even greater preparation. To the extent that Columbia is intolerant of prejudice rather than of one another, we have served our children well.[3]

In 2003, David A. Rakes, an African-American, was a member of the Columbia Council. At a conference on "Columbia: Yesterday and Today," at Howard County Community College, Rakes said he was very happy with Columbia: "Columbia has made me a better person. . . . It's a place where people can live and grow together. . . . My grown children continually thank me for deciding to live in Columbia."[4] Columbia is a place where white people, more than in any other place, do not judge people by the color of their skin but by their character.

The majority of the public elementary, middle, and high schools in Columbia are regarded as being among the best in Maryland and, indeed, among the best in the nation—for black students, for white students, for all students. One of the effects of having such good schools is that couples with children want to move to Columbia. Once out of the dismal 1970s, the demand for housing in most of Columbia has been very strong. And when the demand for Columbia housing exceeded the supply, the price went up—considerably. The hunch of TIAA executives in the 70s that they would have a hard time finding within Columbia, female clerical help has turned out to be correct. The socio-economic makeup of the city has moved upward. The percentage of professionals and business people has steadily risen. By the turn of the century there was relatively little "affordable" housing left. In most of the villages,

Rouse's ambitions for both excellent public schools and housing for a range of income levels have clashed, and the people with more money have won. By 1986, only 13% of Columbia's residents could afford to buy the average-priced single-family home then up for sale.[5] And since then the percentage has dropped.

Columbia's middle-class blacks are for the most part homeowners. Its low-income blacks are mostly renters. Still, during Columbia's first two decades low-income blacks with steady work were able to move up into homeownership and grow a middle-class state of mind. But the application of Rouse's ideal of income-mixing as well as race-mixing has brought trouble to Columbia. As rental units opened up in Columbia's older villages, a stream of low-income blacks who were helped by federal Section 8 rent subsidies moved from Baltimore to Columbia, and some brought with them the pathology of inner-city neighborhoods. Their younger children attended the schools in the older villages, did not do well—and their parents did not mind. Their older children were often undisciplined and irresponsible and fell into patterns of anti-social behavior. Anti-social acts that were never seen in Columbia during its first twenty-five years began to occur in its cul-de-sacs and village centers. With the 1990s in Columbia's older villages came rowdiness, intimidation, vandalism, graffiti, pit bulls, and lower school-wide achievement levels. There also were drug dealing, stabbings, shootings, armed robberies, burglaries, and murders. In 2000, one resident of the village of Owen Brown summed up the situation this way, "The problem properties are not always Section 8, but they usually are. . . . We're being ghettoized, and Columbia will develop pockets of higher-crime areas"[6]

Within Columbia there was white flight from what some called "Inner Columbia." Families moved from older villages to villages with higher-performing schools. If they were unable to move, they got their children transferred to the better schools in other villages. Some parents unable to afford the price of a home in a newer village moved out of Columbia altogether. This is exactly what happened in cities across the country as low-income black children began to attend predominantly middle-class schools. The tipping point seems to be at about 30% of low-income school enrollment. At about that percentage, discipline in the classroom becomes a major problem and teaching and learning suffer.

In other cities with such problems, the local board of education and municipal government would be pressured to deal with the problems. But Columbia has no municipal government, and the responsible school board is the Howard County Board of Education. This is partly due to Rouse's insistence that the city remain unincorporated but mainly due to Maryland's system of county government. Thus, corrective measures requiring a local focus are difficult to bring about. Rouse was very much in favor of heavy resident participation in the governance of Columbia. Indeed, two representative bodies were set up, the Columbia Council and the Columbia Association. But these bodies do not have law-making authority and cannot make their own policing and educational policies.

The Columbia Association at first was called the Parks and Recreation Association. The Association has its chief executive who, like a mayor, is charged with carrying out the measures adopted by the legislative branch. The legislative branch is the Columbia Council, whose members usually appoint themselves to be members of the Columbia Association's board of directors. In any case, the Association's authority is limited largely to recreational facilities; other functions are the responsibility of Howard County. Resembling the typical homeowners association, the Columbia Association oversees twenty-three outdoor swimming pools, forty or so tennis courts, the two golf courses, the ice rink, the horse center, and a variety of other recreational facilities.[7] The Association is supported by a special tax on all property, with set maximums.

Padraic M. Kennedy was president of the Association for twenty-six years. He saw the significance of the growing problems of the older villages, although he thought they might be over-stated.

> At the risk of sounding dramatic, America [is at stake], because if it can't be done here, it can't be done. . . . What else is at stake is the future and soul of Columbia. If Columbia can't address these issues and it starts to ignore these issues, in a sense, it's no longer Columbia.[8]

Time has chipped away at the soul of Columbia. In a 2002 survey, only 28% of Columbians sampled said they were "very familiar" with Columbia's vision. Location was the reason 31% gave for moving to Columbia. Thus, in 2002, along with adjusting programs and services and giving attention to needed physical maintenance, the Columbia Council made a decision to give attention to maintenance of Columbia's vision. The problem of maintaining Columbia's soul goes back a generation. In 1989, at an Association budget hearing, Columbian Dick Lewis told of an encounter with a teenager for whom Columbia was just another place: "To her, Columbia is just another big place like Rockville and Glen Burnie. . . . To increasing numbers of people, it is just another place. . . ."[9] That Columbia can be regarded as just another place is frightening to most of its early settlers.

With an annual budget that in 2003 hit $50 million, the Association's chief executive is an important person in Columbia. Surveys of residents in 2002 and 2003 showed that 62% of residents approved of the Association's operations but only 52% thought they were getting their money's worth. In 2001, the board gave a three-year contract with a beginning salary of $125,000 to Maggie Brown, an African-American who had previously been the Association's vice president. Rouse had wanted this body to be non-political, but contention over the president's salary produced what amounted to political controversy. The appointment of Brown was preceded by the withdrawal of two white finalists for the position. They claimed that "racial politics" was too much of a factor in Columbia and in the selection of the president. Further controversy ensued when plans were afoot to give Brown a second contract with a substantial raise. A watchdog group of residents—an opposition party—called the Alliance for a Better Columbia (ABC) strongly objected to the raise. Vehemence at meetings led to the hiring of a meetings security guard.[10]

Construction of the last of Columbia's nine villages did not begin until 1990. River Hill was to be built on the western edge of Columbia, adjacent to the still-rural part of Howard County. Many of the pioneers in the city wanted to make River Hill the finest of all the villages, the village that came closest to fulfilling Jim Rouse's notion of the ideal village, including a good measure of income as well as racial diversity. Howard Research and Development, Rouse's subsidiary developer, petitioned for ninety acres to be devoted to apartments. The nearby rural residents outside of Columbia were unhappy with that. They wanted to keep minimal the population density of the new village, which means, in effect, the number of low-income families. The permissible density was decided by the county zoning board, and their decision was that only thirty-three acres would be for apartments. As a result, the newest of the villages has the most open space and the finest homes but the least amount of affordable housing. River Hill is diverse, with many residents of Asian ancestry, but it does not have anywhere near the percentage of African-Americans that the other villages have.[11]

Rouse had envisioned downtown Columbia, the Town Center, as a vibrant place, filled with restaurants, outdoor cafes, nightclubs, shops, a museum or two, and even an amusement park. He foresaw a walkable downtown Columbia drawing thousands of visitors, many taking a tourist's day-trip up the road from Washington. Several forces prevented the growth of the urban core—the layout of downtown, the mall, and the automobile. The original planning called for roadways to follow the natural contours of the land. As a result, most of Columbia is a jumble of curving roadways. It is not easy to get from one village to another by car. To do so usually requires that part of the trip be made on one of the main parkways. To get downtown, most residents have to get onto a parkway. Except for the relatively few walkers and cyclists, the parkways are essential for mobility within Columbia. And the main parkway separates the area that Rouse wanted to become the urban core from Columbia's beautiful high-end mall. The Mall in Columbia is a combination of European plaza and American Main Street. It's the biggest attraction around, which you get to by car. At the mall in 2007 were *five* department stores—Nordstrom, Lord & Taylor, JCPenney, Macy's (formerly Hecht's), and Sears. There's also an L. L. Bean store. Thus, the other side of the parkway, even with its lakefront, offers no real competition. It is simply not interesting enough.

While Rouse was enormously disappointed by the refusal of TIAA to relocate to Columbia, the Rouse Company succeeded in bringing in lots of businesses that provided work. In 2004, besides the stores in the village centers and in the mall, there were employers in fourteen office/industrial/research and development parks housing 3,500 businesses. Among recognizable names were Allied Signal, Blue Cross Blue Shield, CIGNA, Wachovia, Honeywell, NCR, State Farm Insurance, TRW, and Sun Microsystems. In 2004, the Rouse Company said, there were 89,700 jobs in Columbia.

Back in the planning stage of Columbia in the early 60s, Rouse was told by his friend John Gardner, then Secretary of Health, Education and Welfare, that Columbia could turn out to be too good. "This city could be so good that people could become very comfortable in it and not fulfill their responsibilities" That story was told in 1987, and in the years since, the great majority of people living in Columbia have become even more comfortable—and are even less likely to fulfill the responsibilities of citizenship. Gardner said further, "Everybody who lives in that city ought to pay a toll. The toll ought to be to each other, to the County, to the State, to the Country and the world."[12] The toll would be the price paid for the opportunity to live in such a wonderful place.

Gardner was more than right in the comfort level he foresaw. And his prediction that such comfortable people would involve themselves less in the affairs of their neighborhood and city also was right. Even before its twentieth birthday, Columbia was in danger of losing its special identity, a large component of which includes caring about neighbor, village, and city. While it is a place of unusual racial harmony, gradually it has been losing what was once an abundance of community feeling. The anti-social behavior in the older villages has not helped. The pioneers came to Columbia looking for community, and they found it. Then Columbia gained a reputation as a good place to live and new generations of expatriates from the rest of America began to move in. The city that billed itself as The Next America began to take on the values of the rest of America. The lament of Columbian Dick Krantz in 1987 is even more true at the beginning of the twenty-first century:

> We live only with our immediate families, or alone, following divorce. We keep cool in our centrally air-conditioned houses. We're entertained alone in front of TV sets. We dry our clothes alone. We travel alone in our cars. There are fewer opportunities to know our neighbors. So we often don't know their needs and problems.[13]

On November 9, 2004, the Rouse Company sold itself. The Rouse Company and all its properties in Columbia and elsewhere became the property of General Growth Properties of Chicago, which, as the second-largest mall owner in America, owned more properties than the Rouse Company. People in Columbia who cared about more than just what is happening on their own doorstep regarded the transaction as a betrayal of Jim Rouse by the Rouse Company. Some old-timers, though, had grown so used to the company's movement away from Jim Rouse's principles that they would not have been surprised at anything the company did. From the time Jim Rouse resigned as CEO in 1979, the Rouse Company began to deviate from the distinctive way of thinking Rouse had said characterized the company. It became more and more like other companies, making the bottom line its top concern. The company bore the founder's name but acted in ways the founder never would have sanctioned. It drifted away from the three basic goals Rouse enumerated in his final address to the annual meeting: improving the physical environment and quality of urban life, providing opportunities for the personal growth of company employees, and increasing company earnings—but only "at a rate sufficient to provide *adequate* rewards to our stockholders."

The people in Columbia who had a broader vision and cared about the quality of life of the whole community did not make life easy for the successor company. They resented the arranged death of the company that represented the city and did not make profit-making its top priority. Within a few months of its purchase, General Growth encountered resistance to its plans to take more profit out of Columbia.

The Merriweather Post Pavilion is in a section of downtown called Symphony Woods. It is one of Columbia's jewels, beloved especially by old-timers. Among the city's first structures, located in a spacious, woods–like setting, it was intended to be the summer home of Washington's National Symphony Orchestra. Its name was chosen to honor Merriweather Post, the Post Cereal heiress who had been a substantial benefactor of the orchestra. Over the years, as the reputation of Frank Gehry, the pavilion's architect, soared, the pavilion came to be regarded as a significant cultural artifact, one of four structures Gehry designed in Columbia's early days. Over the years too, the offerings at the open-air venue became more diverse, with more and more bookings aimed at a young audience.

At one point, fifty concerts a year were held at Merriweather. In recent years, with competition from new nearby venues, the number of concerts per year dropped to around twenty. The Rouse Company had a tentative plan to get a bigger payoff from the pavilion and its grounds. When General Growth took over, it picked up on the plan and pressed to enclose the pavilion and turn it into a small theatre, in order that housing could be erected on a section of the parking lot. When Columbians learned of General Growth's plans, they swung into action.

Two groups were formed. Save Merriweather, Inc. focused on grass roots organizing and outreach. Save Merriweather Political Action Committee raised money to support county candidates who agreed with its position on Merriweather. Faced with this resistance, five months into its ownership General Growth dropped its plan for changes. It promised to keep Merriweather as it is and make it an essential part of an expanded downtown.[14]

Having put an end to the Merriweather issue, General Growth came out for mixed-use development for all of downtown, which is what Jim Rouse had originally wanted. Integral to the further development of downtown would be more condos and apartment buildings. General Growth made prime downtown land available to WCI, a company that describes itself as "the prime creator of luxury towers." WCI proposed to build a 23-story luxury condominium with individual units selling from $600,000 to $2 million. It would provide many luxurious amenities: a rooftop pool and spa, a theatre, a fitness center, billiards room.[15] Would Jim Rouse have approved?

Rouse would not automatically have disapproved. The basic question for him would have been whether the residents of the towers would contribute to the life of the community. Would they leave their luxurious units and stroll the streets and lakefront as Manhattanites stroll the streets of the Upper West Side? Or would the towers be an enclave for rich people who would leave their units only to hop into their cars and drive off from Columbia? Believers in the desirability of more downtown density think the Plaza can only benefit downtown. But there are many who are offended by the idea of a 23-story building at the very heart of the city, and they are trying to scale down the towers through legislation limiting the height of buildings.

Chapter 21 Columbia Fully Grown

1. Quoted by JWR in commencement speech, May 24, 1992.
2. Quoted by Susan Thornton, "Warn kids of racism, study says," *Columbia Flier,* July 4, 1991, 40.
3. Susan Hlesciak, "Now this I love," *Columbia Magazine,* June 1987, 43.
4. David Rakes, "Columbia: Yesterday and Today," Conference at Howard Community College, April 26, 2003.
5. Steve Kelly, "The end is near," *Columbia Magazine,* Fall 1989, 27-28.
6. Gady Epstein, "Two cities emerge in Columbia," *The Sun,* November 26, 2000,1A and November 28, 2000, A1. Epstein is the source for most of what is said here about "the other Columbia."
7. "Columbia, Maryland," Rouse Company brochure, March 2002.
8. Epstein, November 26, 2000, A1.
9. Testimony at Columbia Association budget hearing, February 13, 1989.
10. Laura Cadiz, "Columbia: an experiment that grew into reality," *The Sun,* March 23, 2003, T8.
11. Kelly, 27-28.
12. Dick Krantz, "The Challenge of Columbia," *Columbia Magazine,* June 1987, 46.
13. Krantz, 46.
14. Larry Carson, "Merriweather Post Pavilion," *The Sun,* April 27, 2005, 2B. 15. WCI advertisement in *Baltimore Sun.*

Chapter 22
Legacy

When Jim Rouse died, the Governor of Maryland, William Donald Schaefer said Rouse's legacy required no discussion; his legacy was obvious. Schaefer meant that Rouse's legacy was all the places he had built: the Cherry Hill and Mondawmin malls, the Village of Cross Keys, Faneuil Hall Marketplace and Harborside, the refurbished streets of Sandtown, and, most of all, the city of Columbia. These places, and others, are Jim Rouse's tangible, visible legacy. But Rouse also has passed on intangibles—his values and distinctive ways of thinking and doing. Still, the matter of Rouse's legacy is not all that simple. In the real world conditions change. Things happen that are beyond any individual's or group's control, and what had been reality becomes something unexpectedly different.

If Jim Rouse had lived ten more years, his habitual optimism might have been deflated. He would not have liked the state of the world and his country in 2006. He would have thought his country's involvement in the killing in Iraq totally irrational; he would have been constantly aware of the parallels to the Vietnam War. He would not have been happy with the new threats to poor black neighborhoods. The scourge of drug use and gun-toting drug suppliers, the spread of gangsta culture and its disregard of basic morality—these problems, often matters of life or death, had an urgency that Rouse did not know. It was all so irrational. It was making the good work of so many good people look futile.

In inner-city Baltimore, and especially in Sandtown-Winchester, much had been done to improve education and to provide housing, services, and jobs, and yet from year to year the inner-city murder count did not go down and stay down. The forward momentum in Sandtown was checked. In one post-Rouse year, 2005, the 72-square-block area had eleven murders.[1] Displaced from other neighborhoods, criminal activity in Sandtown was on the rise. According to the Baltimore police, stepped-up enforcement to the south had the effect of pushing drug dealing north into Sandtown. A generation that was in its childhood in the 90s when Rouse was roaming Sandtown streets had grown up, and the streets had become less safe. The drug trade was moving in, and more than a decade of progress in Sandtown was being eroded.

A Baltimore *Sun* article on the first day of 2006, prompted by the great interest Baltimore has in the city's annual murder count, assessed the condition of Sandtown-Winchester. Quoted in the article was 18-year-old Towanda Williams, who was a child during Rouse's time there. She said that ten years ago "'it was all right; kids used to walk outside and play, and whatever. As they got older, they started seeing other people [committing violent acts] and getting away with it, and they started doing it.'" A male of about the same age reported that teens and pre-teens "aren't reluctant to carry out drug deals within vicinity of the police cars and surveillance cameras overhead." He said he thought there were more murders than the number reported. "'For a lot of people my age, to be twenty-one is old.'" Rouse had gone to the bottom in singling out Sandtown for rehabilitation. A lot of progress had been made, but police department efforts elsewhere were taking their toll. With Sandtown, the legacy is muddled. Even so, Enterprise Foundation continues its work, faithful to Rouse's original intentions.

Since Rouse's retirement from the Rouse Company, a new trend developed in the suburbs of big cities. Close to the cities, they had become more like the cities; farther-out exurbs were springing up, and they were like the old suburbs used to be. Exurbs, mainly communities of the well off, have a lot to offer, but they don't offer the community spirit that was so important to Jim Rouse. In Rouse's time, home-building was the work primarily of local and regional builders. Their basic product was not isolated McMansions. That has changed. By 2005, more and more expensive homes were being mass produced and put up by publicly traded companies with a national market. The companies, of course, are profit driven, and the idea of doing well by doing good is not comprehensible to them; the bottom line is the most important line. The philosophy, for example, of Toll Brothers, one of the country's leading builders of upscale homes is simple. The company doesn't get into the question of whether what it does will lead to the improvement of mankind. Instead it asks: "What's selling out there, and how can we do it better?"[2]

Toll Brothers has bought the land and put up houses in more than 800 developments. One of its most notable is The Estates at Princeton Junction in West Windsor, New Jersey, where the number of Toll Brothers homes ultimately will exceed 1,000. The company bought the land, fought the inevitable legal battles with locals who objected—and then proceeded. The company did not collaborate with, or even consult with, town officials. The town would have preferred a mixed-use development, a community in which there would be offices and stores as well as homes. It also would have wanted more open space. According to the mayor, The Estates at Princeton Junction ultimately "will be a big lonely island of suburbia, bound by train tracks on one side and farm fields and woods on the others, a place connected to nothing else in town, leaving its residents largely in thrall to their automobiles"—a town of sprawl and no center.[3] Just what Rouse hated.

On the other hand, another planned city is being developed that would not have come into being if there had been no Jim Rouse. Summerlin, Nevada, exceeds Columbia, Maryland, in scope. One phase of Howard Hughes's multi-faceted entrepreneurial career was the accumulation of real estate in southern Nevada. In 1996, twenty years after Hughes's death, his Summa Corporation, which owned the real estate, was acquired by the Rouse Company, and the Rouse Company moved ahead with plans to make Summerlin, Nevada, a sunland Columbia. The growth of Summerlin, comprised of 22,500 acres, would be guided by the same principles that followed by Rouse and his associates in building Columbia. Unlike the few other planned communities that have been built in recent times—for example, Seaside, Rosemary Beach, and Watercolor in Florida—Summerlin would be a primary-home community, not a resort, second-home community. Like Columbia, Summerlin would be a full-scale, mixed-use city. It would be developed in phases; in 2005 it already had a population of 92,000. The target population is 160,000 to be achieved by the year 2020. That would give it a population about the same as Reno's.[4]

In planning Columbia, Rouse wanted to have a population of mixed incomes. He wanted low-income people to make up 10% of the population.[5] Most of the low-income people would be former residents of inner-city Baltimore. Based on the 2000 census, Summerlin had a population that was 4.1% black, 7.8% Hispanic, and 74.6% white non-Hispanic, with the remainder being made up mostly of people of Asian ancestry. As the growth of Columbia played out, the black and mixed-race population approximated about 20% by 2000. Racial integration in Columbia is more advanced than it is in Summerlin.

On the other hand, Columbia has experienced an educational and income compression that makes it more homogeneous than Summerlin. In 2002, the average household income in Columbia was $90,500, and 70% of adults had a college degree.[6] In Summerlin, in 2000, the median household income was $64,784, and only about one-third of the adults had at least a bachelor's degree.[7] Columbia's population contains a much higher proportion of professionals than Rouse wanted, and they are more inclined to raise their families in a suburban environment than an urban one. Summerlin, especially because of its proximity to Las Vegas, has a relatively high proportion of service workers. As was the case in early Columbia, Summerlin has a variety of housing prices, styles, and densities. And the available recreational amenities in Summerlin are very similar to Columbia's. While Summerlin's proximity to Las Vegas would have given

Jim Rouse shudders, its physical planning is very much in accord with Jim Rouse's principles.

There is, though, the matter of the spirit of community. If it has become more and more remote in Columbia, it has never been promoted in Summerlin. It's doubtful that there's more community in Summerlin than in a typical Toll Brothers development. When the Rouse Company was sold in 2004, General Growth Properties became the Summerlin developer. General Growth is not a rapacious company, but it is not run by visionaries; when it took its first actions after it became Columbia's primary owner, it seemed to have little awareness of that city's special history. Summerlin will be built out and undoubtedly will become a very desirable place to live, but, in typical American fashion, people will go their own way and not care about community.

One important component of Jim Rouse's legacy of intangibles is his ideas about how to run a company. Most notably those ideas manifested themselves in the companies run by Willard G. Rouse III (1942-2003)—the son of Jim's older brother Willard. As a young man, Willard III had worked part-time for the Rouse Company, and at the age of thirty he founded Rouse & Associates. The company had three major accomplishments: the development of Great Valley Corporate Center, twenty-five miles west of Philadelphia; the development of the Philadelphia Stock Exchange Building; and the building of Liberty Place, a mixed-use skyscraper, taller than any other in downtown Philadelphia. In 1994, the company was transformed into Liberty Property Trust, which, specializing in office and industrial properties, became one of the country's largest real estate investment trusts. In a speech about the building of Liberty Place, Willard touched on an odd topic: the importance of having quality restrooms in a building. Restrooms were a symbol. It's in the quality of the restrooms that the common person will make his or her judgment of a building—an idea of Willard's that just as likely could have been his uncle's.[8]

Like Jim Rouse, Willard Rouse III offered himself for numerous roles in voluntary public service. Among other roles, he served as chairman of the Pennsylvania Convention Center Authority; as director of the committee that orchestrated Philadelphia's bicentennial celebration of the Constitution; and as chairman of the Regional Performing Arts Center, with foremost responsibility for the construction of the acclaimed Kimmel Center for the Performing Arts. When Willard died in 2003, Governor Ed Rendell of Pennsylvania, who previously had been mayor of Philadelphia, said that nowhere in his experience with American cities had he ever "seen any individual have as significant an impact on the direction of a city and region" as Willard Rouse had.[9]

Willard followed Jim in his extraordinary leadership qualities. In 1979 Jim Rouse said this about his company:

> It is the pervasive concern for the quality of all the company does; the attention to detail; the respect for the importance and dignity of those we serve; the bright sparks of creativity; the struggle for right answers; the anguish suffered

in the strain; the laughter, the kindness, the caring that abounds among our people that give this company its unique distinction.[10]

When Willard died in 2003, Bill Hankowsky, Liberty Trust's CEO, said this about him:

> It is impossible to express the loss our employees are feeling, . . . Bill was, simply, our hero. . . . The culture of this company is indelibly stamped with his uniquely moral view of the individual's place in the corporation, and the corporation's responsibility to the world. We will strive to emulate his values, his ideals, and his fierce commitment to leaving his piece of the world better than he found it.[11]

Wonderful testimony to the influence of Jim Rouse on his nephew.

Rouse has acolytes throughout the development industry. His younger son, Winstead (Ted) carries on the legacy in Baltimore's Struever Brothers, Eccles & Rouse. In Charlotte, Cincinnatti, Washington, D.C., and elsewhere there are proud acolytes. A comment that is not untypical was made by Martin Millspaugh, who worked with Rouse as an executive in Enterprise Development.

> He's impossible but true, [he said of Rouse]. When I started to work closely with Jim on a daily basis I thought I would at last begin to see the clay feet of the great man. What happened was that he only got better every day: more perceptive, wise, and unselfish—he was truly one of a kind, above the normal run of men.[12]

Chapter 22 Legacy

1. Joe Burris, *The Sun*, January 1, 2006, 1. All that is said about Sandtown-Winchester in 2005 is based on Burris's article.
2. Jon Gertner, "Chasing Ground," *The New York Times Magazine*, October 16, 2005, 68.
3. Gertner, 81.
4. www.summerlin.com/menu.html. Accessed January 2006.
5. www.nbm.org/blueprints/80s/cover/cover.htm. Accessed May 2003.
6. According to the Rouse Company fact sheet on Columbia in March 2002.
7. According to a "city data" fact sheet, accessed at www.city-data.com. Accessed January 2006.
8. John P. Claypool, "Philadelphia citypaper.net," June 5, 2003.
9. www.paradox1x.org. Accessed January 2006.
10. JWR speech, May 23, 1979.
11. Quoted by Natalie Kostelni, "Philadelphia Business Journal," www.bizjournals.com. Accessed January 2006.
12. Quoted by Olsen, 370.

Bibliography

Bloom, Nicholas Dagen. *Suburban Alchemy: 1960s New Towns and the Transformation of the American Dream.* Columbus: Ohio State University Press, 2001.
—. *Merchant of Illusion: America's Salesman of the Businessman's Utopia.* Columbus: Ohio State University Press, 2004.
Bradfield, Kristin. "The First 'Holistic' Approach to Neighborhood Revitalization Is Still Bearing Fruit After 10 Years." *Affordable Housing Finance,* 2001.
Brown, Prudence, Benjamin Butler and Ralph Hamilton. *The Sandtown-Winchester Neighborhood Initiative: Lessons Learned About Community Building Implementation.* Baltimore: Anne E. Casey Foundation and Enterprise Foundation, 2001.
Costigan, Patrick. "A Comprehensive Approach to Rebuilding Poor Neighborhoods." *Georgia Academy Journal,* 1999.
Ditch, Scott, ed. *A Larger Vision: Jim Rouse and the American City.* The book contains excerpts from a selection of speeches by Jim Rouse. Privately printed for Patty Rouse on the occasion of Jim's eightieth birthday, April 26, 1994.
Domhoff, G. William. *Who Rules America Now?* Edgewood Cliffs, New Jersey: Prentice Hall, 1983.
Durr, Kenneth D. *Behind the Backlash: White Working-Class Politics in Baltimore, 1940-1980.* Chapel Hill: University of North Carolina Press, 2003.
Edelman, Peter. *Searching for America's Heart: RFK and the Renewal of Hope.* Boston: Houghton Mifflin, 2001.
Fingerman, Susan. "Sandtown-Winchester: Then and Now." A report to be found at the Enterprise Foundation Resource Center, Columbia.
Gibbons, Boyd. *Wye Island.* Washington: Resources for the Future, 1987.
Hardwick, M. Jeffrey. *Mall Maker: Victor Gruen, Architect of an American Dream.* Philadelphia: University of Pennsylvania Press, 2004.
Harvey, F. Barton. "Community Rebuilding: A Quiet Revolution." *National Civic Review,* Winter 1996.
Herman, Arthur. *Joseph McCarthy: Re-examining the Life and Legacy of America's Most Hated Senator.* New York: The Free Press, 1999.
Holechek, Jim. *Two Cross Keys Villages.* New York: iUniverse, Inc., 2003.
Isaacson, Walter. *Benjamin Franklin: An American Life.* New York: Simon & Schuster, 2003.
Jamison, Kay Redfield, *Exuberance: The Passion for Life.* New York: Knopf, 2004.
La Noue, Patricia J. *Oral History Interview with Jim Rouse.* Baltimore: Maryland Historical Society, 1974.
Lewis, Sinclair. *It Can't Happen Here.* New York: Signet Classic, 1993.
Mark, Michael L. *But Not Next Door.* Baltimore: Baltimore Neighborhoods, Inc., 2002
McFarland, M. Carter. *Federal Government and Urban Problems.* Boulder, Colorado: Westview Press, 1978.
Morgan, Edmund S. *Benjamin Franklin.* New Haven: Yale University Press, 2003
O'Connor, Elizabeth. *Call to Commitment.* New York: Harper & Row, 1963.

Olsen, Joshua. *Better Places, Better Lives: A Biography of James Rouse.* Washington: Urban Land Institute, 2003.

On the Ground with Comprehensive Community Initiatives. Columbia: Enterprise Foundation, 2000.

Rouse, James W. Unfinished and Unpublished Autobiography, with Scott Ditch. Available in Columbia Archives.

Smith, C. Fraser, *William Donald Schaefer,* Baltimore: Johns Hopkins University Press, 1999.

Stillman, Joseph, Benjamin Butler, Prudence Brown, and Lenneal Henderson. "Sandtown-Winchester Community Building in Partnership, 1990-1994: Interim Evaluation Report," Enterprise Foundation Resource Center, Columbia, ca. 1995.

Straight, Michael, *After Long Silence.* New York: W.W. Norton, 1983.

Tennenbaum, Robert, ed. *Creating a New City: Columbia, Maryland.* Columbia, MD: Perry Publishing, 1996.

Thernstrom, Abigail and Stephan Thernstrom. *America in Black and White: One Nation Indivisible.* New York: Simon & Schuster, 1997.

Trump, Donald J. *The Art of the Deal.* New York: Random House, 1987.

Tygiel, Jules. *The Jackie Robinson Reader.* New York: Dutton, 1997.

Index

6th Street Marketplace [Richmond], 191, 193
21st Century Waterfront Plan [Chattanooga], 193
Akers, John F., 196
Alder, Louise, 181
Alexander, Bruce D., 181, 183
Alliance for a Better Columbia, 224
American City Corporation, 158-59
American Council to Improve Our Neighborhoods (ACTION), 80
American Institute of Architects [Baltimore Chapter], 180
Anne Arundel County Council [Maryland], 73
Antioch College, 134-140, 148
Architectural Heritage, 172, 174
Askew, L.B. (Monk), 180
Astor, Mrs. Brooke, 197
Bacon, Edmund, 95
Balch, Margaret Robinson Rouse [sister], 16, 35, 36
Balch, William [brother-in-law], 36
Baltimore, 2, 22, 24, 28, 37-38, 39, 49-50, 66-67, 83, 85, 101, 206, 208
Baltimore City Coalition for Fair Property Taxes, 215
Baltimore City Community College, 69
Baltimore Country Club, 102, 109
Baltimore Neighborhoods, Inc., 85
Baltimore Plan, 51, 52

Baltimore Real Estate Board, 105
Baltimoreans United in Leadership Development (BUILD), 201-202, 206, 208
Bamberger's, 91
Bart, Harry, 63-64, 65, 67, 78
Basildon New Town [England], 104
Bass, Robert M., 196
Batchelor, Harry, 45, 47
Battle Creek [Michigan], 193, 195
Belfast [Northern Ireland], 194
The Belfry Bat, 25
Bellamy, Ralph, 58
Belluschi, Pietro, 68
Bender, Sue, 202
Bendix, 157
Bergen Mall [New Jersey], 70
Berkeley. *See* University of California at Berkeley.
Berman, Mel, 4, 120, 122
Birenbaum, William, 139
Block One [Baltimore], 50
Bloom, Nicholas Dagen, 8-9, 51, 56, 83, 210
Board of Design [Mondawmin], 68
Bon Marche, 89-90
Boston, 180, 181
The Boston Globe, 173
Boston Landmarks Commission, 174
Boston Redevelopment Authority (BRA), 172-74

Boston Society of Architects, 173
Boucher, William III, 85
Boulton, Edward, 111
R. M. Bradley Company, 172
Bradshaw, Thomas, 202
Bridges, Styles, 57
Brodie, M. Jay, 180, 181
Brophy, Paul, 206, 207, 213, 214
Brown, Alexander, 66
Brown, Margie, 224
Brown Memorial Presbyterian Church, 154
Buffet, Warren, 4, 197
Building Inspection of the Department of Public Works [Baltimore], 84
Call to Commitment, 154-55
Calvert School, 21
Camden County Economic Development Commission, 95
Carey, Churchill G. (Tink), 44, 78
Center for the Advancement of Social Entrepreneurship, 197, 198
Charles Center [Baltimore], 7, 84, 85
Charles Stewart Mott Foundation, 193, 204
Charlottetown, (Charlotte, N.C.), 82, 89-90
Chase Manhattan Bank, 121
Chataqua, 24
Chattanooga, (Tn.), 191, 194, 201, 205
Chattanooga 10 Year Plan, 192
Chattanooga Neighborhood Enterprise, Inc. (CNE), 192, 193, 202
Chattanooga Venture, 191-192
Cherry Hill High School West, 94
Cherry Hill Mall [New Jersey], 80, 101
  community response to, 94-95, 99
  design of, 91-92
  early attempts to develop, 90
  financing of, 91
  and Victor Gruen, 91-93
  long-term impact of, 95-96
  opening of, 94
  Rouse's pride in, 90
  sale by Rouse Company of, 96
  skepticism about, 95, 101
  tenants for, 91-92
Church of the Saviour, 154-56, 165, 188, 190

Citizen's Advisory Committee on the Baltimore Plan, 52
Citizens for Harborplace, 182
Citizens for the Preservation of the Inner Harbor, 181
Citizens Planning and Housing Association [Baltimore], 49
City Council [Baltimore], 180, 181, 182
City Council [Boston], 174-75
City Planning Commission [Baltimore], 68
Cochran, Peyton S., Jr., 142-43
Colean, Miles L., 66
Columbia [Maryland], 1, 5, 7, 8, 18
  5th anniversary of, 153
  10th anniversary of, 166
  and Antioch College, 134-140, 148
  as community, 1, 3, 5-6, 221, 225, 234
  county negotiations re, 132
  design and layout of, 125-129, 134
  European models and, 103-105
  expansion of, 225, 227-28
  financing for, 119
  under General Growth Properties, 226-27
  and Gruen, Victor, 127, 129
  Hochschild, Kohn, negotiations with, 142-44
  income diversity of, 3, 126, 141, 142, 144-45, 222-23, 225, 232
  Lake Kittamaquandi in, 129, 134
  land acquisition for, 2, 105, 120-124
  loss of original vision of, 7, 144-45, 223-225
  naming of, 131
  nature, love of, and 24
  opposition to, 5-6, 123, 132
    and TIAA, 121, 134, 140-42
  as Rouse priority, 8, 112, 156
  and racial diversity of, 1, 4-5, 133, 221-22, 223, 225
  rents raised in, 144-45
  retail tenants of, 225
  tenants' problems in, 144-45
  Town Center of, 128, 143
  unprofitable times for, 153
  village model for, 106-7
  vision of Rouse for, 3, 119-120

under WCI, 227-28
Work Group for, 125-127
Columbia Association, 127, 223-34
Columbia Council, 222, 223-34
Columbia Medicine, 128
Columbia Pavilion of Music, 128
Community Building in Partnership, 208
Community Research and Development (CRD), 3, 79, 81, 91, 101, 109, 121
Congress of Racial Equality (CORE), 113
Connecticut General Life Insurance, 44, 46, 70, 85, 121, 05, 157, 164
Constellation, 179, 180
Continental American Life, 44
Cook, G. Yates, 49-50
Coors, William, 202
Corcoran Art Gallery, 129
Corker, Bob, 192, 193
Cornelison, Alice, 222
Cosby, [Newton] Gordon, 155, 171, 191
Costigan, Pat, 217
Cranston, Alan, 58, 59, 204-05
Cross Keys, Village of [Baltimore], 2, 8, 18, 124,
  naming of, 110
  popularity of, 114, 115-116, 117
  racial issues and, 113
  rental issues at, 112, 114
  and Roland Park community, 111-112, 116
  tenant complaints at, 115, 116
  vision of, 110
Cross Street Market [Baltimore], 183
Crouse, Russel, 58
D'Alesandro,Thomas, Jr., 51-52, 54
Daley, William, 135
Daniels, Ned, 5, 6, 71, 90, 112, 114, 171
Darling Harbour [Sydney], 195
Dartington Hall Trust, 189
Dasher family, 122
Dayton [Ohio], 69
DeVito, Mathias J., 64, 163, 187
Ditch, W. Scott, 7, 113, 180
Dixon, James T., 135
DuBois, Irwin J., 180

Dugan, Daniel B., 59
Duhl, Leonard J., 150
Duke University, 198
Eastern Shore [Maryland], 2, 12-13, 16-17, 22, 39, 65, 203. *See also* Easton, Talbottown, Wye Island
Easton [Maryland], 11-14, 21-22, 28, 31, 53, 126
Easton High School, 25, 28, 31
Easton National Bank, 38
Eastpoint Shopping Center [Baltimore], 64
Echelon Mall [New Jersey], 94
Edina [Minnesota], 69
Edmondson Village Shopping Center [Baltimore], 64, 80
Eisenhower, Dwight D., 53-55, 57, 80
Elmhirst, Leonard, 189
Elmhirst, Michael, 189
Enterprise Development Co. (EDC), 189, 190, 191, 192-93, 195-197
Enterprise Foundation (EF), 205
  fundraising for, 190-91, 196, 197, 202
  inspiration for, 188-89
  as model for entrepreneurs, 8, 198
  projects of, 193-94, 202, 206-08,
  successor for, 204, 213-14
  vision of 5, 59, 189, 191, 214, 215, 232
Estates at Princeton Junction [West Windsor, N.J.], 232-33
Exton Square Mall [Pennsylvania], 94
Falzarano Construction Company, 172
Faneuil Hall Marketplace [Boston], 5, 8, 171
  design and vision for, 173-176
  early development attempts at, 172
  financing and leasing of, 174, 175
  history of site of, 172
  minority hiring for, 181
  praise for, 177-79
  small shops and, 176-77
  surburban takeover of, 176-77
Fantus, 140
Farmers Market [Los Angeles], 171
Farsta [Stockholm], 104
Federal Housing Administration (FHA), 2, 38-39, 43, 44, 47, 55, 65, 133, 188, 193

242 Index

Fight Blight Fund [Baltimore], 51
Finley, William E. (Bill), 112, 124, 127, 158
Fire Department [Baltimore], 84
First National Bank of Boston, 91
Flint [Michigan], 191, 193-94, 195, 196
Food Fair, 63, 65, 70
Fosdick, Harry Emerson, 154
Frederick Douglas High School, 68
Froelicher, Hans, 49
Gallery at Market East [Philadelphia], 94, 166
Gardner, John W., 191, 225
Gehry, Frank, 116, 134, 227
General Electric, 157
General Growth Properties of Chicago, 69, 226-27, 234
General Motors, 194
Golden Triangle [Pittsburgh], 83-84
Goldsborough, Bolton, 13
Goldsmith, C. Oliver, 122
Gonzalez, Henry, 205
Gorman, Aubrey, 195
Gould, Kingdon, 122-23
Graham, Katharine, 196
Great Valley Corporate Center [Pennsylvania], 232
Greater Baltimore Committee (GBC), 82-84, 85
Greater Hartford Development Corporation (DevCo), 156, 158
Greater Hartford Process, Inc., 158-59
Greenough, Bill, 134-35, 140, 164
Grieves, James R., 180-181
Griswold, Alexander Brown, 66, 67
Gruen, Victor, 69, 71, 73, 91-93, 97-98, 127, 129
Gudelsky, Isadore, 122-23
Guirlinger, Austin, 197
H&R Block, 69
Hamilton, Wallace, 128
Hamilton, William, 135
Hammerstein, Oscar II, 58
Hankowsky, Bill, 235
Harborplace [Baltimore], 8, 182, 183, 184
   design of, 183
   minority hiring and rental, 181-82
   and open space, 181
   opening of, 182

   opposition to, 180-182
   Mayor Schaefer and, 179, 180-81
   and small business vendors, 182
   suburban takeover of, 182-83
   vision for, 179, 181,182
Harbourside [Sydney, Aus.], 194
Hardy, Bill, 161, 163
Hardy, Frank, 161, 163
Harford County [Maryland], 15-17
Harper House, 116
Harper, Robert Goodloe, 116
Harper's Cleaners, 145
Harriman, Pamela, 202
Hartford [Connecticut], 158-59, 171
Harundale Mall [Baltimore], 70-73, 79, 89
The Harundale Study, 72
Harvard Business School, 198
Harvard Center for Business and Government, 190
Harvard Graduate School of Design, 94
Harvard Univ. Design Conference, 72
Harvey, F. Barton III, 204, 213, 214
Hawaii, 32-33, 35, 45-46.
Hayson, Thomas, 194-95, 196
Head Ski & Sports, 157
Health Dept. [Baltimore], 49, 52, 84
Hechinger, John W., 196
Hecht's, 65, 73
Heiskell, Andrew, 191
Herter, Christian A., 58
Hicks & Ingle, 89-90
Hirsch, Charles L., 196
Hochschild, Kohn, 64, 70, 71, 127, 155
Holland, Al, 33
Hollander, Sidney, Jr., 66, 70, 114
Hollyday, Guy T.O., 43, 50, 51, 82
HOME Investment Trust Fund, 206
Hoppenfeld, Morton, 8, 124, 127
House Ways and Means Committee, 191
Household Finance Company, 70
Housing Act of 1949, 55
Housing Act of 1954, 55-56, 80
Housing Advisory Committee [U.S.], 54
Housing and Community Development Commission [Baltimore], 180
Housing and Home Finance Administration [U.S.], 55, 56

Housing and Urban Development (HUD), U.S. Department of, 205
Housing Bureau [Baltimore], 52
Housing Court [Baltimore], 52
Housing Opportunity Program (HOP) [U.S.], 205
Houston, 71
Howard County [Maryland], 120
Howard County Board of Commissioners, 124-125
Howard Co. Board of Education, 223
Howard Co. Citizens Association, 132
Howard Co. Community College, 222
Howard Research and Development Corporation, 121, 157, 159, 225
Howell, Roger, 38
Hurricane Agnes, 153
Hutzler's, 64
Ichan, Carl, 197
Inner Harbor [Baltimore], 179, 181, 183, 184. *See also* Harborplace.
Interdenominational Ministerial Alliance, 182
The Ireland Fund, 195
James W. Rouse & Company, 67, 80. *See also* Community Research and Development; Rouse Company
JCPenney, 73, 91, 225
Jerome, Judson, 138
Johns Hopkins Hospital, 23-24, 218
Johns Hopkins University, 15, 22, 25, 29, 31-32, 39
Jones, John Martin (Jack), 5, 122
Jones, Paul, 155
Jubilee Housing, 156, 188, 205
Keeton, Morris T., 135-137, 139-140
Keeton, Ruth, 136
Keidel, Albert, Jr. (Bob), 65, 78
Keith, Nathaniel, 83
Kellogg Foundation, 194
Kemp, Jack, 205
Kenney, Robert T., 172
Ketchum Company, 202
King, Peter, Jr., 139
King's Contrivance, 123
Kresge, 70
Krummeck, Elsie, 71
Lassiter, Robert Jr., 89-90
Lee's Pharmacy, 65
Lemkau, Paul, 126

Levin, Susan Bass, 96
Lexington Market [Baltimore], 183
Liberty Medical Center [Baltimore], 69
Liberty Place [Philadelphia], 232
Liberty Property Trust, 232
Long Island [New York], 65
Longfellow, Henry Wadsworth, 66
Los Angeles, 208
Louie's Bookstore Café, 152, 215
Lowe, Ed, 196
MacArthur Foundation, 202
B.H. Macomber Co., 172
Macy's, 65, 73, 91
Madison National Bank, 123
Madison Square [Charlotte, N.C.], 90
Manufacturers Hanover, 157
Marchi, John, 159
Marcus, Stanley, 202
Marley Station [Maryland], 73
Marshall, George C., 57
Marshall, Wink, 33
Maryland Institute of Art, 128, n-4
Maryland Science Center, 180
Mason, Sidney, 103
Mathias, Charles McC., 191
Mayor's Advisory Council on the Housing Bureau [Baltimore], 52
McCamly Place [Battle Creek], 195
McCann, Bob, 136, 137
McCarthy, Joseph J., 54
McDermott, Jerome S., 90
McFarland, M. Carter, 55
McKeldin, Theodore R., 53, 59
McNally, William J., 194-95
McNamara, Robert S., 191
Memphis [Tennessee], 160-61, 171
Merchant's Association [Charlottetown], 90
Merck, Sharp & Dohme, 157
Merlin International Properties, Ltd., 195
Merriweather Post Pavilion [Columbia], 227
Metropolitan Research and Development, 65, 82
Metropolitan Structures, 86
Meyerhoff, Harvey M. (Bud), 202
Meyerhoff, Jack, 63-64, 65, 78, 80, 88, 90
Meyerhoff, Joseph, 64-65, 80

Meyner, Robert B., 94
Michael, Donald N., 124, 127-28
Miller, J. Jefferson, 86
Millspaugh, Martin, 179, 235
Molinaro, Leo, 158
Mondawmin [estate], 66
Mondawmin Corporation, 67
Mondawmin Mall [Baltimore], 66-69
Montclair Shopping Center [Houston], 71
Morgan Guaranty, 157
Mori, Eugene, 90
Mortgage Bankers Association, 51, 58
Moss, Hunter, 43, 44, 47, 78-79, 142-43, 153-54
Moss-Rouse Mortgage Company, 4, 44, 45, 47, 65, 67, 68,
Motor Vehicle Administration [Maryland], 69
Mott Foundation. *See* Charles Stewart Mott Foundation
Mott, Seward H., 66, 68
Moxley, Robert, 122-23
Mutual Benefit Life Insurance Company, 63
The Myth that Threatens the World, 58
Nash, Ogden, 114
National Affordable Housing Act, 206
National Capital Planning Commission, 126
National Housing Task Force, 204-206
National Life of Vermont, 43
National Mortgage Bankers Association, 2
National Recovery Act, 38
Naylor, Lawrence P., 78
Nehemiah Program, 206
Neighborhood Progress Administration [Baltimore], 201
New Communities Corporation, 164
New Deal, 37, 38, 43
New York City Panning Department, 159
The New York Times, 149
Newark [New Jersey], 80, 196
Nippard, Lewis S., 132
Nix, Russel, 71
Nixon, Richard B., 148-49
No Slums in Ten Years, 83
Norfolk [Virginia], 192, 195, 197

Norfolk Redevelopment and Housing Authority, 165
North Star Mall [San Antonio], 82
Norton, Edward [grandson], 151
Norton, Edward B. [son-in-law], 150-51
Norton, Lydia Robinson (Robin) Rouse, [daughter], 44, 46, 138, 148-50, 156
Nuveen, John, 58
Ober Law, 58
O'Connor, Elizabeth, 154
Ontario Place [Toronto], 129
Orchard Village [Chattanooga], 194
Palmer, Edward L., Jr., 44
Peabody Conservatory of Music, 128
Peace Bottom Creek, 24
"Peckham Experiment," 103, 107
Pei, I.M., 65
Pennsylvania Real Estate Investment Trust, 94
Pensacola [Florida], 46
Perot, H. Ross, 197
Petrie, Milton, 197
Philadelphia, 94, 101
Philadelphia Stock Exchange Building, 234
Phillips, Wendell, 182
Pilot Area [Baltimore], 50, 52
Pines, Marion W., 201
Piper & Hill, 78
Piper and Marbury, 122
Pittsburgh, 83-84
Plain and Simple, 203
Planning Council [Baltimore], 85
Plumer, Steven B., 148
Plymouth Meeting Mall [Pennsylvania], 94
Pollin, Abe, 197
Portside [Toledo], 192
President's Special Message to the Congress on Housing (1954), 55
Pride of Baltimore, 183
Prime Time [ABC-TV], 210
Princeton University, 25
Progressive Architecture, 71
Pryor, Mary Day Rouse [sister], 16, 32, 36
Pryor, William Lee [brother-in-law], 36

Quincy Market [Boston], 171, 172, 175, 176, 179, 181
Quincy, Josiah, 172
Radical Students Institute [Antioch College], 137-38
Ratner, Albert, 202
Ravitch, Richard, 197
"Reilly's Law of Retail Gravitation," 68
Review of Life's Meaning, 155
Richmond [Virginia], 192, 194, 196
Rite-Aid, 69
Riverside Church [Manhattan], 172
Robin Hood Trust, 189, 191
Robinson, Jackie and Rachel, 67
Rockefeller, David, 197
Roland Park, 110-112, 113, 114, 117
Roosevelt Field Shopping Center [Long Island], 65
Rosemary Beach [Florida], 233
Rouse & Associates, 234
Rouse, Anne Stump Webster [father's first wife], 16
Rouse, Bill [brother]. *See* Rouse, Willard
Rouse, Buddy [half-brother]. *See* Rouse, John Goldsmith II
Rouse, C.C. [uncle], 16-17
Rouse, Christopher Chapman [great-grandfather], 15
The Rouse Company, 6, 68, 95, 113-1114, 115, 116, 147, 153, 157, 171, 175, 180, 181, 184, 187, 188, 190. *See also* Community Research and Development; James W. Rouse & Company
Rouse, Dia [sister], 32
Rouse, Elizabeth (Libby) Jameson Winstead [wife], 44, 45, 46, 67, 135, 136, 147, 150, 151, 153-54, 156-57, 159
Rouse, James (Jim)Wilson Richardson
and American City Corporation, 158
and American Council to Improve Our Neighborhoods, 82
and Antioch College, 134-139, 148-49
Australia trip of, 195
and Baltimore Neighborhoods, Inc., 84-85

and Battle Creek, 191, 193, 195
boyhood of, 11, 21-29
and brother Bill: business relationship with 64; as surrogate father, 31-40 passim.
and Buffet, Warren, 4
and capitalism, 4-5, 6, 96, 103
as card player, 45
character and personality of, 4-5, 7-9, 47, 112
and Charles Center, 84-85
and Chattanooga [Tn.], 192-93, 194
and Cherry Hill Mall: 90, 93, 96: conflicts concerning, 92-93; design details for, 92, 93, 94; financing obtained for, 89;
and Columbia, 157: Antioch College negotiations re, 134-139; community support for, 131-132, design details for, 134; financing for, 121, Hoschild, Kohn negotiations re, 142-144; land acquisition for, 120-21, 123; tenant response policy in, 144-45; TIAA negotiations re, 134, 140-142; Tivoli in, 127; Town Center in, 128; Work Group for, 125, 127; vision and design of, 1, 119-120, 124, 128, 129
and community, vision of, 3, 69-70, 72, 95, 104, 106, 110, 221
and Community Research and Development, 78-81
conflicts in professional life of, 52, 84, 89-90, 92-93
and Cross Keys, Village of: goals for, 110; land acquisition for, 109; rental policies of, 113, 114; tenant complaints handled for, 115 zoning changes for, 111
defeats and disappointments (professional) of, 7, 71, 85, 116, 125, 127, 142, 144, 163-64, 179, 195, 217
divorce of, 5, 156-57
as employee, FHA, 38-39, 43
as employee, Title Guarantee & Trust, 43
and Enterprise Development, 195-96
and Enterprise Foundation, 190-91,

197, 202
European trip by, 1, 102-105
and Faneuil Hall, 171-172, 174, 176
father's influence on, 14, 28, 36, 40
and Flint, 191, 193-195
genealogy of, 15, 22
and Greater Baltimore Committee, 82-85
and Gruen, Victor, 71, 90-92, 100
and Harford [Ct.] planning, 158-59
and Harundale Mall, 70-73
Hawaiian experiences, influenced by, 35
and the homeless, 215
with infantile paralysis, 23-24
and James W. Rouse Company, 76
Jewish community, opposing discrimination against, 105
and jobs as young man, 37-38
and Jubilee Housing, 188
and McKeldin, Theodore, 53
marriage to Libby of, 44, 153-54
marriage to Patty of, 171
military service of, 44-46
and misjudgment of center city impact of suburban malls, 79-81
and misjudgments of deterioration of cities, 100, 101, 106
and Mondawmin Mall, 66-68
on National Housing Task Force, 204-05, 206
and Norfolk, 195
as peace advocate, 2, 56-57, 148-49
philosophy (personal and business) of, 3-4, 6, 8, 9, 59-60, 79-80, 84, 99, 110, 153, 157-58, 187, 189-91, 214, 215, 218, 226-27, 234-35
and political campaigns, 53-54
and poverty as young man, 2, 17, 31-40 passim
and public affairs, interest in, 1, 2, 5, 6, 147
public service of, municipal, 51-52
public service of, national, 54-55, 204-205
and racial attitudes of early environment, 2, 13-14, 32
and racial equality, commitment to, 1-2, 4-5, 6, 13, 53, 84, 105, 113-114, 118, 133, 190, 192, 221
as recipient, Bronze Star, 46
as recipient, Johns Hopkins University acclaim, 39
as recipient, Legion of Merit, 46
as recipient, Presidential Medal of Freedom, 5
religion in life of, 14, 136, 154-56, 187, 202
retirement as Rouse Co. CEO of, 6, 187-88
and Richmond, 191
Rouse, Jimmy [son], relationship with, 150, 151-52
and Sandtown: hands-on involvment with, 207, 218; and Schmoke, 206; vision of, 6, 201-202, 206
sensitivity in business relationships of, 5-6
and Shelby Farms [Tn,], 160
and shopping centers/malls, philosophy and design of, 69-70, 79-80, 94-95, 101, 176, 177, 189-90, 191, 194, 195
and slums, vision and revitalization for, 5, 6, 49-53, 55-56, 82-83, 118, 189, 192-93, 201
social conscience of, 5, 6, 8, 26-27, 34-35, 53, 190, 215
speeches by, 2, 8, 84, 93, 94-95, 105-106, 124, 190, 191, 204, 208, 221
sports interests of, 7, 24, 25, 28, 33-34, 36
and Staten Island plan, 159-30
and Strawbridge, G. Stockton, 91-94
as student, college, 2, 33-37
as student, elementary school, 21, 23, 24
as student, high school, 25-28
as student, law school, 37-39
as student, prep school, 31
and suburbia development, scorn for, 1, 2, 5, 119
and Talbottown, 65
and Toledo, 191, 195
Trump, Donald, contrasted with, 3, 35
and urban design, vision of, 99-100, 106, 110, 120

and urban revitalization: 170, 176, 189, 191, 193-93, 194, 196. *See also* and slums . . . *above.*
and villages as model, 106-105, 110
and Waverly Tower, 64
as workaholic, 77-78, 112, 132, 156, 204
as world government advocate, 2, 57-60
and Wye Island plan, 161-63
Rouse, James (Jimmy) [son], 147, 149-53, 209, 215
Rouse, John Goldsmith [grandfather], 15, 22
Rouse, John Goldsmith II (Buddy) [half-brother], 2, 16, 25, 29. 33
Rouse, Libby. *See* Rouse, Elizabeth.
Rouse, Lydia [sister], 16
Rouse, Lydia Robinson [mother], 16, 17-18, 21, 23, 24, 28, 40
Rouse, Lydia Robinson (Robin) [daughter]. *See* Norton, Lydia.
Rouse, Margaret Robinson [sister]. *See* Balch, Margaret.
Rouse, Mary Day [sister]. *See* Pryor, Mary Day.
Rouse, [Myrtle] Patricia (Patty) [wife], 6, 165, 177, 184, 188, 202, 210
Rouse, Patty. *See* Rouse, Myrtle Patricia (Patty).
Rouse, Robin [daughter]. *See* Norton, Lydia Robinson.
Rouse, Teddy [son]. *See* Rouse, Winstead
Rouse, Willard (Bill) [brother], 2, 16, 22, 28, 29, 31-32, 34, 35, 37, 38, 40, 63, 64, 65, 68, 91, 91, 94, 111, 112, 120, 123, 202
Rouse, Willard G. III [nephew], 94, 234-35
Rouse, Willard Goldsmith [father], 8, 11, 14-18, 25, 28, 29, 36
Rouse, Winstead (Ted, Teddy) [son], 28, 135, 147, 215, 235
Ryan, Jim, 133-34, 201
Ryland Modular Homes, 134, 201
St. Paul Garage, 38
Salisbury [Maryland], 39
Sandtown-Winchester [Baltimore], 6, 7, 8, 188

and BUILD, 208
city involvement with, 206-208
conditions, pre-rehab, of, 188, 206, 208, 209
contrasted with other projects, 201
outcome of, 7, 210, 231-32
on *Prime Time,* 210
Rouse's view of, 6
Karl Schmoke and, 201-02, 206, 207
Save Merriweather, Inc. 227
Save Merriweather Political Action Committee, 227
Schaefer, William Donald, 180, 181, 182, 183, 231
Schmoke, Karl, 201-202, 206, 207
School of Christian Living, 157
Schuttler, Barry, 72-73
Sears, 68, 73
Seaside [Florida], 233
Security Life of New York, 43
Security Realty Company, 120
Shallcross, John, 123-24
Shelby Farms [Memphis], 11, 160-61, 163
Sherman, Mal, 133
Sherwood, Robert E., 58
Shopping Town USA, 72
Sigler, Andrew C., 197
Smith, Larry, 71, 90, 143
Social Ventures Network, 217
South Baltimore Business Association, 180
Southdale [Minnesota], 69, 71
Spear, Michael D., 158
Spencer, Duncan M. 58
Springfield Mall [Neshaminy, Pa.], 94
Stark, Albert, 63-64, 67, 78
Staten Island, 159-60, 171
Stevenson, Adlai, 53, 54
Stewart, Albert, 135
Stop, Shop & Save, 69
Stout, Rex, 58
Straight, Dorothy Payne Whitney, 188
Strawbridge & Clothier (S&C), 90
Strawbridge, G. Stockton, 91-93, 94, 109
Streuver Bros., Eccles & Rouse, 215, 235
Summerlin [Nevada], 232-34
The Sun [Baltimore], 34, 232

248 Index

Sun Ray Drugs, 63
Swett, Paul, 151
Sydney [Australia], 194
Talbot County [Maryland], 11, 12
Talbottown Shopping Center [Easton, Md.], 65, 78, 79, 161
Taylor, Telford, 58
Teachers Insurance and Annuity Association (TIAA), 7, 121, 140, 164, 222, 225
Temerlin, Maurice, 150
Tennessee Riverpark [Chattanooga], 194
Thompson & Associates, 175
Thompson, Benjamin (Ben), 171-72, 175, 183
Title Guarantee and Trust Company, 43
Tivoli (Columbia), 127-29
Tokyo, 190
Toledo [Ohio], 192, 194, 196
Toll Brothers, 232
Tome School, 31-32
Towers, J. H., 46
Town Center [Columbia], 127-29, 225
Traugatt, [Myrtle] Patricia (Patty). *See* Rouse, Myrtle Patricia (Patty).
United Church of Christ, 72
U.N. Conference on Human Settlements, 194
U.S. Department of Housing and Urban Development (HUD), 205
U.S. Naval Reserve, 44
U.S. Public Health Service, 52
U.S. Social Security Administration, 69
United World Federalists (UWF), 58-60
University of California at Berkeley, 105-6, 124, 208
University of Hawaii, 33
University of Maryland, School of Law, 2, 15, 38
University of Virginia, 36
Urban Growth and New Community Development Act, 164
Urban Life Center, 159
Urban Renewal and Housing Agency [Baltimore], 84-86
Vacation Cottage Program [Rouse Co.], 113-114
Value City, 73

Van Arkel and Moss, p2
Van Leuven, Karl, 91-92
Village of Cross Keys. *See* Cross Keys, Village of
Wallace, McHarg, Roberts and Todd, 162
Wanamaker's, 91
Washington (D.C.), 81, 83
Washington National Symphony, 128
The Washington Post, 149
Waterfront Urban Renewal District, [Boston], p-2
Water Street Pavilion [Flint], 193-94
Watercolor [Florida], 233
Waterside [Norfolk], 192, 194, 196
Waverly Realty Corporation, 63, 78-79
Waverly Redevelopment Corporation, 63
Waverly Tower Shopping Center [Baltimore], 63, 65
WCI, 227
Webb, Roger, 173-74
Webster, Anna Stump. *See* Rouse, Anna Stump Webster.
Weill, Sanford I., 202
Welch, Kenneth C., 68
Wesray Capital Corporation, 197
Western Auto, 63, 90
Westview, 71
White Coffee Pot, 68
White, Kevin H., 173, 174, 175
White Tower, 63
White, William S., 193
Wiggins, Willie (Wiggins Home Improvement), 145
Wilde, Frazer B., 121
Wilkie, Wendell, 53
Williams, Huntington, 52
Williams Roy E., 175
Winstead, Elizabeth Jameson, *see* Rouse, Elizabeth.
Wolfson, Louis, 197
Woodward & Lathrop, 143, 171
Work Group [Columbia]), 107, 125-26
WWIN, 63
Wye Island [Eastern Shore, Md.], 7, 161-63, 171
Youth Center [Harundale Mall], 73
Zeckendorf, William, 65
Zeidler, Frank, 5

About the Author

Paul Marx is Professor Emeritus of English at the University of New Haven. In retirement, he lives in Towson, Maryland. He is the author of *The Modern Rules of Style* (American Bar Association Publishing, 2007) and *Utopia in America* (Burke Publishing, 2002). He is the editor of *Modern and Classical Essayists* (McGraw-Hill, 1996) and *Twelve Short Story Writers* (Holt, Rinehart & Winston, 1970). As a freelance writer, he has had articles in The New York Times, The Los Angeles Times, The Washington Post, The Baltimore Sun, The New Republic, The Nation, The New Leader, Commonweal, The St. Louis Post-Dispatch, Houston Chronicle, Dallas Morning News, Hartford Courant, New Haven Register, Yankee, Education Week, The Chronicle of Higher Education, and elsewhere.